THE 1964 REPUBLICAN
CONVENTION

ALSO BY JOHN C. SKIPPER
AND FROM MCFARLAND

Frank Robinson: A Baseball Biography (2015)

*Billy Southworth: A Biography of the Hall of Fame
Manager and Ballplayer* (2013)

*Showdown at the 1964 Democratic Convention:
Lyndon Johnson, Mississippi and Civil Rights* (2012)

*The Iowa Caucuses: First Tests of Presidential
Aspiration, 1972–2008* (2010)

*A Biographical Dictionary of the Baseball
Hall of Fame,* 2d ed. (2008; softcover 2015)

*Charlie Gehringer: A Biography of the
Hall of Fame Tigers Second Baseman* (2008)

*Dazzy Vance: A Biography of the
Brooklyn Dodger Hall of Famer* (2007)

*Wicked Curve: The Life and Troubled Times
of Grover Cleveland Alexander* (2006)

*The Cubs Win the Pennant!: Charlie Grimm, the Billy
Goat Curse, and the 1945 World Series Run* (2004)

*A Biographical Dictionary of Major League
Baseball Managers* (2003; softcover 2011)

*Take Me Out to the Cubs Game: 35 Former
Ballplayers Speak of Losing at Wrigley* (2000)

*Umpires: Classic Baseball Stories from the
Men Who Made the Calls* (1997)

The 1964 Republican Convention

Barry Goldwater and the Beginning of the Conservative Movement

John C. Skipper

McFarland & Company, Inc., Publishers
Jefferson, North Carolina

LIBRARY OF CONGRESS CATALOGUING-IN-PUBLICATION DATA

Names: Skipper, John C., 1945–
Title: The 1964 Republican Convention : Barry Goldwater and the beginning of the conservative movement / John C. Skipper.
Description: Jefferson, North Carolina : McFarland & Company, Inc., Publishers, 2016. | Includes bibliographical references and index.
Identifiers: LCCN 2016008460 | ISBN 9780786498086 (softcover : alkaline paper) ∞
Subjects: LCSH: Goldwater, Barry M. (Barry Morris), 1909–1998. | Goldwater, Barry M. (Barry Morris), 1909–1998—Political and social views. | Republican National Convention (28th : 1964 : San Francisco, Calif.) | Presidents—United States—Election—1964. | Presidential candidates—United States—Biography. | Conservatism—United States—History—20th century. | United States—Politics and government—1963–1969.
Classification: LCC E748.G64 S55 2016 | DDC 324.2734—dc23
LC record available at http://lccn.loc.gov/2016008460

BRITISH LIBRARY CATALOGUING DATA ARE AVAILABLE

ISBN (print) 978-0-7864-9808-6
ISBN (ebook) 978-1-4766-2419-8

© 2016 John C. Skipper. All rights reserved

No part of this book may be reproduced or transmitted in any form or by any means, electronic or mechanical, including photocopying or recording, or by any information storage and retrieval system, without permission in writing from the publisher.

On the cover: *Mr. Conservative: Goldwater on Goldwater,* HBO documentary, 2006 (Photofest)

Printed in the United States of America

McFarland & Company, Inc., Publishers
 Box 611, Jefferson, North Carolina 28640
  www.mcfarlandpub.com

For Larry and Patty Hiatt
In honor of our friendship

Table of Contents

Introduction	1
1—Thirty Words	11
2—A Tale of Two Tafts	18
3—Filling the Vacuum	26
4—The Contenders	35
5—The Clandestine Meeting	45
6—Feeling the Draft	58
7—The Rockefeller Campaign	64
8—November 22, 1963	72
9—The Goldwater Kitchen Cabinet	82
10—The Rocky Road	88
11—Lyndon Johnson	94
12—New Hampshire	103
13—Scranton and Romney	115
14—The Eisenhower Factor	122
15—The Battlefields	128
16—California	142
17—Cleveland	149
18—The Civil Rights Bill	155
19—San Francisco	165
20—The Acceptance Speech	180

21—Convention Myths	187
22—The Lion and the Lamb	192
Epilogue	199
Appendix A—1964 Primary Election Results	207
Appendix B–Total Primary Popular Vote	208
Appendix C–1964 Convention First Ballot Vote Count	209
Appendix D–Goldwater Acceptance Speech, July 16, 1964	209
Chapter Notes	219
Bibliography	231
Index	235

Introduction

The 1978 movie *Same Time, Next Year* has a telling scene. The movie is about a couple, George and Doris, both married to other people, who have a chance meeting at an inn. They chat, hit it off and wind up spending the night together. They enjoy each other's company so much that they agree to meet again next year—and that leads to many more years of having a weekend rendezvous.

In one scene in the movie, presumed to take place in 1965, George, played by Alan Alda, and Doris, played by Ellen Burstyn, are catching up on what each has done in the past year as they prepare to retire for the night. George mentions in passing that he voted for Barry Goldwater.

Doris is shocked. She tells him, "If you think I'm going to bed with any son of a bitch who voted for Goldwater, you're crazy."

George pleads with her: "Doris, don't do this to me." But any hope for a romantic interlude has been stifled.

"How could you vote for a man like that?" asks Doris. "Yuck!"

Such was the feeling about Barry Morris Goldwater, the venerable United States senator from Arizona, at least in the minds of liberals, even 14 years after he became the ringleader of an ambitious conservative drive to elect him as president of the United States. He lost in a landslide to President Lyndon Johnson as the American public offered a resounding "yuck" to a possible Goldwater presidency.

The "son of a bitch" reference was often directed at him, toward him—and even by him. When supporters of his met in a hotel room in 1961 to talk about his possible candidacy, they were frustrated by his unwillingness to run. At one point, one of the men in the room said, "Let's draft the son of a bitch" and they launched one of the most successful draft efforts in American history.[1]

Later, when Goldwater became a candidate, he expressed his displeasure at how he was being portrayed by other Republicans and the press. He said if he believed everything he read and heard about himself, "I wouldn't vote for the son of a bitch either."[2]

Such was the tone of an improbable candidate in an improbable campaign that had a predictable outcome—Goldwater was trounced in the presidential election.

But historians point to that election as the start of what developed into a successful conservative movement that helped elect Ronald Reagan as president in 1980, propelled Newt Gingrich to speaker of the House of Representatives in 1994 and gave rise to the Tea Party movement in the 21st century that essentially espouses the same principles that Goldwater endorsed. J. William Middendorf, who worked in the Goldwater campaign, wrote a book about it many years later and aptly titled it *A Glorious Disaster*.[3]

Goldwater was at first a reluctant candidate in an election he didn't think he could win but subsequently was willing to fall on his sword for a cause he believed in so deeply. His followers began planning his candidacy, without his consent or approval, not long after the 1960 election in which John F. Kennedy, the Democrat, narrowly defeated the Republican, Vice President Richard Nixon.

What began as an idea tossed around by about 20 men in a Chicago hotel room mushroomed into a national conservative movement to nominate Goldwater at the 1964 Republican convention in San Francisco and then get him elected in November. They succeeded in everything except getting him elected but their efforts along the way are a remarkable political road map on how to draft a candidate.

The 1964 Republican National Convention provides a unique look into the tawdry world of hardball politics. The convention was more like a bar fight that lasted four days instead of a celebratory family reunion of members of the Grand Old Party.

But to understand what happened as Republicans gathered at the Cow Palace on the outskirts of San Francisco for their convention, it is necessary to look at what life was like in America in 1964 and the political forces that were at work.

It was a year that marked the debut of the Ford Mustang, Bubble Wrap, the VCR and a delicacy produced in a kitchen in New York consisting of chicken wings and a special sauce. The latter came to be known as Buffalo wild wings.

In the same year that Dr. Martin Luther King won the Nobel Peace

Prize, race riots took place in New York, New Jersey, Chicago, Philadelphia and many other cities across the United States. Sidney Poitier became the first black actor to win an Academy Award in the same year he was providing financial support to black people in Mississippi who were banding together to demand equality with whites in their everyday lives.

The most powerful earthquake in U.S. history, with a magnitude of 9.2, struck Alaska. Thousands of miles away, Albert DeSalvo, who was known as the Boston Strangler when he was on the loose, was finally arrested.

In the entertainment world, the Beatles, a British singing quartet, made their first appearance in the United States at a time when they had 13 of the top 100 hits on Billboard, the music sales tracker. Elizabeth Taylor and Richard Burton, icons of the movie industry, got married, and *Hello Dolly*, *Funny Girl* and *Fiddler on the Roof* opened on Broadway.

The New York Yankees won their fifth straight American League championship while the St. Louis Cardinals won the National League title. The boxing world was introduced to Cassius Clay, a young black fighter from Louisville who beat Sonny Liston for the heavyweight boxing championship and would later change his name to Muhammad Ali.

The tobacco industry was thriving and advertising agencies were busy trying to outdo one another with jingles and catch phrases promoting cigarettes with such ditties as "Winstons taste good like a cigarette should" and "L.S.M.F.T—Lucky Strike means fine tobacco," not to be outdone by the rough-and-tumble "Marlboro Man." But 1964 was also the year that the surgeon general issued a report linking cigarette smoking to lung cancer.

In the midst of all of this, 1964 was a presidential election year. The nation was still reeling from the assassination of President John F. Kennedy in Dallas on November 22, 1963, and all the questions about it that were still unanswered fueled speculation, theories and many books. President Johnson appointed a commission headed by Supreme Court chief justice Earl Warren to investigate the assassination. The Warren Commission Report, which concluded that Lee Harvey Oswald acted alone in killing Kennedy, would be a topic of dispute for the next half-century and beyond.

The political fallout from the assassination, like ashes from a volcano, spread far and wide. Johnson, who as vice president was suddenly thrust into the role of leader of the free world, benefited politically from having the sympathy and support of a grieving nation and would have no opposition at his party's convention in Atlantic City in August.

Republicans had the challenge of coming up with a viable candidate and, whoever it might be, had to convince the American people that having three different presidents in the span of about a year was okay.

The following pages will show it is impossible to accurately report on the happenings at a political convention without a thorough examination of the events leading up to it. And as the old adage goes about sausage, it may be something to appreciate in its final form as long as you don't see how it is made.

Sometimes, the person who emerges as the presidential candidate is the sausage, acceptable in its final form, brutal in its production. The Democrats met in Atlantic City in August in what President Johnson hoped would be more like a coronation than a convention—a testimonial to how he led the nation through a period of immense grief. He sought not only the approval but the appreciation of his party for what he had accomplished.

In his early days in politics, Johnson was a disciple of Huey Long, the Louisiana governor and senator, who was loved by the people in his home state for all that he had done for them. Johnson craved adulation and, in studying Long, realized that success started with power. With power, a leader could create jobs, create commissions, create boards, appoint friends and political allies to fill those jobs and serve on those boards and commissions. In return, he would have their love, their gratitude—and their vote—in the next election. But it started with power. Without it, nothing could be accomplished.

Historian Nick Kotz said Johnson "had both an ego and insecurities as outsized as his extraordinary talent, an intense desire to be loved by everyone and a burning need to be in control of the action."[4]

So while Republicans were holding their convention in San Francisco, Johnson and his aides were plotting behind the scenes to thwart a possible floor fight at their convention a month later over the seating of the Mississippi delegation.

Mississippi was perhaps the most segregated state in the nation, with black citizens being denied many basic rights, including the right to vote. Mississippi Democrats had elected an all-white delegation to the convention, like they always did, because black people were prohibited from taking part in the process.

In 1964, a freedom movement emerged in which blacks held their own state convention, elected their own slate of delegates and, helped financially by Poitier and singer Harry Belefonte, took a bus from Mississippi to Atlantic City where they went before the Credentials Committee demanding to be seated in place of the all-white delegation.

Historian Theodore White described it as a classic dilemma—the white delegation was legally right but morally wrong; the challenging black delegation was morally right but legally wrong.

President Johnson was more concerned about it politically than morally or legally. He did not want a floor fight at the convention that would be nationally televised and would ruin his "coronation." He knew, too, that if the black delegation, or any part of it, were seated, the regular Mississippi delegation would walk out—and so would the delegations from Alabama, Louisiana, Georgia, Florida and perhaps even Texas. And they might stay home on election day. The president was not about to let that happen.

So in classic Johnson style, he arranged for the FBI to bug hotel rooms and tap telephones of the black insurgents. He dispatched Minnesota senator Hubert Humphrey, who wanted to be Johnson's running mate, to be a mediator and meet with the blacks to work out a compromise that would avoid the floor fight. And he arranged to have one of his advocates on the Credentials Committee, Minnesota Attorney General Walter Mondale, help stave off trouble during the committee hearings.

All the pieces were in place. A "compromise" was reached, much to the dissatisfaction of the black contingent, that would allow for them to have two at-large delegates and the assurance that reforms would be made to insure fair representation in the future. There was no floor fight at the convention, Johnson got the warm reception he so badly wanted, Humphrey had earned the right to be his running mate, and, after the successful November election, Mondale got the Senate seat vacated by Humphrey.[5]

Republicans had problems far different from the Democrats. If Johnson was king of the hill, and he was, the GOP faced the ominous task of figuring out a way of dethroning him. And while the Democrats had a candidate with no opposition, Republicans had a stable full of ambitious candidates and potential candidates, many of whom not only disagreed fundamentally on the direction the party should be headed, but plainly did not like each other.

While Johnson maneuvered behind the scenes with specific instructions to his staff to keep him out of it—think of me as "Joe Glotz," he told them—the Republicans fought each other openly, slugging it out in state conventions, primary elections, party conferences, platform committee meetings, and even on the floor of the convention in full view of the American public. They wound up nominating Goldwater.[6]

But how they did it—how Goldwater survived vicious attacks from the press as well as from members of his own party, how a dedicated group of volunteers worked for three years on a "Draft Goldwater" movement that seemed doomed from the start, how Goldwater overcame his penchant for saying things that were often rude and inappropriate, and how his campaign bungled one opportunity after another—all of that is how the Republican sausage was made in 1964.

The cast of characters included several East Coast aristocrats. There was New York Governor Nelson Rockefeller, born into a family of immense wealth and privilege, never lacking for anything and who wanted to be president of the United States because it was about the only thing he wanted that couldn't be handed to him.

There was Henry Cabot Lodge of Massachusetts, a third generation politician, statesman and diplomat who had been a U.S. senator, ambassador to the United Nations, candidate for vice president four years earlier and currently U.S. ambassador to South Vietnam. Lodge's position as a diplomat prevented him from engaging in U.S. politics but he did nothing to try to stop write-in campaigns on his behalf, the first of which, in New Hampshire, stunned Goldwater and Rockefeller.

Pennsylvania Governor William Scranton, also born of privilege, whose family name was so prominent in the state that the capital city was its namesake, was a relative newcomer in politics, having served briefly in the U.S. House of Representatives and was in his first term as governor. Scranton had influence because he was considered a rising star in the Republican Party and, like Rockefeller, was governor of a large state that carried considerable electoral weight. Unlike Rockefeller, Scranton publicly shrugged off any notions of wanting to be president but then made a last-ditch effort to try to get the nomination.

Michigan Governor George Romney, like Scranton, was serving his first term and was also considered a shining light into the future of the Republican Party nationally. Romney never touted himself as a candidate in 1964 but had a penchant for showing up at national political gatherings, speaking to organizations with obvious influence such as the National Press Club in Washington and never shying away from offering his views on the issues of the day.

Former Vice President Richard Nixon was never a declared candidate but did not resist having his name put on the ballot in states holding primaries nor did he dissuade anyone from mounting write-in campaigns on his behalf. As the party's most recent presidential candidate, Nixon could have expected to be the standard bearer for the party, the man who put it all on the line but came up short.

But many Republicans felt Nixon sold out to the Eastern Establishment elitists in 1960 and bungled his chance to be president by trying to be all things to all people. So Dwight D. Eisenhower, the most recent Republican president—the only Republican president since 1932—was the man most Republicans held in highest respect. In 1964, Nixon was simply a man in the doorway of the ballroom, hoping someone would invite him in to the dance.

All of these men, self-righteous, self-serving and ambitious, but so different in personality and temperament, had one thing in common as the 1964 Republican Convention beckoned. They all had a hearty disdain for Barry Goldwater.

The convention, at which Goldwater was nominated easily on the first ballot, was the most raucous Republican gathering since 1912 when Theodore Roosevelt, by then a former president, tried to snare the nomination from President William Howard Taft and, failing to do so, bolted the party and ran as an independent Progressive Party candidate. He took enough votes away from Taft in November to hand the election to Democrat Woodrow Wilson.

There was no third-party movement in 1964, but the convention was filled with floor fights over provisions of the platform; behind-the-scenes efforts to dump Goldwater; loud, spiteful, disrespectful booing of Nelson Rockefeller as he tried to speak to the delegates; harsh treatment of people believed to be anti–Goldwater people; and obvious disharmony that led Goldwater to believe he lost the election even before he was formally nominated.

In 1964, Congress passed and President Johnson signed into law a civil rights bill that provided equal access for all Americans to most public accommodations. Barry Goldwater was one of the few senators to vote against it, not because he was against racial equality but because he thought some of its provisions were unconstitutional. Nonetheless, his vote was ammunition not only for Democrats but for liberals within his own party.

The Goldwater forces at the convention made sure his opponents and the rest of America knew where they stood on the issue. Delegates voted down a proposed platform plank that, in effect, would have endorsed the Civil Rights Act. They also rejected a proposal denouncing "extremism." This was the plank proposed by Rockefeller that drew the jeers of the delegates.

A byproduct of the convention's attitude on civil rights was displayed in two ugly ways. Broadcaster John Chancellor, covering the convention for NBC, said he personally witnessed shabby, almost criminal treatment of black people attending the convention.

He said he came across an elderly black delegate, leaning against a back wall, weeping. When Chancellor asked him what the trouble was, he pointed to the suit he was wearing. "The Goldwater delegates had put their cigarettes out all over his suit," said Chancellor. "There were certainly some nasty edges to that convention."[7]

At one point in the convention, security officers, at the behest of Goldwater's supporters, demanded that the aisles be cleared and began to forcibly move people to outside the convention arena. Chancellor was on the air, live, when security people picked him up and carried him out. "This is John Chancellor reporting from somewhere in custody," he told his audience as he disappeared from view.[8]

Jackie Robinson, the Hall of Fame baseball star who in 1947 became the first black major league ballplayer, was a delegate to the convention and was appalled at what he witnessed.

Robinson later wrote that as the Republican Party began to swing philosophically toward Goldwater conservatism, he began to realize what life must have been like as a Jew in Hitler's Germany.

"A Barry Goldwater victory would insure that the GOP could be completely the white man's party," he wrote. "What happened at San Francisco when Senator Goldwater became the Republican standard-bearer confirmed my prediction."[9]

Robinson, one of a handful of black delegates at the convention, was there in support of Rockefeller. The abuse he saw directed at Rockefeller and anyone who did not support Goldwater surprised and disappointed him.

The man who withstood prejudice and hatred on the baseball diamond 17 years earlier, said, "That convention was one of the most unforgettable and frightening experiences of my life."[10]

The following pages will lead the reader on the trail to the convention—the emergence of the Draft Goldwater movement; the importance of knowing how each individual state selects its delegates; the significance of "favorite son" candidates as part of campaign strategy; the grueling nature of campaigning, from going from one town to another in the dead of winter; and the necessity of having an experienced staff that knows what it's doing in a national campaign.

It is a trail filled with improbables—the first woman candidate for president, Senator Margaret Chase Smith of Maine; the unannounced and yet potent candidacy of Henry Cabot Lodge who was 10,000 miles away and never campaigned; the carefully planned emergence of "favorite son" candidates in Ohio, Pennsylvania and other states; cross-over voting in Wisconsin that allowed Democrats to vote in a Republican primary; arbitrary counting of write-in votes in Illinois; the requirement in Oregon for men and women to sign declarations of candidacy, forcing them to be on the ballot or be ignored.

Successful candidates had to know the nuances of each state—and each state had them—or face almost certain defeat at state conventions or primary elections.

New terms became part of the American political vocabulary—"stop light issues" in small-town America; "me-too-ism," which is how conservatives branded the philosophy of liberal Republicans; "choices" rather than "echoes" which is how conservatives believed their philosophy was different and superior to others; and "extremism," a word that was hung on Goldwater like a noose around his neck, a noose that he subsequently tightened by his own, often careless rhetoric.

All of this led up to nominating a person to potentially be the leader of the free world, perhaps the most powerful person in the world.

Goldwater did not speak reverently about the process of picking a president. "In no other nation on earth will you find anything comparable," he wrote. "It is a spectacle unsurpassed. Those uninformed, indifferent citizens emerge from their cocoons of apathy prodded by their fears of what one candidate might do to them and by their hope of what another candidate might do for them."[11]

The reader of the following pages is likely to conclude that, even at its best, politics can be aptly described as glorified sausage making. Herewith is the grinding of the Republicans in 1964.

Chapter 1

Thirty Words

It was all over before it had hardly begun. A moment of instant despair.

The people who had worked so hard to get this far were stunned.

Politics is often a shabby, unwholesome business with its only justification being that it is a means to an end. Whether the ends justify the means is a question in which the answer is the essence of democracy because the citizens, through their votes, provide the answer. That makes the system tolerable to the public and admired in many parts of the world.

Nomination of men or women to be the leaders of the free world is part of that process, and the person who receives that honor has the opportunity, through his or her acceptance speech, to energize the party and the nation, unite them by espousing common goals and the ways to achieve them, to proclaim the importance of working together to defeat the candidate of the other party.

The speech offers the opportunity for the candidate to lead an optimistic march to the future.

In 1900, President William McKinley, nominated for a second term, touched on both domestic and foreign policy challenges, saying, "We have been moving in untried paths but our steps have been guided by honor and duty. There will be no turning aside, no wavering, no retreat."

Twenty years later, Republican nominee Warren Harding stressed the importance not only of America's strength but of its honor when he told delegates, "The Republic can never be unmindful of its power and must never forget the force of its example."

Dwight Eisenhower told the convention in 1952 how important it was for Republican contenders to mend fences and work together in unity for the cause they all believed in and said he appreciated the words of support from Senator Robert Taft of Ohio and Governor Earl Warren of California who had opposed his nomination.

Then Eisenhower offered these words of encouragement to the party and to the country: "Where ever I am, I will end each day of the coming campaign thinking of millions of American hones, large and small; of fathers and mothers working and sacrificing to make sure that their children are well cared for free from fear, full of good hope for the future, proud citizens of a country that will stand among the nations as the leader of a peaceful and prosperous world."

Barry Goldwater had that opportunity on the night of July 16, 1964, and his speech had moments of optimism and enthusiasm. But a half-century later, it is remembered best for 30 ominous words.

Speaking to thousands of excited, cheering delegates as he accepted the Republican presidential nomination at the Cow Palace in San Francisco, there was a need for some encouraging words, ones that would heal the wounds of a deeply divided Republican party.

The task was going to be tough enough in the fall, trying to defeat President Lyndon Johnson, who had been thrust into office nine months earlier upon the assassination of President John F. Kennedy. Would the American public, in many ways still reeling from the tragic events of November 22, 1963, be willing to have a third president in the space of about a year?

The nominating process of the Republican and Democratic parties couldn't have been more different in 1964. The Democrats had the president, Lyndon Baines Johnson, who had taken over in tragedy and now was looking forward to a convention that he envisioned as being a coronation of sorts, a political lovefest for the man who took the reins for a nation in shock.

Republicans were still licking their wounds politically from their narrow loss in the 1960 presidential election in which Kennedy defeated Vice President Richard Nixon. They were deeply divided as conservative, moderate and liberal candidates emerged for the next presidential election. In some cases, the rancor was often on public display. They didn't like each other, they didn't trust each other and they didn't hide their feelings. But, as always, much of the storm could be calmed by the words of the eventual winner of the nomination with his words of reconciliation in his acceptance speech.

It was not unusual after an acceptance speech for all the rivals during the campaign to join the candidate on stage and to join hands, at least figuratively, in a show of unity. It was not to happen on this night.

Elsewhere in the country on this day, Americans were going about their business, enjoying their morning coffee, going to work, reading their newspapers, mowing their lawns, putting hamburgers on the grill and perhaps talking politics with their neighbors over the fence post.

Little League baseball was incorporated by federal charter in Congress on this day, while in the Major Leagues, Ernie Broglio, recently traded to the Chicago Cubs from the St. Louis Cardinals, was the winning pitcher in an 11–1 win over the New York Mets. Elsewhere in New York, three youngsters made national news when they gave police and their parents a vivid account of their encounter with a spaceman in a field near their home. *The New England Journal of Medicine* featured a story headlined, "Hazards to Health: The Puss Caterpillar, Alias Wooly Slug."

In the south, black Americans struggled to win basic rights afforded to white Americans. In Greenville, Mississippi, and surrounding towns, "Freedom Day" was held in which black citizens turned out in mass to register to vote. Few were allowed to register and 110 were arrested for trying. A month earlier, three civil rights workers had been murdered after they were ushered out of town by a sheriff's deputy who led them into the path of waiting Ku Klux Klan members.

Perhaps symbolically, the number one song in the country on July 16 was "Where Did Our Love Go?" by the Supremes, a trio of black women from Detroit, while the Beatles, the British singing sensation, were near the top of the charts with "Hard Day's Night."

This was all part of the backdrop of life in America as Barry Goldwater took to the podium in the Cow Palace to accept his party's nomination for president.

It had been a raucous convention—some said the most uproarious since 1912—with bitter disputes between conservatives led by Goldwater and the old-guard Eastern Establishment liberals such as New York's governor Nelson Rockefeller, who was booed and jeered so loudly earlier in the week when he tried to address the convention that he could not be heard above the noise of the crowd.

Political infighting is common at conventions as professional politicians and delegates do everything they can to round up votes for their candidates. But when the nominating process is over and a candidate is chosen, the combatants usually rally behind the winner—and the winner does his best to rally the troops, put aside past transgressions and be united in the effort to elect a president.

Mahatma Gandhi, the Indian theologian and philosopher of a generation past, said eloquently, "A small body of determined spirits fired by an unquenchable faith in their mission, can alter the course of history." Such is the stuff that American political campaigns are capable of being.

And on that hot night in San Francisco, with the bright glare of television lights shining on him, and red, white and blue balloons bouncing around him, after having been introduced by Nixon, Goldwater began his speech in traditional form.

"From this moment, united and determined, we will go forward together, dedicated to the ultimate and undeniable greatness of the whole man," he said, and the crowd roared its approval. "And I promise you tonight that every fiber of my being is consecrated to our cause, that nothing shall be lacking from the struggle that can be brought to it by enthusiasm, by devotion and plain hard work."

He had begun, as so many had done before him, by extolling the greatness of America and its people and his pledge to work unceasingly to move America forward. He then spent several minutes chastising the Democrats and particularly the Lyndon Johnson administration, calling them "false prophets" of freedom as he identified what he thought separated Democrats from Republicans in this election year.

The language was curt, in typical Goldwater style, but the message was predictable for a presidential candidate—patriotic and purposeful in promoting common goals and unity within the party.

Then, toward the end of the speech, Goldwater seemingly could not help himself from taking a jab at the moderate and liberal wings of his own party, the very people whom he needed to invite and welcome and invigorate.

"I would remind you," he told the delegates in the Cow Palace and millions watching on television, "that extremism in the defense of liberty is no vice. And let me remind you also that moderation in the pursuit of justice is no virtue."

Goldwater's handlers had worked for months to try to shed the extremist image that Democrats, some Republicans and the media had bestowed upon him because of his caustic, shoot-from-the-hip comments that did more damage than good in terms of advancing a candidacy.

He had voted against the civil rights bill earlier in the year, not because he was opposed to civil rights but because he questioned the constitutionality of some of its provisions. He was accused of being a warmonger and someone who would be quick to start a nuclear war. In short, he had been painted by his opponents, the media and by virtue of some of his own statements as an extremist—an image his aides worked day and night to refute.[1]

And now he had just given that very label not only legitimacy but something to be worn as a badge of honor.

Frederick Clifton White, who had organized the first group of Goldwater supporters three years earlier and built it into a nationwide movement, heard the speech from his trailer outside the Cow Palace, where he was carefully monitoring all activities inside and relaying instructions to Goldwater team members.

Senator Barry Goldwater won the Republican nomination but passed up the chance to unify the party in his acceptance speech (U.S. Senate).

White, known by everyone as simply "Clif," was stunned by his candidate's statement, which he said caught him totally by surprise. "This was the time for magnanimity, the time for building bridges across the gulfs that separated Republicans from one another and from countless thousands who were not Republicans and probably never would be. But now the magic moment had passed. There would be no recapturing it."[2]

As the delegates cheered wildly, White said he wondered if they realized they were reveling in the outskirts of pending disaster. "With those fateful words, 'extremism in the defense of liberty is no vice,' Senator Goldwater had seemed to identify himself with the very groups that the public had been led to believe would drive us into nuclear war with world Communism."[3]

"Why had Goldwater turned his back on millions of Americans who would be needed to win the presidency? To the Americans who had previously viewed Goldwater as a 'kook' or simply misguided, this one phrase seemed to confirm their every fear of his vision for America."[4]

The national media had a feast chewing on what Goldwater had fed them. James Reston, veteran reporter and columnist for the *New York Times*, wrote, "If extremism in the defense of liberty is no vice, then surely the Negro extremists are justified in their civil disobedience. And if moderation in the pursuit of justice is no virtue, then obviously, Negro moderate leaders are to be condemned."[5]

The *Washington Post* said in an editorial, "If a party so committed were to gain public office in this country, there would be nothing left for us to do but pray."[6]

Historian Robert Novak, reporting on the convention, said Goldwater had several chances to extend the olive branch to disgruntled Republicans. "But Goldwater did not. For the first time in memory at a contested convention, the victor had no words of kindness or praise for the vanquished.... These words shattered the last flickering hope that party unity would come out of San Francisco."[7]

Even the conservative publication *National Review* chimed in, saying Goldwater would have been better off doing the cautious thing instead of providing such a big bulls'-eye for his opponents.

White said later there was some confusion and disagreement as to who wrote what instantly became the two infamous lines in the speech. But Steve Shadegg, a close Goldwater adviser said the way the acceptance speech was written, by a handful of writers and editors, "produced a document that became a pattern in the Goldwater campaign, a series of ideas and phrases gathered together until all unity of thought and style was completely destroyed."[8]

By some accounts, Harry Jaffa, a political science professor at Claremont College, is said to have inserted the extremism phrase into a speech that was crafted by Karl Hess but Jaffa said later the speech was "my work from beginning to end."[9]

For all the clamor over 30 words, the idea that sprung them was not original. Almost 200 years earlier, Thomas Paine wrote, in *Rights of Man*, "A thing moderately good is not so good as it ought to be. Moderation in temper is always a virtue, but moderation in principle is always a vice." In a letter to Clif White years later, Jaffa acknowledged Paine's contribution to the speech, saying "Neither I nor Aristotle could have said it any better."[10]

Paine was writing at the time of the American revolution. The ardent followers of Senator Goldwater two centuries later thought they too were on the cusp of a revolution.

In some parts of San Francisco that night, after the crowds had

1. Thirty Words 17

left the convention center, now strewn with broken balloons, crumpled banners and all manner of trash, a group on a street corner could be heard singing in unison, "We Shall Overcome."

In contrast, historian Theodore White said when he left the Cow Palace and returned to his hotel room, he was awakened in the middle of the night by Goldwater supporters jubilantly singing "Dixie."

It had been that kind of a night, an omen of sorts of what would become the ongoing struggle to get everybody singing from the same song book.[11]

A reporter in the press gallery may have summed it up best when, reacting to those 30 words he had just heard in the acceptance speech, he turned to the person next to him and said, "My God, he's running as Barry Goldwater."[12]

Chapter 2

A Tale of Two Tafts

Don't trust anyone.

That was the message Clif White sought to convey to the hundreds of delegates from around the country arriving in San Francisco in July of 1964 for the Republican National Convention.

With good reason.

Many of the delegates were professional politicians well-seasoned at both glad-handing and back-stabbing and making connections that would further their ambitions.

But others were political novices who worked in their hometown banks, bakeries and car dealerships, came home after work and read the afternoon newspaper, had dinner with the family, and watched *Bonanza* or *The Fugitive* or *The Andy Griffith Show* on television. For many, their social life never strayed too far beyond the Chamber of Commerce annual dinner, the Rotary steak fry or having dessert with friends after Wednesday night Bible study.

They had a genuine patriotic spirit about them. Some dressed in red, white and blue, and many waved tiny American flags and wore campaign buttons attached with pins to their coat lapels, shirts and blouses. Their goal was to take part in the ultimate political experience—nominating the candidate they believed would be the next president of the United States—and they were going to have a good time too.

For them, it was exciting to see the sights on the streets of San Francisco, to ride the cable cars, shop for souvenirs and travel across the Golden Gate bridge. At the convention hall, they could catch a glimpse of some of their heroes—maybe former President Dwight D. Eisenhower or Senator Barry Goldwater of Arizona or Governor Nelson Rockefeller of New York or Senator Everett Dirksen of Illinois, or maybe even Ronald Reagan, the movie star or Jackie Robinson, the ex-ballplayer who in 1947 became the first black man to play Major League baseball.

The delegates were there to take part in history, yes, but they also wanted to grab as many "Kodak moments" as they could to take back home and share with their friends.[1]

The Republican National Committee had a full week of activities planned for them and provided pamphlets highlighting many festivities guests could enjoy when they weren't on the convention floor.

White, a veteran of four previous conventions, had worked for three years in preparing for this one, and an important part of the preparation was preparing the delegates, or, more to the point, warning them of all the political landmines they could step on.

H. L. Mencken said, "There is something about a national political convention that makes it as fascinating as a revival or a hanging ... a show so gaudy and hilarious, so melodramatic and obscene, so unimaginatively exhilarating and preposterous...."[2]

Candidates all promise they'll help citizens achieve the American dream. Meanwhile, some of their henchmen may be tapping telephones, bugging hotel rooms with hidden microphones and planting spies—people like waitresses, maids, bellhops, delivery people—anyone with easy access to politicians' hotel rooms who were willing to eavesdrop for a price.

There was only one goal in all of this—to collect information on delegates such as any debts they had, weaknesses in their character, skeletons in their closets, old boyfriends or girlfriends—any gems from their past that could be used as blackmail to get the delegate to back a particular candidate.

They could be humiliated publicly if word leaked out about some past indiscretions or were seen at the wrong place at the wrong time. In some cases, the delegates' jobs back home might be in jeopardy or they might be passed over for a promotion if they didn't support the "right" candidate or the "right" proposal on the convention floor.[3]

White had been a witness to past shenanigans—candidates receiving phony messages that the event at which they were to speak had been cancelled; cab drivers getting lost or having their cabs break down, preventing candidates from public appearances where they were expected. Anything to make an opposing candidate look bad. In politics, publicly, there are rules of discretion. Privately, there are none.

"Clif White was a seasoned professional, as wily a political genius as was likely to be found anywhere, one who knew every dirty trick in the book and then some, and yet he scrupulously restrained from using any of them, even in the face of extreme provocation."[4]

He knew how the political game was played and he didn't want anything to get in the way of a project he had been working on for so long, to elevate Goldwater, who 16 years earlier had been running his father's department store in Phoenix, as the next president.

White, 46, was a would-be politician who found his niche as a backroom wheeler-dealer, someone more comfortable as a king maker than as king. He was born in upstate New York and attended Cornell University with a goal of becoming a history teacher. But he was drawn to politics when he became involved in housing issues in Ithaca, urging the City Council there to give breaks to veterans seeking affordable housing.

He became a political disciple of New York Governor Thomas E. Dewey, twice an unsuccessful Republican candidate for president. White's only attempt at seeking public office was when he ran for Congress and lost decisively in the Republican primary. It was then "White recognized his abilities lie in backroom politics [a phrase he used without reservation] rather than as a candidate."[5]

White understood what hardball politics was all about because he had been on the receiving end of it a few times. As a young man, he helped form a chapter of the American Veterans Committee, an advocacy group for veterans in which he led the fight to try to get government assistance for veterans in getting home loans. He became a statewide organizer for the organization and decided to run for state chairman. Prior to balloting at the state convention, opponents spread the rumor that White, a married man, was having an affair with his secretary and was using veterans' committee funds to finance his dalliances.

Anyone who knew Clif White could have assured the veterans that the rumor was preposterous. White was a tall, shy, straitlaced, morally pure individual, whose attire most often included a bow tie, whose friends compared him to Jimmy Stewart, the wholesome movie star with the "gee whiz" personality and the *Mr. Smith Goes to Washington* approach to life.[6]

When Gus Tyler, White's floor manager at the veterans convention, realized what was happening, he withdrew White as a candidate to spare him further embarrassment and offered up someone else in his place. So White didn't lose the election but he lost his political innocence. He learned some valuable lessons on how, in politics, anything goes, and to not stake your future in the trust you place in others.

Tyler offered advice on how to handle adversaries. "Learn from them," he said. "I've been fighting these bastards for a long time. The first thing you need to know is whom you can trust, who will stand up with you, and who you can work with."[7]

Those were the days of Communist threats in America—some perceived, some real—that in few years would usher in the McCarthy era in which U.S. Senator Joseph McCarthy, a Wisconsin Republican, used Senate hearings as a platform to recklessly accuse many Americans in government work as being Communists or having Communist leanings.

F. Clifton "Clif" White was the man behind the plan of the Draft Goldwater movement that resulted in the most successful grassroots draft movement in American history (Ashbrook Center Archives, F. Clifton White Collection, Ashland University, Ashland, Ohio).

Communists were said to have tried to take over the American Veterans Committee—and one way to do that was to stop Clif White from becoming its chairman. Heeding Gus Tyler's advice to learn from them, White not only felt the sting of a political dirty trick but, more important in the long run, he witnessed the method through which the enemy grew. Communists organized by forming cells, small groups, each loyal to a cause and to a leader, and as the cells multiplied, the cause never changed and the loyalty grew until it was one unified effort. It was a lesson he remembered for the rest of his career in backroom politics.

White recalled only too well the convention of 1952 when political maneuvering wrested the nomination from "Mr. Republican," Senator Robert Taft of Ohio, and handed it to General Dwight D. Eisenhower, whom White supported, a war hero who never before had sought public office.

Taft, whose father, William Howard Taft, had been president a half-century earlier, was more eager to be president than his father had been,

Senator Robert Taft is shown in his office in 1952. On the mantle in the background is a photograph of his father, President William Howard Taft (Library of Congress).

and had sought the nomination twice before. In 1952, he had substantial delegate strength going into the convention but the Eisenhower forces challenged the credentials of his delegates in several southern states.

"The manic haggling for delegates took place in rooms that were filled with cigar smoke, whiskey, filthy spittoons and sweaty deal makers."[8]

The Credentials Committee approved the Taft slates but when they came to a full vote on the convention floor, the Eisenhower challenges prevailed. By a 607–531 roll call vote, delegates rejected the Taft slates in Georgia and Texas. The result was that what had been a 17–0 Taft margin in Georgia became a 14–3 Eisenhower majority. In Texas, the shift went from 22–16 for Taft to 33–5 for Eisenhower. With those changes, the Eisenhower bandwagon was rolling and the general won the nomination.[9]

The Eisenhower forces, of course, believed justice had been served whereas the Taft contingent believed they had been swindled.

The battle for delegates on the convention floor was ugly, with some delegates pushing and shoving one another, others vocally showing disdain for their fellow Republicans. At one point, Senator Everett Dirksen of Illinois, speaking from the podium, pointed to Dewey in the New York delegation and shouted, "You led us down the road to defeat twice." He was voicing conservative disrespect for the Eastern Establishment branch of the party and that same rancor would last for years.

Clif White was there. He witnessed what happened. He wanted to make sure there would be no such "stolen delegates" in 1964. He had worked too hard and for too long to get them. He went so far as to set up a "buddy system" in which he tried to arrange to have pairs of delegates stay in the same hotel room, dine together and socialize together—a kind of built-in accountability system to help prevent a delegate from being swayed by opposing forces.[10]

The Republican Party had been struggling for a generation to find one voice, to act in concert as one party capable of captivating the soul of the American voting public. Democrats had controlled the White House for all but eight of the last 32 years, with Republicans electing only one president during that time, Eisenhower for two terms.

Franklin D. Roosevelt defeated President Herbert Hoover in 1932 and won re-election over Governor Alf Landon of Kansas in 1936, Wendell Wilkie of Indiana in 1940 and Dewey in 1944. Dewey ran again in 1948 and narrowly lost to Roosevelt's successor, Harry Truman.

The conservative wing of the Republican Party was convinced the losses were due to what they called "me too" candidates—Republicans who shared many of the views of liberal Democrats. "Me-too-ism" would play a big part in the race for the 1964 Republican presidential nomination as well.[11]

The division within the Republican Party that would soon be played out on the convention floor in 1964 as it had with the Eisenhower-Taft foray in 1952 actually had its roots in a convention about a half-century earlier when Taft's father, President William Howard Taft, was nominated for a second term. He had been President Theodore Roosevelt's close friend for 20 years, served in his cabinet and was Roosevelt's hand-picked candidate to succeed him in 1908.

But Taft, a former judge who later would serve on the Supreme Court, was more conservative than Teddy Roosevelt and had the highest respect for the judicial system in which he had so ably served. Roosevelt was aggressive and preferred to run roughshod over the courts to accomplish his purposes.

"Taft had nothing but disdain for his predecessor's jaundiced view of the judiciary. 'The regret which he [Theodore Roosevelt] certainly expressed that the court had the power to set aside statutes was an attack on our system at the very point I think it is strongest,' wrote Taft."[12]

Historians have pointed out that Theodore Roosevelt always sought public office but public office always sought William Howard Taft. In Taft's long career of public service, the only office he ever ran for was for president.

There were other sore points that shattered the once strong early 1900s Roosevelt-Taft relationship, including some of Taft's appointments and dismissals, one of which was the removal of Gifford Pinchot, one of Roosevelt's closest friends, as chief forester.

Roosevelt, who went on an African safari after he left office to remove himself from politics, was eager to get back to it when he returned as he became more and more disenchanted with his successor. In 1912, he decided to challenge Taft at the convention and once again become the Republican nominee for president. He appeared to have enough delegate strength but the Republican National Committee, controlled by Taft, awarded enough delegates to the sitting president to guarantee his nomination.

An incensed Roosevelt claimed the nomination was stolen from him. He bolted from the Republican Party and ran as a third party candidate on the Progressive or "Bull Moose" ticket. In the November election, Republicans divided their votes between Roosevelt and Taft, thereby handing the election to Democrat Woodrow Wilson. Taft, the incumbent president, actually finished third.[13]

"The convention was not Armageddon but to observers it seemed a close second," wrote William Allen White, the famous Kansas editor. He looked down from the press tables 'into the human caldron that was boiling all around me.'"[14]

With the obvious deep division within, "the Republican Party was descending into minority status, a party that could go to its right but not to its left. That rightward movement was adequate for survival during the post World War I reaction. But when the nation demanded a leftward movement during the Depression, the party of Theodore Roosevelt was immobile."[15]

When Theodore Roosevelt's fifth cousin, Franklin D. Roosevelt, a

Democrat, swept into office during the Depression and offered New Deal policies to heal the nation's wounds, Democrats became the majority party in the United States for the first time in 80 years.[16]

Republicans seemed transfixed in conservatism while the public thirsted for liberalism. And it elected Democratic presidents in 1932, 1936, 1940, 1944 (Roosevelt) and 1948 (Truman). Republicans broke through in 1952, not because of a resurgent conservative movement but because their candidate was a war hero who would have won the election as either a Republican or a Democrat.

Theodore Roosevelt ran as a third party candidate against William Howard Taft in 1913. Republicans were so divided in their vote that Democrat Woodrow Wilson was elected (Library of Congress).

"The break between President Taft and Colonel Roosevelt, the causes of which were never fully explained ... had far-reaching consequences, and the scars of the conflict that was cause for the formation of the National Progressive Party [Bull Moose], under the leadership of Roosevelt in 1912, still remain."[17]

Years later, with the defeat of another Republican presidential candidate, Eisenhower's vice president, Richard Nixon, in 1960, Clif White, the man who reveled in working behind the scenes, decided to mount a conservative movement that was so well conceived, so well planned and so strong in numbers, that it could not be stopped.

It would start with a single cell group with purpose and loyalty being two of the core values, and it would grow not only in numbers but in influence. At least, that was the plan.

Chapter 3

Filling the Vacuum

On Tuesday, November 8, 1960, Senator John F. Kennedy of Massachusetts, the Democrat, defeated incumbent Vice President Richard Nixon in one of the closest presidential races in American history, so close in fact that Nixon did not concede until noon the next day.

Kennedy, who became the nation's first Roman Catholic president, had to convince skeptical voters during the campaign that the Pope would not be running the country in absentia. He also had to shrug off persistent rumors that his father, millionaire Joseph P. Kennedy, had used his wealth to procure votes for his son. A standing joke at the time, which Republicans saw little humor in, was the notion that Joe Kennedy said to his son, "How many votes do you need, Jack? I'm not going to pay for a landslide."[1]

Many things factored into the Nixon defeat. He came across poorly in the nation's first nationally televised debate between the presidential candidates, looking pale, sweaty and sickly compared to Kennedy's tanned skin and calm, cool demeanor. There was also President Eisenhower's less than enthusiastic support for his two-time running mate.[2]

Also, many within the Republican Party felt Nixon had aligned himself too much with the "me-too" philosophy in which he honored principles that did not separate him enough from Democrats. He was perceived as trying to be in synch with the Eastern Establishment old guard moderate-to-liberal Republicans while at the same time attempting to woo Southerners who were unlikely to vote for any Republican under any circumstances.

Moderate and conservative Republicans were incensed when they learned that Nixon had met with Governor Nelson Rockefeller of New

York—Mr. Me-Too, Eastern Establishment in the minds of many—not long before the convention and that Rockefeller had persuaded Nixon to back some of Rockefeller's positions on the GOP platform.

Washington reporter and columnist Robert Novak, in his 1965 book, *The Agony of the GOP 1964*, writes succinctly, "Nixon attempted to appeal to both the left and right wings in a party that is more deeply divided than it cares to admit. Nixon made a bad job of it. He failed to satisfy either faction."[3]

Novak contended Republicans were unsatisfied with Nixon almost from the time he was nominated but were duty-bound to support their candidate.

"Behind-the-back criticism was the order of the day in the Republican Party. Everybody was doing it, including the two leaders who symbolized the opposite poles of the Republican Party: Governor Nelson Rockefeller of New York on the Republican left and Senator Barry Goldwater of Arizona on the Republican right."[4]

Nixon's defeat and the widening division within the Republican Party created a vacuum of leadership that further diminished its influence and prospects for the immediate future.

"The narrow defeat of Richard Nixon in November of 1960 left no apparent heir for the nomination in 1964. Both the liberals and conservatives in the Republican party argued that if Nixon had just followed their advice, he could have easily defeated Kennedy."[5]

J. William Middendorf, who would later play a major role in the Goldwater campaign, described the Republican dilemma this way: "They saw a leadership vacuum in the Republican Party—gentrification at the top—superannunated officials out of touch with the present, let alone the future."[6]

Historically, a basic difference between Democrats and Republicans is that Democrats believe government is an instrument to help the people whereas Republicans believe in more individual responsibility and less government intervention into the lives of citizens.

"Democrats are the party that guarantees government will do things. The Republicans impossible dilemma is that they have never sorted out properly what it is that government should and should not do, and at what level."[7]

Historians trace the problem all the way back to the 1912 rift between Taft and Roosevelt, then moving through the New Deal years when the Democrats pushed through one government program after another and the Republicans had no answer, and advancing to the 1960s squabble between the so-called "me too" politics of the Eastern Establishment and the Robert Taft–brand conservatism.

"In their attempt year after year to solve this dilemma, the Republicans confuse one another and the nation, and, in defeat, distill a bitterness among themselves greater than their bitterness against the Democrats."[8]

That's where the party found itself after the Nixon defeat in 1960 with no clear leader for the future.

Political vacuums don't last long because of what they represent: opportunity. Just as a fledgling local politician sees the chance to jump in when there is an open seat on the City Council or Board of Supervisors, national politicians are quick to spot openings at their level. "Political nature abhors a vacuum. Somebody is certain to try to move into it."[9]

But who would it be? To understand the dynamics of potential Republican Party leadership after the Nixon defeat, it is necessary to assess the motivations of its primary movers and shakers.

There was Rockefeller, a liberal Republican who wanted to be president almost from the moment he became governor of New York in 1958. There was Goldwater, a conservative senator from Arizona who never really wanted to be president except to see conservative principles prevail. There was Nixon who would not object to being nominated again but would have to wait in the wings, a convention deadlock being his only real chance. There was George Romney, governor of Michigan, who could have been a moderate alternative to Goldwater or Rockefeller—except that he wasn't especially well liked by moderates. There was Henry Cabot Lodge, Nixon's vice presidential candidate, former senator, former ambassador to the United Nations, and now an ambassador overseas—a man from a prestigious Massachusetts political family with a glossy resume but who was out of the country and not active in party politics. And there was Pennsylvania Governor William Scranton, a popular Republican but a johnny-come-lately in presidential politics.

"Rockefeller emerged as the most likely Republican candidate for 1964. He possessed all the qualities the Eastern Establishment wanted: he was rich, internationalist and liberal. The old Dewey Republicans thought it was just a matter of time before Rockefeller took his rightful place as the Republican nominee."[10]

Clif White had a front row seat to the Republican circus. He had been around a long time, had seen the party go down twice with Dewey and win with Eisenhower, whom White had supported and worked for, but who made conservatives nervous. Instead of shrinking government—a core value of conservatives—Eisenhower enlarged it with such actions as creating the Department of Health, Education and Welfare, a cabinet level department, and one more bureaucracy in Washington. Goldwater, in his typical caustic manner, referred to Eisenhower as a "dime store New Dealer." It was a typical candid comment from Goldwater. It stung Eisenhower and contributed to the less-than-warm relationship he had with the senator.

"The Eisenhower that emerged after the 1952 elections forced conservatives to sharpen their perceptions of themselves and to understand their own limitations. The debate between Eisenhower and conservatives came over the president's unwillingness to dismantle the New Deal and Fair Deal programs of FDR and Truman."[11]

Eisenhower was by no means a liberal but "the core of his social program was to bring the American people to what he considered a 'legitimate center,'" which did not sit well with conservatives.[12]

But now there was a Democrat in the White House once again, and from White's perspective, the country was in big trouble. Not long after Kennedy took office, the new commander in chief, with the reputation of being a naval hero in World War II, oversaw the botched Bay of Pigs invasion that was intended to help liberate Cuba from the dominance of Communist dictator Fidel Castro but instead was an embarrassment to the U.S. government.

The Bay of Pigs fiasco actually was planned during the Eisenhower administration. Kennedy was briefed on it after his election in 1960 and was responsible for carrying it out. Fidel Castro led the overthrow of Cuban dictator Fulgencio Batista in 1959 and instituted policies in which the Cuban government confiscated private property, including some owned by Americans; established economic and diplomatic ties with Communist countries; and attempted to start revolutions in several Latin American countries to try to engineer Communist takeovers. Castro's renegade policies in a country 90 miles from the U.S. border were a cause of concern.

In the U.S., the Central Intelligence Agency, with Eisenhower's approval, developed a plan in which Cuban exiles, trained in the U.S. and backed by U.S. air support, were to invade Cuba at several ports, including the Bay of Pigs. They were to be joined in the invasion by Cuban militants who opposed Castro. The air support was faulty and weak and the Cuban military easily overtook the exiles and took 1,400 prisoners.

It was a huge embarrassment to the Kennedy administration, which found itself negotiating for the release of the prisoners—a situation Senator Goldwater described as the "disgusting spectacle of Americans groveling before a cheap, dirty dictator."[13]

There were also troubling policies in Southeast Asia in a little country called Vietnam that was in danger of Communist takeover. Kennedy authorized sending military "advisers" to South Vietnam with the hope that American involvement could be kept at a minimum which, as history has shown, did not turn out to be the case.

White saw what was happening with U.S. foreign policy under the Democrats and at the same time was distressed by the lack of leadership and unity in his own party to do anything about it. He felt compelled to try to come up with an answer.

At about the same time, William Rusher, a writer and editor from New York, and John Ashbrook, a congressman from Ohio, who knew each other from their days of being leading members of the Young Republicans for Freedom, had another concern. They had been aggressive conservative leaders in the Young Republicans but the organization, in its most recent election, had turned the leadership over to men who did not share the same principles as Rusher and Ashbrook.

Rusher, 38, publisher of the *National Review*, a leading conservative periodical run by William F. Buckley, was a native Chicagoan whose family moved to New York when he was a youngster. He did his undergraduate work at Princeton and earned a law degree from Harvard. His next stop was Wall Street, representing some influential companies and individuals.

He had become interested in Republican politics in his days at Princeton and stayed politically active through organizations such as the Young Republicans. But instead of falling in line with the Eastern Establishment traditional Republican liberal politics, his political leanings became more and more conservative. In 1957, he made efforts to become the legal counsel for oil interests owned by the family of Buckley, one of the nation's best known conservatives. He didn't get the job representing the oil company. Buckley had another job for him. He asked him to be publisher of the *National Review* and Rusher accepted the position, solidifying his place as a staunch conservative.[14]

Ashbrook, five years younger than Rusher, was from Ohio and, as the son of an Ohio congressman, grew up with politics as part of the family dinner table conversation. He studied law at Ohio State University and spent some time as legal counsel to the state attorney general.

Similar to Rusher, Ashbrook got a chance to get involved with journalism and became publisher of his father's weekly newspaper in his home town of Johnston and also published three other weekly papers. All the while, he immersed himself in Republican politics, eventually becoming president of the national Young Republican organization.

Unlike Rusher, Ashbrook had firsthand knowledge and experience in state and national politics, being the son of a congressman, having served two terms in the Ohio state legislature and being elected to the U.S. House in 1960.[15]

On July 10, 1961, Rusher went to Washington to meet with Ashbrook and talk about ways they could make sure their conservative cronies would stay loyal to the cause, and, more important, be poised for the challenges that lied ahead. As they ate lunch in the House dining room in the Capitol building, one thing led to another and Rusher remarked that their old friends in the Young Republicans probably made up one of the biggest segments of the Republican party, yet had failed to exercise any real influence.

After lunch, they went to Ashbrook's office and continued their conversation. At some point, Ashbrook opened a file cabinet and pulled out a folder of names, addresses and phone numbers of Republicans from all over the country who he met and developed relationships with when he was president of the Young Republicans. "These people still know me," he told Rusher.[16]

Three days later, Rusher was back in New York and made arrangements to have lunch with White. As they dined at the Commodore Hotel above Grand Central Station, Rusher talked about his meeting with Ashbrook and about Ashbrook's file full of names and contact information. White mentioned that he had similar files not only from his days with the Young Republicans but from contacts he had made through his various activities with the Republican party as a whole. They talked about the possibility of merging their files and coming up with a list of Republicans from coast to coast who would be willing to become part of a grassroots conservative organization that might someday take charge of the Republican Party.

A few weeks later, White went to Washington to meet Charles Barr, a Chicago business executive who was also a conservative and a friend. He bounced the idea off of Barr about starting a conservative movement from the ground up because he knew his friend would tell him if it was a foolish idea. To the contrary, Barr told White to count him in.

In the next two months, White met with Rusher again to tell him of Barr's approval. He then met again with Ashbrook so they could take their merged list of conservatives and start culling it down to come up with a core group that could be counted on to be politically smart and trustworthy. It would be the beginning of putting the pieces of the puzzle together out of the glare of any media attention.

On September 7, White and Rusher worked into the night, painstakingly eliminating one name after another, for one reason or another, until they had pared the list down to 23. Including White, Rusher and Ashbrook, the core group would consist of 26 men.

While Goldwater remained reluctant to project himself into the spotlight, others were not hesitant to promote him. In June of 1961, seven months after the Nixon defeat and five months after President Kennedy was inaugurated, *Time* magazine featured Goldwater on its cover and in its cover story, gushed over the senator's rising popularity.

"Goldwater is the hottest political figure this side of Jack Kennedy. No Republican is more in demand. Goldwater's mail runs to a remarkable 800 pieces a day. Visitors crowd around Barry Goldwater's fourth floor suite in the Old Senate Office Building hoping to earn a passing handclasp or a hastily scrawled autograph."[17]

White, Rusher and Ashbrook all thought Goldwater was the ideal person to carry the flag for the conservative movement and be the Republican Party presidential candidate in 1964. His conservative credentials were impeccable.

A book, *The Conscience of a Conservative*, published in 1960, became the political Bible of the movement. The book credited Goldwater as being the author but it was actually written by L. Brent Bozell, one of Goldwater's speech writers and was, in fact, a collection of conservative thoughts on various topics such as education, state's rights, civil rights, welfare, foreign policy, government spending and the perils of power, culled from speeches Bozell had written for the Senator over the years. Years later, Clif White claimed there was a good chance Goldwater not only had not written the book but had not read the manuscript before it was published.

Nonetheless, the book espoused the Goldwater philosophy—the conservative philosophy: "I have little interest in streamlining government or in making it more efficient, for I mean to reduce its size.... My aim is not to pass laws but to repeal them. It is not to inaugurate new programs but to cancel old ones that do violence to the Constitution."[18]

3. Filling the Vacuum

He said he wanted to do away with laws that failed in their purpose and that he would first determine whether a law was constitutional and then determine whether it was needed.

"And if I should later be attacked for neglecting my constituents' interests, I shall reply that I was informed their main interest is liberty and that in that cause, I am doing the very best I can."[19]

The book was a runaway bestseller and firmly established Goldwater as the icon of conservatism, the Robert Taft of the '60s with respect to the national following he was developing but oozing with candor to get his points across. It was not in Goldwater's political nature to try to make people feel good or kowtow to those who disagreed with him, even within his own party.

Goldwater had given one of the speeches at the 1960 convention that nominated Nixon. In it, he said, "Let's grow up, conservatives. If

Clif White speaks to supporters of the Draft Goldwater movement while William Rusher, another of the early conservative leaders, watches in the background (Ashbrook Center Archives, F. Clifton White Collection, Ashland University, Ashland, Ohio).

we want to take this party back, and I think someday we can, let's get to work."

That was a clarion call for conservatives and Goldwater seemed an obvious standard-bearer who could provide Republicans with a strong, dynamic alternative to Rockefeller. Goldwater was more interested in advancing the movement, rather than promoting himself, while others, including White, Rusher and Ashbrook saw him as the answer to their conservative prayers.

"In Goldwater's actions and rhetoric, conservatives found validation for their belief that big government, created by The New Deal, was taking away individual liberty and replacing the rule of law by rule of men. These beliefs were sanctified by Goldwater's ardent anti-communism and the conviction that the nation must be returned to its philosophical foundation."[20]

White, Rusher and Ashbrook knew it was too early to back a candidate for 1964 even though Goldwater was the obvious choice. Too many things could happen in the next three years that could change the dynamics. And besides, Goldwater had made it clear he had no interest in being a presidential candidate.

He could discourage talk about him being a candidate but he could not or would not stop the movement that White, Rusher and Ashbrook wanted to start. And it did start, on October 8, 1961, in what historian Robert Novak was to call "one of the most remarkable clandestine meetings in American political history."[21]

Chapter 4

The Contenders

As White, Rusher and Ashbrook prepared for their first organizational meeting of what they envisioned would become a national tidal wave of conservative values, most Republicans sought to fill the vacuum left by Nixon's loss to Kennedy the traditional way—by taking a good look at potential candidates as they emerged over the next three years. And Goldwater was certainly among them, but he was not the only one.

Barry Morris Goldwater was a senator from Arizona who, in the early 1960s, was primarily known for two aspects of his personality—his conservative political views centered on strict adherence to the U.S. Constitution; and his off-the-cuff remarks, often witty, often brazen, often unconstructive.

He was born in 1909 and had lineage that included his grandfather, known as "Big Mike," a Jew who came to America from Poland and got involved in retail sales and politics. Young Barry Goldwater sometimes fell victim to anti-semitism because of his Jewish heritage. It is said he was once prohibited from playing golf at a private golf course because of his ancestry and asked the manager if he could just play nine holes because "I'm only half Jewish."[1]

Goldwater's father, Baron, and uncle, Morris, were heavy into Arizona politics. Morris was elected mayor of Prescott nine times and was someone young Barry admired for his tenacity in politics.

Big Mike started a department store in Phoenix that his son, Baron, eventually took over. When Baron died, Barry dropped out of the University of Arizona to take over the store. He was popular with the employees, providing advances on their paychecks when they needed them and bonuses for work well done.

Goldwater was a lifelong tinkerer at home and at his store. He loved gadgets and clever innovations and products. He developed a product line in men's underwear called "Antsy Pants"—boxer shorts with imprints of ants—that became a huge hit.

In 1948, he was elected to the Phoenix City Council. In 1950, he decided to run for governor and made an agreement with a political cohort, Howard Pyle, for each to support one another as Pyle intended to run in an upcoming race for the U.S. Senate. But Pyle upstaged Goldwater, allowing himself to be drafted as a candidate for governor. He eventually ran and lost. It was an early lesson in the frailty of political loyalty for Goldwater.

The next year, Senator Everett McKinley Dirksen of Illinois came to Phoenix for a speaking engagement. Dirksen was one of the icons of the Senate and easy to spot with his curly, often unkempt hair and his soft, mellow voice in which words seemed to roll out of his mouth like those of a midnight radio announcer. While in Phoenix, Dirksen met with Goldwater and urged him to run for the Senate the following year.

Goldwater decided to do it. Despite the support of people like Dirksen, who didn't live or vote in Arizona, the odds were against the young city councilman from Phoenix. He would be up against the incumbent Democrat, Senator Ernest McFarland, who was the minority leader of the Senate. Helped by the coattails of General Dwight Eisenhower at the top of the Republican ticket, Goldwater scored a stunning victory. Goldwater had shrugged off the thought of being an underdog in the race, claiming he could win "because I can call 10,000 people in this state by their first name."[2]

That win had major political significance that no one could have known at the time. With McFarland's defeat, Senator Lyndon Johnson was elected by his colleagues as Senate minority leader. When Democrats took over control of the Senate, he became majority leader and built up enormous political influence. He was elected vice president in 1960 and became president upon Kennedy's assassination. None of that probably would have occurred had not Goldwater defeated McFarland in 1952.[3]

The polar opposite of Goldwater was Governor Nelson Aldrich Rockefeller of New York, a liberal Republican who represented the Eastern Establishment "me too" philosophy that was abhorrent to moderates and liberals within the party.

Rockefeller was the grandson of John D. Rockefeller, one of the nation's first billionaires, and while he was growing up, young Nelson was the beneficiary of the family fortune in most everything he did. Financially, he never had a worry.

Goldwater had respect for Rockefeller but not for his political philosophy. He considered him a charming, urbane person who was a good public speaker and an excellent politician. "But he was the spokesman for an ideological grouping within the party which I call the 'Me Tooers.' They embraced most of the objectives of the New Deal and the Fair Deal and were asking for voter support on the claim Republicans could do it better and perhaps a little cheaper."[4]

Rockefeller was born in Bar Harbor, Maine, on July 8, 1908, and was named after his maternal grandfather, U.S. Senator Nelson W. Aldrich of Rhode Island. He was one of six children of John D. Rockefeller, Jr., and his wife, Abby Aldrich Rockefeller. He wanted to join his older brother John at Princeton but was not accepted. So he enrolled at Dartmouth, where he excelled, becoming president of the senior honor society and earning a Phi Beta Kappa key for academic excellence.

Shortly after graduation, Rockefeller married Mary Todhunter Clark and, for their honeymoon, took a trip around the world. Armed with a degree in economics from Dartmouth, Rockefeller set out into the work world as a clerk at the Chase National Bank in New York (now known as Chase Manhattan). Before long, he got involved in the family businesses, serving as the rental agent for what was then the new Rockefeller Center in the heart of Manhattan.

Later, he worked for another family company, Creole Petroleum Co. This job required him to make many trips to Venezuela where he learned firsthand about the problems of people living in Latin American countries; this experience forged many of his views on American foreign policy.

He had occasion to meet President Franklin D. Roosevelt when Roosevelt was in New York for a museum dedication. Rockefeller talked to the president briefly about his concerns of growing Nazi presence in South America. The president was impressed with Rockefeller's knowledge and passion. It led to Roosevelt's naming him to a new government position, coordinator of Inter-American Affairs.

He served on advisory boards for President Harry S Truman, primarily related to help with under-developed nations. He was also active with domestic policy and with Republican administrations. When President Eisenhower created the Department of Health, Education and Welfare, he appointed Rockefeller as an undersecretary.

Rockefeller enjoyed the opportunity to help others through work with federal programs but came to the conclusion he could have far more impact as an elected official. In 1958, he ran for governor of New York and defeated the incumbent Democrat, W. Averill Harriman, the multimillionaire son of a railroad tycoon. Because of the personal fortunes of both candidates, the race became known as the "Battle of the Millionaires." His victory established him as a future major player in Republican politics.[5]

Unlike Goldwater, who was a reluctant candidate more interested in advancing the conservative movement than becoming president, Rockefeller wanted the presidency passionately, not only to promote his political agenda but also because it would be something he would have to earn rather than something bestowed upon him because of his wealth.

Once, while flying over Washington, D.C., in one of his family's planes, someone asked him when he first thought about running for president. He said, "Ever since I was a kid. After all, when you think of what I had, what else was there to aspire to?"[6]

Michigan Governor George Romney, like Rockefeller, was a man of extraordinary wealth. Unlike Rockefeller, he wasn't born with it. George Wilcken Romney was born in Chihuahua, Mexico, in 1907. His parents were devout Mormons, a characteristic their son carried on for his entire life. His parents were American citizens and, though they were not polygamists, they joined other Mormons in moving to Mexico after Congress passed a law outlawing polygamy in the United States 20 years before George Romney was born.

They moved back to the United States when Romney was a child and he grew up in Idaho and Utah. He enrolled in several colleges but never earned a degree. True to his faith, he served two years as a Mormon missionary in England and Scotland. When he returned to the United States, he worked in Washington, D.C., and got his first taste of politics and its inner workings when he worked as a speech writer for Massachusetts Senator David Walsh and later as a lobbyist for the aluminum industry and for the American Automobile Association.

He became interested in the automobile industry and went to work for the Nash-Kelvinator Corporation in 1948. In 1954, Nash-Kelvinator merged with the Hudson Motor Car Company and was renamed American Motors. By that time, Romney had developed an extensive working knowledge of the industry from the standpoint of both labor and management because of his days as a lobbyist and his experience working for Nash-Kelvinator. He was named president of the newly formed American Motors. He helped the company become successful with the development of the Nash Rambler. It was a small car compared to its competitors but it was marketed as more efficient and cost-saving because it was not a "gas guzzler."

By this time, Romney was married, had a family and was living in Michigan where he became heavily involved in civic affairs, including the formation of a political group called Citizens for Michigan. In 1962, he decided to take a leap into politics by running for governor. True to his faith once again, he made the decision only after a time of prayer and fasting.[7]

Running as a Republican, and, unusual for a GOP candidate, appealing for the vote of organized labor, Romney defeated John R. Swainson, the Democratic incumbent. In a relatively short period of time, he not only was a dominant force in Michigan politics, he was looked on as a possible rising star in the Republican party nationally.

The national media made comparisons of Romney to Warren G. Harding because of his good looks, to French President Charles de Gaulle because of his sense of almost endowed leadership, to evangelist Billy Graham because of his faith that he expressed openly and unabashedly and to former President Dwight D. Eisenhower because of his charm and also his ability to sometimes lull his audiences to distraction with vague generalities about government policy.[8]

But he was quick to find out that running a state was not the same as running a company where a boss isn't always right, but he's always the boss. He had to learn to work with the state legislature to get things done and his background had not included much room for compromise when he thought his way was the right way. "He's not the kind of guy who will sit and chin things out with you," said a Michigan legislator.[9]

Even his friends kidded that Romney's real aspiration was to someday take over the leadership of the Mormon Church or perhaps an even loftier religious goal. A joke that made the rounds in Michigan had it that "Romney might make a pretty good President but I'd hate to have anyone use the White House as a stepping stone to higher office."[10]

Like Rockefeller, William Warren Scranton, governor of Pennsylvania, was born of privilege on July 19, 1917, at his parents' summer home in Madison, Connecticut. He was the son of Worthington Scranton, a descendant of a pioneer family for whom the capital of Pennsylvania was named, and Mary Warren Scranton, whose lineage traced back to families who came over to America on the Mayflower in 1620.

Mary Scranton was a Republican political activist who served as a national committeewoman for several decades. She reared her son to appreciate the finer things in life, including Republican principles and ideals.

"Commissions from Abraham Lincoln hung over the mantle of the family manse where Bill Scranton grew up—tokens of a family history that perfectly described the arc of the Republican Party's northeastern wing."[11]

At the age of nine, he was helping his mother take precinct election returns over the telephone and at age 11, he accompanied her to the Republican National convention that nominated Herbert Hoover for president.

He attended private schools and graduated from the Yale University in 1939. At Yale, he joined a fraternity that came to be known as "Destiny's Men" for it included future Supreme Court justices Byron "Whizzer" White and Potter Stewart, future Secretary of State Cyrus Vance, future Peace Corps head and vice presidential candidate Sargent Shriver and future president Gerald R. Ford.[12]

Scranton was in the Yale Law School when he left to join the Army Air Corps where he became acquainted with a young pilot by the name of Barry Goldwater. He became a pilot but never flew in combat during World War II.

After the war, Scranton returned to Yale Law School and then joined the family law firm in Pennsylvania. With the help of his family's influence and connections, Scranton landed a job in the Eisenhower administration as a special assistant to Secretary of State John Foster Dulles and to Dulles' successor, Christian Herter.

In 1960, he ran for Congress and won in a heavily Democratic district in a heavily Democratic state in a year in which a Democrat was elected president. He quickly established himself as part of the more liberal wing of the Republican party, supporting legislation on civil rights, on President Kennedy's foreign aid policies and on creation of the Peace Corps.

In 1962, Eisenhower, now out of office and living in Gettysburg, kept an eye on his fellow Pennsylvanian and urged him to run for governor. "What it boils down to, Bill," the old general told his political protégé, "is duty." That was a word that was sacred to the old general and had great influence on Scranton as well.[13]

Scranton ran and defeated the Democrat, Richardson Dilworth, the mayor of Philadelphia. In the space of a few short years, Scranton had established himself as a major player in Republican politics and, like Rockefeller, was now part of the Eastern Establishment core that eventually would try to stop the conservative tidal wave led by Goldwater. As Scranton's political star continued to rise, he felt confident he would always have the support of Eisenhower.

Another potential Republican candidate with an establishment aristocratic heritage wasn't even in the country. Henry Cabot Lodge, former U.S. senator, former U.S. ambassador to the United Nations and Nixon's vice presidential candidate, was serving as Kennedy's ambassador to Saigon in South Vietnam.

Lodge came from a family with an imprint on American history in which government service was the family business. He was born July 5, 1902, in Nahant, Massachusetts. His grandfather and namesake was a United States senator who fought President Woodrow Wilson's plan for a League of Nations and did not live long enough to see his son at work in what would have been the next generations' counterpart to the League, the United Nations.

Lodge was the great-grandson of U.S. Senator Elijah Mills and the great-great-grandson of U.S. Senator George Cabot. On his mother's side of the family, he was the great-great-grandson of U.S. Senator John Davis.

Lodge graduated cum laude from Harvard University and was elected to the Massachusetts House of Representatives in 1933. In 1936, he continued the family tradition when he was elected to the U.S. Senate. He was in the military overseas in World War II and gave up his Senate seat in 1944 to devote his time to the war effort. When the war ended, he returned home and regained his Senate seat in 1947. He lost his bid for another term in 1953 when he was defeated by John F. Kennedy.[14]

Lodge had served as Eisenhower's campaign manager and the new president rewarded him by naming him as U.S. ambassador to the United Nations. Unlike his grandfather, who vigorously opposed President Woodrow Wilson's plan for a League of Nations, Lodge strongly supported the United Nations but knew its limitations. He said, "This organization is created to prevent you from going to hell. It isn't created to take you to heaven."

In 1960, Nixon selected Lodge as his running mate, leading to the second time in eight years Lodge would lose to Kennedy. But Kennedy had respect for Lodge's experience with the United Nations and his knowledge of international politics and named him as ambassador to Saigon.

When the Republican Party found itself in a vacuum after Nixon's loss to Kennedy, Lodge's name came into the political dialogue for 1964. Among others, Eisenhower encouraged him to run. Since he was now in the foreign service, he was prohibited from engaging in American political campaigns but that did not stop others from touting a possible Lodge candidacy.[15]

And then there was Nixon, the man who narrowly missed being president four years earlier and was vice president for eight years before that, and yet, had lost the respect of many within his own party. Still, he was a loyal Republican who had been through the rigors of the last three national political campaigns. In 1964, he was a longshot to be sure, but he was there for the asking.

Richard Milhous Nixon was born in 1913 in Yorba Linda, California, and grew up in nearby Whittier. His personal life was marred early on by the deaths of two of his brothers, Arthur and Harold, both from illnesses several years apart from one another. Nixon graduated from Whittier College in his hometown and then went cross-country to Duke University Law School, where he excelled.

He returned to Whittier where he practiced law and became involved in community activities including the local community theater. It was there he met Thelma "Pat" Ryan. They married in 1940.

On the recommendation of one of his old law professors, Nixon landed a job in Washington with the Office of Price Administration. When the war broke out after Pearl Harbor, he enlisted in the Navy. After the war, Nixon was looking for work when he was approached by a group of California Republicans who were seeking a candidate to run in the 12th Congressional District against five-term Democratic incumbent Jerry Voorhis.

It was in this race that Nixon not only discovered his lifelong career but a hard-core political persona that remained with him the rest of his life. He rarely engaged in any activity or struck up a personal relationship with anyone where he did not consider the political consequences first. In that regard, he was much like a future political nemesis, Lyndon Johnson. Historian Theodore White said of Johnson (and could easily have said of Nixon), "Those who come in contact with him are accepted generally as cronies or partners or supplicants—or men he could use, as servants. But of real friends, he had few, for, above all else, he lacks the capacity for arousing warmth."[16]

The late 1940s and early 1950s were times of growing fear of Communism and its potential infiltration in the United States and fueling

4. The Contenders   43

that fear was politically easy. Voorhis made it clear in his campaign that he would not accept money or endorsement from any organization that had Communist ties. When a newspaper accused him of doing exactly that, Voorhis vehemently denied it. But the Nixon campaign claimed it had proof and produced a document which Nixon displayed during a debate with Voorhis. Though the document was false, the damage was done and Nixon was elected.[17]

Nixon became a member of the House Un-American Activities Committee where he was instrumental in revealing that Alger Hiss, who worked for the State Department, had passed on sensitive information to the Communists.

The congressman's reputation for hunting down Communists in the U.S. helped his political career. In 1950, he ran for the U.S. Senate and defeated incumbent Helen Gahagen Douglas, accusing her of having a voting record that was in line with Communist ideals.

A year later, when General Eisenhower was a candidate for president and California Governor Earl Warren was a possible candidate, Nixon worked hard to sway delegates to the upcoming convention to support Eisenhower. In part as a reward for his efforts and because California was a crucial state in the election, candidate Eisenhower picked Nixon as his running mate. During the campaign, when he was accused of living well beyond his means because of a secret slush fund, Nixon went on national television to defend himself and declared one campaign gift he would never give up was a cocker spaniel puppy his daughter Tricia loved, a dog named Checkers. The speech became known as the "Checkers Speech" and not only saved Nixon's political career but enhanced it with a sympathetic public.

In 1960, when Eisenhower hurt Nixon's presidential campaign by lightheartedly saying he'd need a week to recall any major decisions Nixon had been involved in, it took away from some genuine contributions he made as vice president such as traveling around the world promoting democracy and administration policies and twice filling in responsibly for the president after Eisenhower's two heart attacks.

But Nixon lost favor with many in his own party, particularly with conservatives, when he met with Governor Nelson Rockefeller in New York shortly before the convention and came away with what came to be known as the "Fifth Avenue Compact"—an agreement to support some of Rockefeller's wants on the party's platform. Conservative Republicans thought Nixon has fallen into the "me-too" syndrome of accepting liberal doctrine.

Goldwater characterized Nixon as cool and calculating, "a loner, a cold man with great self confidence and a one-track mind centered on the advancement of Richard Nixon."[18]

After the close loss to Kennedy in the 1960 presidential election, Nixon returned to California and ran for governor against incumbent Edmund "Pat" Brown. When he lost, he held a press conference in which it seemed he was writing his own political obituary, telling the media, "You won't have Dick Nixon to kick around any more."

As 1964 approached, Nixon was viewed as damaged goods politically but still had the distinction of having participated in three consecutive presidential campaigns, one running for vice president, one as vice president and one as the presidential candidate. If the convention deadlocked, Nixon would not have minded being a compromise candidate as he waited in the wings.

Chapter 5

The Clandestine Meeting

On the morning of October 8, 1961, Barry Goldwater appeared on the ABC television news program *Issues and Answers* and proclaimed "I am not interested in 1964, at all, in any way."

In Chicago that morning, Clif White was preparing to oversee a meeting involving 22 men from around the country who had agreed to meet at Chicago's Avenue Hotel to begin important discussions. None knew precisely what they were going to discuss or who besides themselves would be there. But they knew Clif White and what his passion was, so they could surmise that they'd probably be talking about the conservative movement in the United States—and how to get it moving. It is not known how many of them, if any, had heard Goldwater's declaration that morning that he had no interest in running for president.

The Avenue Hotel was at 7154 Michigan Avenue on the northwest corner of Michigan and Roosevelt Road. Opened in 1960, it boasted air conditioning and televisions in each of its 100 rooms and a dining room just off the lobby. It was nondescript compared to other Chicago hotels and, in fact, had more of the look of a bland motel. It certainly lacked the ambiance of the Palmer House or the Sherman House with all of their charm and elegance, but that may have been the very reason Clif White chose it for his meeting. It was a place in which some of the rooms may have rented by the hour by some of its patrons, but it was not a place where people would be easily recognized, a place big enough to hold a large group and yet keep a big secret.

Those attending came from the merged lists of Bill Rusher, John Ashcroft and White, most of them products of the Young Republicans, some of whom were still active in the organization.

The Avenue Motel in Chicago was the site of the first meeting of a group of men in 1961 who would form the Draft Goldwater movement that led to Goldwater's nomination in 1964 (author's personal collection).

In his planning for the meeting, White wanted to be careful to explain a course of action that would be slow, methodical, purposeful and, he hoped at this early stage, enticing to this group of conservatives who had agreed to come to Chicago, all at their own expense, to hear the plan. Twenty-three had been invited. Four could not make it, not for lack of interest but because of prior commitments. All four would be at the next meeting. So the assembled group consisted of 19 invited guests along with White, Ashbrook and Rusher.

Among them were White's friend and adviser, Charlie Barr of Chicago, a lobbyist for Standard Oil and a man who possessed the most political shrewdness of anyone in the room, in White's estimation, the man White consulted before following through with setting up the meeting. Others attending came from diverse backgrounds.

James "Jimmy" Boyce of Baton Rouge, Louisiana, was a wealthy dealer for the Caterpillar Tractor Company and a Democrat-turned-Republican. He worked in the Nixon campaign in 1960 where he met White but didn't actually switch political parties until 1963. So he was still a registered Democrat when White invited him to the meeting in Chicago.

Congressman Don Bruce of Indiana was a young man who could be spotted across the room because of his dark, horn-rimmed glasses. Bruce was a radio announcer in Indianapolis when he got involved in politics and eventually became chairman of the American Conservative Union, an organization he helped found.

Another Hoosier was Robert E. Hughes, of Greenwood, who was Indiana state treasurer and had been active in the Young Republican national organization for many years. A third Hoosier was a former state GOP chairman, Robert Matthews of Indianapolis, who, like Charlie Barr in Illinois, had a good grip on the inner workings of Midwest Republican politics and whose opinions were valued by White.

Gerrish Milliken and his brother Roger, of Spartanburg, South Carolina, were executives of family businesses that made up the world's largest privately-owned textile and chemical textile industry of which their grandfather was a co-founder.

Greg Shorey of Greenville, South Carolina, was founding president and chairman of the board of Style-Crafters Inc., manufacturer of marine safety and water sports equipment. He later served in leadership capacities with two other companies. He was active for years in South Carolina Republican politics and gave a seconding speech for the nomination of Goldwater at the 1960 Republican convention. Shorey loved to tell the story about how his father got him interested in politics. In an interview with the *Greenville Times-Examiner*, he said his father told him, "Son, you can choose to leave the government alone but it will never leave you alone. It affects the water you drink, the roads you drive on and the schools you attend. It affects every facet of your life. It will be the single biggest expense you ever have, even after you are dead."[1]

Another South Carolinian, Robert Chapman, also of Spartanburg, had long been active in Republican politics and succeeded Shorey as state chairman.

Roger Moore of Massachusetts, at age 28, was the youngest man in the room that day and one of the smartest. He was a graduate of Harvard University and Harvard Law School and had become publisher of the *National Review*. In 1956, when he was just 24, he led the Eisenhower campaign in Massachusetts and would become general counsel for the Goldwater campaign.

Charles "Charlie" Thone, a future Nebraska governor and congressman, was a lawyer who served as deputy secretary of state in Nebraska and then as administrative assistant to U.S. Senator Roman Hruska. Thone's biggest achievements in politics were still ahead of him but he arrived in Chicago with keen insights into the workings of Midwest politics.

Frank Whetson of Cut Bank, Montana, brought a western flavor to the meeting room and had expertise in media and big business. He was a media executive, having served as publisher and president of the Cut Bank Pioneer Press and chairman of the board of KLCB radio in Libby, Montana. He was a former president of Lack Jack Gas & Oil Company and president of IMPEX, an import-export firm. Cut Bank was a town of only 4,500 but Whetson had such influence within the Republican Party that every Republican presidential candidate for the past 28 years had paid a visit to the little town.

Charles "Ned" Cushing of Lawrence, Kansas, was president of the University State Bank in Lawrence and was a former chairman of the Young Republicans through which he became friends with White, Rusher and Ashbrook and was a natural fit for the group gathering in Chicago.

Samuel "Sam" Hay of Elm Grove, Wisconsin, was director of labor relations and public affairs for Allen Bradley, a manufacturer of factory automation equipment in Milwaukee. He had a passion for politics and would serve as Midwest campaign chairman for Goldwater.

Robert Morris, president of the University of Dallas in Texas, brought a unique perspective. He was a former lawyer for the U.S. Senate Internal Security Subcommittee with a reputation for having insight into the Communist movement within the United States, a movement Morris believed had a mission to influence U.S. foreign policy and ultimately trample democracy.

Dave Nichols, the state Republican chairman from Maine was there, as were John Keith Rehmann of Iowa, who later would be a consultant and contributor to the Ashbrook conservative think tank; Speed Reavis, Jr., of Arkansas, whom White had met four years earlier when Reavis was a volunteer for the Nixon campaign; and Leonard Pasek, a businessman from Milwaukee, Wisconsin, whom White had met in his business travels and been impressed by with his conservative ideals.

The assembled group represented quite a cross-section of Republican America—an all-white, all-male consortium of wealthy businessmen and political activists who came from 16 states. There was one congressman, one university president, one newspaper publisher, two state officials, three tycoons and a smattering of citizens involved in local Republican politics in their respective states.

White presided over what he would later describe as several hours of frank and open discussion about the fate of the Republican party. "Everyone agreed that our principal goal should be to re-establish the Republican party as an effective conservative force in American politics."[2]

5. The Clandestine Meeting

Most in attendance agreed that the eight years of the Eisenhower administration had been an era of stability but without any significant progress toward the conservative level of government that these men preferred. And now, there was a Democrat in the White House and the political philosophy of government had taken a definite shift to the left.

If it continued, they believed, it would destroy a meaningful two-party system in the United States and be replaced by two brands of politics that were not far enough apart to make a difference. "There would ultimately be established a monolithic state with at best two factions, erroneously labeled Republican and Democrat, going through the motions of fighting a rubber-stamp election every four years for control of an all-powerful federal government."[3]

The discussion eventually led to who would be best to lead the charge to save the two-party system and have the guts to stand up for conservative principles and constitutional values. They wanted Goldwater to be the standard-bearer, the same Goldwater who hours earlier had appeared on national television to say he wasn't interested in running in 1964.

White cautioned the men not to look too far ahead and not to focus on any particular candidate—yet. It was more important, at this point, he said, to concentrate on recruiting conservatives at the grassroots level in their cities and counties and states. When the time came, they could mobilize the forces they had organized to support a particular candidate. But there was much work to do before that could happen.

The seed had been sown that afternoon in Chicago, and like the Biblical mustard seed, it would grow. All agreed that White should be the chairman and that they should meet again in two months, giving him time to draw up a plan and a budget.

The group had no name but it had a purpose. White was not concerned with names or labels. His concern at this point was anonymity because if word leaked out as to what they were doing, he believed the powerful Eastern forces of the Republican party would do everything they could to crush them.

Their next meeting was on December 10, again at the Avenue Motel in Chicago in the same conference room in which they met two months earlier. There were ten new men added to the original group, but because of a snowstorm that shut down O'Hare airport, four from the first group were unable to make it. In all, 28 were in attendance at the December meeting.

Joining the group were Sam Barnes, the Republican chairman in Orange County, California; Tad Smith of El Paso, state GOP chairman in Texas; another Texan, Albert Fay of Houston, a Republican national committeeman; Donald Nutter, governor of Montana; John Lupton, a state senator from Connecticut; William McFadzean of Minneapolis, a business colleague of White's; Edward Ethell, administrative assistant to Colorado governor Gordon Allott; John Tope of Birmingham, Alabama, a past chairman of the Young Republicans; and Sullivan Barnes of South Dakota, who now worked for former governor Joe Foss with the American Football League and who also was a past chairman of the Young Republicans.

White presided and reported on a meeting he and Charlie Thone had with Goldwater in which they informed him of what occurred in Chicago in October. He said Goldwater seemed pleased that conservatives were organizing and said he would do what he could to help. But he gave no indication that he was interested in running for president.

White proposed a modest budget of $65,000 that would include a $24,000 salary for himself with the rest going toward office rent and equipment and travel expenses. The budget was, as White put it, "laughably low. If Nelson Rockefeller had learned about it, I'm sure he would have sneered us right off the political map."[4]

But White was convinced the movement could survive because of the number of people who would gladly volunteer their time for the cause and for the free-will donations that would come in from people who believed in the cause. Before the day was done, Roger Milliken pledged to raise the first $30,000.

The rest of the meeting was devoted to the hard work that would have to be done just to set the wheels in motion for 1964. The name of the game was delegates, said White. When all the campaigning is done, when all the balloons are popped, when all Lions Club guest appearances are over and there is no more posing for pictures and baby kissing and eating hot dogs at state fairs—when all of that is past history—the winner will be the person who has the most delegates on the night of the presidential nomination.

And the time to start lining up delegates is now, said White, three years in advance. It would be tedious, unexciting work, most of it behind the scenes in living rooms, coffee shops and many back rooms and it would be complicated because there was no such thing as one size fits all. Most of the states had their own specific procedures for selecting delegates. It was important for everyone in that room in

5. The Clandestine Meeting

Chicago to know the rules of their states and make sure the people they recruited knew them as well.

"There are 50 independent systems of law on delegate choice, and as they change from year to year, only a political technician with staff can keep in mind all their intricacies, dates, sharp and pointed legal distinctions and dominant personalities."[5]

The system as a whole was complicated; it was White's job to figure it out. The individuals he recruited had to know how the system worked in only one state, the state they lived in, and then work the system to perfection for Goldwater. Some of the smaller states selected delegates through a series of caucuses, almost by process of elimination, starting with precinct caucuses that were sometimes as small as neighborhoods, leading to county or district caucuses, all leading to state conventions where the final vote on delegates was taken.

"The laws governing these tiny precinct gatherings of citizens [were] very fuzzy; and these grass-roots meetings, so lavishly praised in textbooks on democratic practice [were] precisely the kind that can be dominated by the energetic, the motivated, the dedicated."[6]

Republicans honored party loyalty in the delegate selection process. Each state automatically got four at-large delegates plus an at-large delegate for every Republican congressman from the state. They were awarded six at-large delegates if the state supported Nixon in 1960 or elected a governor or senator in that year. In addition, they got one delegate for each congressional district that supported Nixon in 1960 by at least 2,000 votes and the same held true for support of their congressional candidate.

Sixteen states held primary elections which provided delegates to the convention. But most states chose their delegates the old-fashioned way, at state conventions where political bosses could put overbearing pressure on potential delegates—or simply bribe them with the promise a patronage job or cash for aligning themselves with the right candidate.

White's plan was to thwart all of those shenanigans by taking care of business well in advance of party conventions. "White's plotters would search for conservatives who were more interested in saving Western civilization than gaining a spot on the streets and sanitation commission. The rules were often so obscure and complex that just knowing them would give the insurgents an enormous advantage."[7]

White was a master strategist not only because of what he learned from winning over the years but also from when he lost. And in putting together a game plan aimed at a conservative victory three years in the making, he drew from his experience when he lost out on his bid to become head of the American Veterans Committee. He was a fervent anti–Communist but he understood how its movement grew, moving outward like the ripples in a pond.

"A single, small organization, from a distance and with minimal resources, working in stealth, could take on an entire party. They didn't need the big fish, the governors, senators, mayors. They didn't need the little fish, the individual voters. They just needed enough middling fish."[8]

At the end of the meeting, Governor Nutter stood up and gave a rallying cry to the rest of the assembled group. He spoke with passion about the difficult road ahead and the importance of what they were doing, which he said was preserving the nation.

With that, the men got up, said their good-byes and left in a spirit of conservative euphoria as they headed home, out of the Chicago winter and into what they all knew would probably become a political hurricane. But for now, their task was simple, at least in definition. They had to start recruiting.

White returned to New York, rented an office on the 35th floor in the Chanin Building near Grand Central Station, hired a secretary and scrounged up some secondhand furniture. His office was in Suite 3505 and that became the code name for the still-secret operation.

He had a cause, he had ground troops, he had an office and a place to sit inside the office. What he didn't have, at the moment, was a willing candidate.

On January 25, 1962, Governor Nutter, who six weeks earlier had so eloquently and enthusiastically lifted the spirits of everyone as they ended their latest meeting, was on his way to a speaking engagement in Cut Bank, the hometown of fellow conservative Whetson, when his plane crashed, killing him and four others aboard. The crusade had lost one of its most ardent soldiers.

Their next meeting was on April 13, 1962, in the unlikely setting of a hunting lodge in northern Minnesota. The lodge had several cabins where the men paired off and spent the night. The one exception was Rita Bree, White's secretary who made the trip and had a cabin all to herself. White purposely wanted the meeting to be held in a more informal setting than the first two, where this band of conservative brothers could get to know each other better in a relaxed atmosphere while still attending to the business at hand. When the day's work was done, many of them stayed up and chatted over coffee or drinks and some engaged in a friendly poker game.

During their meeting, White emphasized the importance of conservatives having a presence at the many primaries and state conventions that would be held in the spring and summer, stepping stones to the delegate selection process that was critical to any success in 1964. By the end of the year, White wanted each state to have a chairman hand-picked from this group of conservatives whose job would be to oversee and influence the selection of delegates.

There would be 16 presidential primary elections in 1964, he told them, which were basically beauty contests in which candidates got a lot of media attention, boosting their name recognition and fundraising—if they won or did better than expected. But if the delegates in those states were already committed, the primaries lost a lot of their political importance. In states where the projected delegate count didn't favor the right candidate, conservatives were to cozy up to the political bosses and urge one of them, probably a governor or senator, to run as a "favorite son" candidate in their state. For the "favorite son," the value was being able to release his delegates to whomever he chose, when the time for it came at the convention. For the conservatives, who by this time would hope to be backers of a Goldwater candidacy, having enough "favorite sons" could prevent other presidential candidates from securing precious delegate votes.

Momentum was building and, incredibly, all of the organizational work and traveling and meetings had been done without the scrutiny of the me-too Eastern Establishment politicians or the probing eye of the press. The one thing that wasn't going as well as planned was fundraising. White had budgeted $65,000 for the first year and had taken in about $43,000.

Meanwhile, Goldwater, who had made a lot of contacts throughout the country as chairman of the Republican Senatorial Campaign Committee, was one of the most sought after speakers on the GOP circuit. And his backers often held their breath because of his penchant to "shoot from the lip," sometimes offending the very people he was supposed to be wooing.

Goldwater had accepted an invitation to speak at a rally at Madison Square Garden in New York. It was sponsored by the Young Americans for Freedom, a group founded by William F. Buckley, a conservative author, philosopher and publisher, and comprised of conservative firebrands who were, in essence, a constituency in search of a candidate.

As Goldwater stood at the podium, after being introduced as "the conservative's choice for president," an estimated 18,000 spectators cheered and chanted "we want Barry, we want Barry, we want Barry." This went on for, some say, at least 20 minutes—a politician's dream in terms of its ego-building, its energizing force and its expression of adulation. But Goldwater had a different reaction. As they continued to shout, "we want Barry," he said into the microphone, "Well, if you'll shut up, you'll get him."

The next meeting of the still-secret group was again in Chicago on December 2, 1962. The meeting was a turning point for two main reasons. First, Clif White minced no words in telling the group its mission. "We are going to take over the Republican Party," he said. Secondly, as he was to discover, the secret group wasn't so secret any more.[9]

By this time, the group had expanded to 55 members, more than twice the number that had originally gathered earlier. Among the newcomers were Jeremiah "Jerry" Milbank and J. William "Bill" Middendorf, two wealthy businessmen from Connecticut; and J.D. "Stets" Stetson Coleman, the Fannie May candy entrepreneur from Chicago.

White said he had met with Goldwater several times and while Goldwater endorsed the group's efforts to promote conservative principles and conservative candidates at all levels of government, he still had no interest in running for president.

There was much work to do in the next 18 months before the convention and the stakes were high, not only politically but financially. White said it would take $3 million to get the job done. While the organization had no official treasurer, Middendorf, Milbank and Coleman agreed to be trustees until a treasurer could be named. (Eventually, it would be Middendorf).

The men talked about the challenges of raising the money and, as the conversation progressed, Coleman said he would pledge $25,000. Middendorf said he would donate $10,000. Fred LaRue of Mississippi also pledged $25,000. By the time the meeting ended and everyone headed back home, a total of $285,000 had been pledged—nearly 10 percent of the goal.

One thing none of them counted on, yet they shouldn't have been surprised, is that word leaked out about their meeting and, within a day, it was national news. The Associated Press picked up on it first and before long, it was headline material from coast to coast—and the headlines varied from one extreme to another. The *San Francisco Examiner* proclaimed "Secret Move to Push Goldwater in 1964" while the *New York Herald Tribune* approached it from an angle closer to home to its readers: "Move to Block Rocky."[10]

White said he first discovered there had been a leak when he received a phone call from Carl DeBloom, the Washington correspondent for the *Columbus (Ohio) Dispatch* who heard that Ohio Congressman Ashbrook had been at a meeting of political operatives in Chicago. White did not deny that a meeting had taken place because he did not want to get caught in a lie. But he also declined to provide any details. He called Goldwater in Phoenix to alert him that the press was on the trail. Goldwater said if he was asked, he would tell reporters he knew nothing about it, which was accurate in the sense that he knew next to nothing about it and certainly did not know details as to what had taken place.

Not long after White phoned Goldwater, he got a call from Arthur Edson from the Associated Press's Washington bureau. White tried to fend Edson off as he had DeBloom but Edson kept calling back with more information he had picked up, including a list of names. He had enough to publish the first story about the meeting. It began, "A secret, highly confidential meeting of leading Republicans who want Senator Barry Goldwater for president was held in Chicago Sunday. Their objective is to get, as one put it, 'an honest-to-God conservative Republican candidate for president' and, incidentally, to try to block the road for Gov. Nelson Rockefeller of New York."[11]

So, the word was out and it made for good coffee shop conversation for political junkies and fodder for journalists and political operatives of other potential candidates. But it did nothing to stop the enthusiasm or momentum of the Goldwater brigade. That occurred on the morning of January 14, 1963, when Clif met with Goldwater to bring him up to date on the group's activities.

Goldwater was in a bad mood. He had crisscrossed the country in the past year as chairman of the GOP Senatorial Campaign Committee, speaking on behalf of Republican candidates and doing whatever he could to help their campaigns. In some cases, he was singing the praises of candidates he had never met until the day of his appearance. He had developed contacts throughout the country—hundreds of new friends for him and his party. So he was shocked on the morning of January 14 when fellow Senate Republicans failed to elect him to the party's Policy Committee. It was a move he thought was engineered by Senator Jacob Javits of New York, who represented the liberal wing of the party and was a supporter of Governor Rockefeller for president.

White and the senator talked about the snub for a few minutes and then White began talking about the conservative movement that was steadily growing. He gingerly mentioned his group's enthusiasm for Goldwater to be the Republican nominee in 1964 but Goldwater stopped him cold. "I'm not a candidate and I'm not going to be," he said. "I have no intention of running for the presidency."

White teased him a little, saying he might have to be drafted. Goldwater replied, "Draft, nothing. I told you I'm not going to run. And I'm telling you now, don't paint me into a corner. It's my political neck and I intend to have something to say about what happens to it."[12]

Goldwater's cold water on his presidential run may have been a bit of a ruse on his part because he really didn't want to jeopardize his chances of being re-elected to the Senate. "He was willing to keep his options open. He just wanted to retain stewardship of his own political neck."[13]

He also brought an old Arizona friend and adviser, Denison Kitchel, to Washington to manage his Senate campaign. But any mail Goldwater received from organizations and individuals touting his presidential possibilities was automatically sent over to Kitchel to sort through.

Meanwhile, White returned to New York and told his office staff and a few others about his latest meeting with the senator. Someone said he should just tell Goldwater to go to hell and to forget trying to get him to run. White said the advice was tempting but he just couldn't throw away all the time and effort and work that had been done in the past year to energize the conservative movement.

He learned through the political grapevine—a powerful force in Washington–that Goldwater had two concerns. One was obvious. He intended to run for re-election to the Senate in 1964—it would be his third term—and he didn't want to run for president at the same time. In fact, in 1960, he had been a critic of Lyndon Johnson who ran for vice president and for re-election to the Senate from Texas at the same time.

The other concern was not as obvious, and it was hurtful. White was told Goldwater suspected that White might be using the potential Goldwater candidacy to line his own pockets. That was never the intention—in fact, White had given up a lucrative public relations career to spearhead the conservative movement. But he chose not to confront Goldwater about the rumors, because that's what they were—rumors—and to continue with the tasks at hand.

On Tuesday, February 5, White met again with Goldwater but this

5. The Clandestine Meeting

time he brought Charlie Barr with him, someone Goldwater had known for years and respected. White purposely let Barr take the lead in the conversation, but the result was the same. Goldwater said he had no interest in running.

The two men decided it was time to start breaking the news to the scores of individuals who had signed on as volunteers. But first, they thought it would be best to meet with a smaller group, an executive board of sorts, to get a feel from them as to what they should do next.

On February 17, they met at the O'Hare Inn near the airport in Chicago. Not everyone who was invited chose to come because they sensed it was the beginning of the end. But Frank Whetson was there from Montana, and Bob Matthews and Bob Hughes from Indiana, and Tad Smith and Peter O'Donnell from Texas and Andy Carter from New Mexico as well as Ashbrook and Rusher.

They talked about all that had been accomplished, how far they had come since the first meeting involving just 22 men in October of 1961. The troops had been recruited and mobilized and now everything was in danger of disintegrating. As the meeting took on the atmosphere of doom and gloom and defeat, Hughes finally said, "There's only one thing we can do. Let's draft the son of a bitch."

Some in the group reminded him that Goldwater wanted no part of it. But Hughes was insistent. "I mean, let's really draft him." In other words, if the best way to push the conservative movement forward was to elect Goldwater for president, then the thing to do was to put together an organized, nationwide effort that he would not be able to stop or ignore. And all the pieces were in place to make it happen.

Whether he liked it or not, they were going to draft the son of a bitch.[14]

Chapter 6

Feeling the Draft

The Draft Goldwater movement had a body—a multitude of believers all over the country; and it had a soul, F. Clifton White, who represented the essence of the conscience of a conservative. What the movement needed was a head, a front man to be the public face of the organization while White continued to do what he did best, and what he enjoyed most, working behind the scenes.

Whoever led the organization had to be someone Goldwater respected, someone he would not repudiate, someone who could control without seemingly be controlling. Two names rose to the top—Senator Peter Dominick of Colorado and Peter O'Donnell, a philanthropist and chairman of the Republican party in Texas.

Dominick was the first choice. He was a fellow senator, he was a conservative, he appealed to the younger generation—something that wasn't well represented in the leadership group, and he had proven to be a good campaigner. He took office in Colorado by defeating liberal incumbent Democrat John Carroll. In addition, as White pointed out, Dominick was not the kind of person Goldwater was likely to publicly humiliate when he found out what was going on. Everything seemed to fit—except Dominick said no.

He explained he was a freshman senator, just getting his feet wet, and he would not feel comfortable taking on such an awesome responsibility while at the same time trying to represent his constituents in Colorado. In effect, he said it was too early for him to start picking presidents.

White's leadership team had originally thought of Dominick and O'Donnell as being co-chairs, but now there was only one baton and it was being passed to O'Donnell if he agreed to accept it. He had excellent credentials. He was a partner in his family's investment business and was a well-known philanthropist in Texas. He had a master's degree in finance and earned a Phi Beta Kappa key for academic excellence.

In 1960, he managed the Nixon campaign in Dallas County, which Nixon won by 60,000 votes. Republicans took note of that accomplishment since the county was in the heart of Lyndon Johnson territory. Most recently, O'Donnell had managed the campaign of John Tower, a conservative who became the first Republican senator from Texas since the Civil War.

O'Donnell was hesitant at first, but after thinking it over for a couple of days, he enthusiastically accepted his newest challenge.

Bill Middendorf, the Wall Street tycoon who had joined the ranks at the December 1961 meeting, agreed to be treasurer. The leadership team was in place. The cause was clear. The constituency was growing every day. And, at this point, the challenge hadn't changed. Early in 1963, Barry Goldwater, the man they wanted in the White House, was not only being reluctant; he was being the often annoyingly candid Barry Goldwater. Asked about his potential presidential candidacy, he replied, "I'm doing all right just pooping around."[1]

Historian Theodore White, assessing the situation at the time, wrote, "Essentially, Goldwater thought of himself, not as a man prepared to or even desiring to run and administer the government of the United States, but as a leader of a cause; this cause is precious to him. His loyalty to it is sincere and unblemished."[2]

Four governor's races in 1962 helped shape the Republican presidential landscape, for some better than others. Nixon, who had fallen from grace with many Republicans for the manner in which he ran his 1960 campaign, fell even further when he lost in California to Governor Edmund "Pat" Brown and conceded with his infamous verbal political obituary: "The last play. I leave you gentlemen now and you will now write it. You will interpret it. That's your right. But as I leave you, I want you to know—just think how much you're going to be missing. You won't have Nixon to kick around anymore, because gentlemen, this is my last press conference."[3]

Rockefeller won re-election in New York by defeating Robert Morgenthau, an able U.S. district attorney for the southern district of New York but an inept campaigner who was no contest for the incumbent governor. But Rockefeller's victory was tainted by the fact that his margin of victory, 529,000 votes was less than his victory margin of 1958 and less in 1962 than that of Jacob Javits, a Republican who won re-election to the U.S. Senate.

In Michigan, Romney, the American Motors executive who introduced compact cars to America, and who had never before sought public office, beat the incumbent Democrat John B. Swainson. The new governor instantly was looked at as a rising star in national Republican politics even though his popularity in Michigan, even among Republicans, lessened as election day drew near because of his penchant for being argumentative when people disagreed with him.

Scranton in Pennsylvania, who had served one term in Congress, defeated Richardson Dilworth, a former mayor of Philadelphia, in a race that became testy more than once. In one scenario, Scranton took on Dilworth in a televised debate and clearly was the victor. Dilworth demanded a second debate but Scranton turned him down. So Dilworth decided to pull the old political trick of debating an empty chair. As a statewide television audience watched, Dilworth was sitting next to the empty chair, denouncing his opponent, when Scranton walked in and sat down, clearly upstaging his opponent. Like Romney, Scranton was now looked on as a Republican on the rise.

While all of these governors' elections were going on, Clif White was traveling throughout the country, linking up with the many conservative friends he had met over the years, and his remarkable ability to work behind the scenes was paying dividends. By the spring of 1963, there were Draft Goldwater chairpersons in 33 states and each of them had committees and subcommittees working for them. The plan had not changed. The volunteers were attending local public meetings, holding their own meetings, educating people on the importance of county and state precinct caucuses and how the presidential nominating process begins well before the convention.

Bill Middendorf had a theory that at the local level, citizens could argue for hours about the need for a stoplight at a particular intersection but pay little attention to big-picture politics and therefore squander opportunities to make a difference nationally. Clif White's strategy was to engage these stoplight citizens and transform them into Goldwater advocates, and it was working.

White and others determined the time had come to make a public announcement about the Draft Goldwater movement, with or without the senator's blessing. On April 8, 1963, Peter O'Donnell and his co-chair, Ione Harrington of Indiana, met with a smattering of reporters in a small meeting room of the Mayflower Hotel in Washington to announce the formation of the National Draft Goldwater Committee, P.O. Box 1964, Washington, D.C.[4]

O'Donnell told those assembled that the committee had been formed to help organize and mobilize the enthusiasm that was being shown throughout the country for a Goldwater candidacy. He said he thought a contest for the nomination would strengthen the party, rather than divide it and that competition for the nomination had not hurt the Democrats in 1960.

He talked a little bit about areas of the country in which Goldwater would be strong but emphasized no part of the country would be ignored or written off. The main thing, he said, was that Senator Goldwater would offer the American people a definite choice between the policies of the New Frontier and the principles of conservatism.

Goldwater continued to remain ambivalent and sometimes hostile toward the movement. He told reporters after the announcement that the committee was acting on its own, with its own people and its own money but without any direction from him. He could not have been unaware of his growing popularity.

A week later, in an interview with the *New York Times*, he was quoted as saying, "I don't want the nomination. I'm not looking for it. I haven't authorized anyone to look for it for me. But who can tell what will happen a year from now? A man would be a damn fool to predict with finality what he would do in this unpredictable world."[5]

A Gallup poll in April had Republican voters favoring Rockefeller with 43 percent, Goldwater at 26 percent, Romney at 13 percent, and Scranton at 7 percent. Nixon was also considered a potential candidate but was below 5 percent in the poll, not surprising for someone who had recently proclaimed that the press "wouldn't have Nixon to kick around anymore."

The Draft Goldwater campaigners continued their quest to show not only the public but their reluctant hero that support for him was solid and growing. On July 4, 1963, when the senator was riding a horse in a parade in Arizona, his backers held a Goldwater Rally at the National Guard Armory in Washington.

Among those in attendance were U.S. Senator John Tower of Texas, Congressman John Ashbrook of Ohio, Governor Paul Fannin of Arizona as well as actors Walter Brennan, one of the stars of *The Real McCoys* television program; Efram Zimbalist, Jr., also a TV star on the hit show, *77 Sunset Strip*; veteran character actor William Lundigan; and entertainer Chill Wills.

More than 9,000 citizens packed the armory and they heard Clif White remind them that this event was not a presidential campaign rally because there was a lot of work to be done in the trenches before there could ever be a presidential candidate.

The Republican political landscape was taking shape. Rockefeller, Romney and Scranton had the advantage of being governors—chief executives overseeing their own bureaucracies with the potential of leading an even bigger one. Nixon was always a factor despite his recent failures at the ballot box. And the momentum for Goldwater was building though American voters had a penchant for not electing senators to the presidency. Kennedy in 1960 was a notable exception. Prior to Kennedy, the only other man to go directly from the Senate to the White House was Republican Warren Harding in 1921.[6]

But it was clear that the front-runner for the nomination was Rockefeller, the epitome of Eastern Establishment me-too liberalism that conservatives despised. And he had something going for him that Goldwater didn't—a burning desire to be president.

But periodically Goldwater showed signs that he hadn't totally dismissed the idea—or at least that the enormous amount of publicity about the conservative movement on his behalf had inevitably made him think about it.

In a conversation with Middendorf one day, he mentioned that a political campaign was like a three-legged stool; you needed a message, a candidate and money behind both of them. He said most campaigns usually have the first two but fail on the third. And if you don't have all three legs, the stool tips over.

Then, as further evidence that he had given a national candidacy some thought, whether for himself or someone else, he asked Middendorf, a veteran of Wall Street and of political financing, what the secret was to successful fundraising. Middendorf gave him a five-minute tutorial. Supporters of the candidate should:

1. Start the fund-raising by making their own contribution to the campaign to demonstrate they mean business.

2. Invite close personal friends of the candidate and, if possible some celebrities or well-known individuals to be on an executive committee that would be created and named to clearly identify these people with the candidate and the cause. Obviously their financial support would be not only encouraged but expected.

3. Have stationary produced with the name of the organization and the names of the executive committee in the letterhead. Send out press releases announcing the formation of the committee with information on how the public can contribute to the cause.[7]

4. Continue to invite supporters to be part of the executive committee and, as they agree, add their names to the letterhead on the stationary to show, in press releases and fundraising letters, the growing number of people who have joined the cause.

5. Encourage executive committee members to sponsor events such as dinners or rallies as a way of drawing more people—and more money. Dinners could be arranged at a set amount—$25 or $50 a $100 a plate, for example, to cover costs and add to the campaign warchest. Rallies could have big-name speakers that the average citizen would love to meet. The rallies could have an admission fee or have a free-will offering—or both.

6. Send thank-you notes to as many people as possible with a personal signature. Add names to the mailing list and to the letterhead whenever possible.

7. Cash the checks.[8]

As the days and weeks passed, it was clear the man to beat for the Republican nomination, Rockefeller, was someone who didn't have to be as concerned with fundraising as other candidates because he could devote his personal fortune to his personal ambition.

Paul Duke, writing in the *Wall Street Journal*, put it this way: "Rockefeller is running so far ahead for the Republican presidential nomination in 1964, he may have an unbreakable hammerlock on the prize.... While there is much speculation about possible challenges from Govs. William Scranton of Pennsylvania and George Romney of Michigan, there is astonishingly little talk about either among party professionals."[9]

The Goldwater people were not distressed that their candidate wasn't even mentioned in the same sentence as the other challengers. They considered Duke's analysis part of the typical East Coast approach of considering only the most liberal wing of the Republican party—the very faction that Clif White and his minions were quietly and carefully plotting to destroy.

Chapter 7

The Rockefeller Campaign

Nelson Rockefeller had lived a privileged life from the time he was born. There had been virtually nothing he couldn't have that money could buy.

His family name, power and influence were also guiding factors that helped open many doors for him including those that led him into politics. When he was elected governor of New York in 1958, he became the icon of the Eastern Establishment liberal Republican politics that had tremendous sway nationally.

Rockefeller's goal of becoming president fed into this political culture and could almost be expected, for being governor of New York had been a mighty stepping stone for many in American politics. Presidents Martin Van Buren, Grover Cleveland, Theodore Roosevelt and Franklin Roosevelt had all been New York governors and, more recently, Thomas E. Dewey had twice been the Republican nominee. Five New York governors had served as vice president and one, Charles Evans Hughes, became chief justice of the United States. Three governors later became secretaries of state.

Rockefeller had some political baggage, even within his own party. Many Republicans remembered how Rockefeller met with Richard Nixon prior to the 1960 Republican convention and convinced the vice president to press for a more liberal agenda in the party platform—and how that concession to the Eastern bloc mentality may have contributed to Nixon's narrow loss to John F. Kennedy.

As 1964 approached, the two main contenders for the GOP presidential nomination were Rockefeller, who really wanted it, and Goldwater who really didn't want it. Despite the fact the two men couldn't have been more opposite in their political philosophies, they had similar shoot-from-the-hip personalities and had a cordial relationship with one another.

During the winter of 1962 and early spring of 1963, Goldwater was a frequent breakfast guest of Rockefeller where the two men talked about a goal that they had in common—party unity. A central theme they agreed on, and what they thought could be and should be the focus for all Republicans, was the dismal record of President John F. Kennedy. In their minds, he had botched the Bay of Pigs invasion in Cuba in 1961, had gotten the U.S. involved in the political and military struggles in North and South Vietnam and had a poor domestic record as well.

In the interest of party unity, Goldwater helped to avoid a couple of embarrassing situations for Rockefeller. On March 9, 1963, Rockefeller was scheduled to give a speech in Milwaukee and Goldwater heard he might be treated rudely by some in the audience.

In Goldwater's travels across the country as chairman of the Republican Senatorial Campaign Committee, he had made a lot of contacts. He called one of his Milwaukee acquaintances, Claude Jasper, the Wisconsin state chairman, and urged him to keep the crowd under control. Jasper came through for Goldwater and Rockefeller was the beneficiary. His appearance went off without a hitch.

On April 5, Rockefeller was scheduled to be a guest in Omaha, Nebraska, at a testimonial dinner and fundraiser for Senator Roman Hruska. Conservatives threatened to boycott the event. Goldwater learned of their intentions and contacted Nebraska's other senator, Carl Curtis, a fervent Goldwater supporter, and told him, in the interest of party unity, to make sure there was no boycott. Curtis came through, just as Jasper had in Wisconsin. There was no disruption of any kind. The next day, Rockefeller phoned Goldwater and thanked him.

Rockefeller seemed to have everything going in his favor. Even his political opponents were helping him. Then, a change in his personal life created a major change in how America considered him politically.

He divorced his first wife, Mary Todhunter Clark, in March of 1962 amid rumors there was "another woman." On May 4, 1963, Rockefeller, 54, married Margaretta Fitler Murphy, 36, a former member of his office staff who went by her nickname, "Happy." Mrs. Murphy had been married for 18 years to Dr. James Slater Murphy, a virologist who worked with the Rockefeller Institute and who considered Nelson Rockefeller a good friend. The Murphys divorced in 1963 and Happy married Rockefeller a month later. In marrying Rockefeller, Happy agreed to give up custody of her four children.

By 1963 standards, the situation was scandalous and had influential people rethinking their evaluation of Rockefeller, his judgment and his political future. Republican Senator Prescott Bush of Connecticut, father and grandfather of two future presidents, said, "Have we come to a point in our life as a nation where a governor can desert a good wife, mother of his grown children, divorce her, then persuade a mother of four youngsters to abandon her husband and their four children and marry the governor? Have we come to the point where one of the two great political parties will confer its greatest honor on such a one? I venture to hope not."[1]

No divorced man had ever been elected president. The most recent divorced presidential candidate, Illinois Governor Adlai Stevenson, a Democrat, was divorced in 1949. He ran against Dwight Eisenhower in 1952 and 1956 and lost both times. His divorce was not necessarily a factor in his two defeats because neither election was close and he had the disadvantage of running against a war hero and one of the nation's most popular individuals.

In Britain, Rockefeller was being compared to King Edward VIII who in 1936 abdicated his throne to marry Wallis Simpson, a twice-divorced American socialite. In Rockefeller's case, the perception was that his love life may have caused him to abdicate his chance at the throne.[2] A high-ranking Republican in Michigan, Romney's home state, was quoted in the *New York Times*: "The rapidity of it all," he said. "He gets a divorce, she gets a divorce—and the indication of the breakup of two homes. Our country doesn't like broken homes."[3]

A few days after the wedding, 28 women were to pay a visit to Congressman (and later U.S. senator) Charles "Mac" Mathias of Maryland to discuss a local issue of concern to them. But they spent most of their time with him chastising Rockefeller for his behavior. Because of this and comments from other constituents, Mathias concluded Rockefeller's presidential hopes were dead in Maryland and probably nationally.[4]

Senator Hugh Scott of Pennsylvania received a letter from a Presbyterian minister who wrote, "This may all go over with the jet set, but it will not go over with many decent-thinking persons like myself."[5]

President Kennedy is said to have weighed in on the Rockefeller remarriage in a conversation with some of his aides. Puzzled by how the governor had apparently bungled his presidential chances, Kennedy reportedly said, "No man would ever love love more than politics."[6]

About a week after the wedding, Republicans held a $1,000-a-plate testimonial for Goldwater at the Sheraton-Park Hotel in Washington. Rockefeller, who was to be one of the speakers, sent a note of apology from "Mrs. Rockefeller and me" from Venezuela where the couple was honeymooning. When the host for the dinner, Senator Thruston Morton of Kentucky, read the message from the Rockefellers, the place erupted in horse laughs.[7]

Politicians weren't the only people who reacted to Rockefeller's remarriage with surprise and disdain.

New York Governor Nelson Rockefeller was the early favorite for the Republican presidential nomination until events in his personal life turned many voters against him (Library of Congress).

A Gallup poll taken a month before the nuptials had shown Rockefeller with 43 percent support among likely Republican voters to 26 percent for Goldwater. Goldwater had fared well but Rockefeller obviously had a commanding lead. At that point, it looked as if it was his nomination to lose.

"Only an act of incredible naivete could stop him. Rockefeller provided it by marrying Happy Murphy, fast upon the heels of his divorce from Mary Todhunter Clark. Virtually overnight, his lead over Goldwater reversed itself."[8]

The next Gallup poll, taken shortly after the remarriage, showed Goldwater with 40 percent support to 29 percent for Rockefeller. Romney and Scranton remained about the same. The Republican mainstream, showing its moral fortitude, had clearly spat in the face of the newlywed.

Goldwater, who had been the breakfast buddy of Rockefeller's and considered him a friend, felt sorry for the public rebuke of the governor. And he was surprised that he, and not Romney, was the beneficiary of Rockefeller's fall from grace. While he remained a noncandidate, he was not blind to the groundswell of support that was growing for him and the ideals of the conservative movement.

Through no effort of his own, he was on a pretty good run. There had been testimonials for him such as the one in Washington and there had been rallies such as the one at the National Guard Armory featuring leading politicians and television and movie stars. And the third leg of the campaign stool—money—was looking better and better.

Clif White and his band of eager volunteers had forged a strategy for victory that was counter to most any other national campaign. They felt strongly that the Goldwater message would carry the South and the Southwest and would resonate well in the West and Midwest as well. They believed Goldwater could win the nomination and, yes, even the election, without carrying the traditional strongholds on the East Coast. The polls were clearly favoring Goldwater now but White knew those were popularity contests that could change overnight, depending on who else got into the race or what gaffes any one of the potential candidates, including Goldwater—especially Goldwater—might make.

White knew the fickleness of polls. He knew what the polls said about the Truman-Dewey race in 1948 and what they showed in Robert Taft's quest for the nomination in 1952. So while White enjoyed his candidate's popularity, he concentrated on securing delegates—for they held the key to the nomination. That was the work being done in the trenches while Goldwater, by his own admission, was still "just pooping around."

Rockefeller had clearly lost his momentum and needed to do something to regain it. On July 14, 1963, he issued a lengthy statement that came to be known as the Declaration of War against what he called the radical element of the Republican party—the conservatives.

He started by outlining what he considered to be "articles of faith" that bound all Republicans together: the importance of freedom throughout the world; equal opportunity for all people; democracy with home rule for municipalities; the free enterprise system; freedom of speech; and fiscal responsibility.

Then he fired the shot heard round the Republican world: "The Republican party is in real danger of subversion by a radical, well-financed and highly disciplined minority," he wrote. "It has now become crystal clear that the vociferous and well-drilled extremist elements boring within the party utterly reject these fundamental principles of our heritage." He claimed that the radical elements of the party were segregationists and that Republicans now had to work to save the party from themselves.

The declaration was an abrupt change in Rockefeller's demeanor. When he was ahead in the polls, he espoused party unity and shared small talk with Goldwater over English muffins and coffee at his home. Now, he was behind in the polls and to hell with party unity. Rockefeller had not mentioned Goldwater by name but, the next day, in a press conference, he challenged Goldwater to dissociate himself from the radical right, describing him as a puppet and dupe of that element.

The following day, the *New York Journal-American* trumpeted the news with the headline, "Rocky Declares War on Goldwater."[9]

New York's two senators, Jacob Javits and Kenneth Keating, praised Rockefeller's forthrightness, although Keating conceded that Goldwater was superior to Kennedy on civil rights issues, in stark contrast to what Rockefeller had said. Nixon was in Germany and, when asked his reaction to Rockefeller's declaration, admitted that the far right was backing Goldwater. But he tempered his remarks by saying he didn't consider the senator an extremist and thought Goldwater probably looked at the right-wingers as a liability, as Nixon did.

But Senator Carl Curtis of Nebraska, a Goldwater supporter, went on the Senate floor the following day to address his colleagues. "It is my considered judgment," he said, "that a man who would take such desperate and destructive measures against his own party in a gamble to gain some temporary political advantage, has already forfeited any claim to loyalty from any part of the party organization."[10]

"Rockefeller was stunned, apparently caught completely off guard to the public reaction [to his remarriage]. He needed a new issue now to get himself back in the race. He discovered this in the 'radical right' of the Republican Party."[11]

Goldwater was deeply hurt that a friend would turn on him with such venom. He also realized that Rockefeller's reckless comments had produced something both men had vowed to avoid—a deeply divided party.

Would 1964 be 1912 all over again—reminiscent of the Roosevelt-Taft tiff—or was it that 1912 had become part of the Republican party's DNA, showing itself in some generations more than others and certainly popping up again now?

"This ideological debate between Goldwater and Rockefeller

descends directly from the great schism that devitalized the Republican Party in 1912 and has been debilitating it ever since."[12]

In a Gallup poll in September asking Republicans which candidate they preferred, 59 percent said Goldwater to 41 percent for Rockefeller. "If Rockefeller had kept his mouth shut, he might very well have won the nomination despite the remarriage. As it was, moderates had no candidate who could present himself as a unifier."[13]

But the poll that included all potential candidates revealed a new circumstance. Goldwater was well ahead of Rockefeller—but Romney, the rookie governor up in Michigan, was gaining in popularity. He had a long way to go, but the nomination process was still a long way away. There was ample time to gain more support.

At the White House, President Kennedy and his closest advisers took notice. They were beginning to discuss strategy for the election that was a little less than a year away. They talked about Goldwater and Rockefeller, the two obvious front runners for the Republicans as well as the up-and-comers such as Romney and Governor Scranton in Pennsylvania. There was even some talk about Henry Cabot Lodge, the former senator, U.N. ambassador and vice presidential candidate who was now JFK's envoy to Saigon. Though he had agreed to serve in a Democratic administration, he had impeccable qualifications to be president. And of course there was Richard Nixon, who barely lost to Kennedy in 1960.

Lodge would have been a longshot because by law, even if he wanted to, as a member of the State Department's foreign service, he was prohibited from taking part in politics. Nixon was thought to be a nonfactor since he had uttered his political obituary a year earlier after losing the California gubernatorial election. But ever the politician, he would be just offstage in case any of the leading men faltered.

Kennedy wanted to run against Goldwater. They had been friends in the Senate and respected each other's political differences. Kennedy envisioned a campaign in which he and Goldwater would travel across the country and engage in lively debates.

Goldwater, the noncandidate thus far, held a similar view. "For Goldwater, John F. Kennedy was history's perfect opponent—they would debate the issues up and down the country. They would draw the line between the conservative and liberal philosophies. Kennedy would probably win," in Goldwater's estimation, but the conservative movement would be a viable political force for many years to come.[14]

Kennedy did not want to run against Romney. Robert Kennedy,

the president's brother, his attorney general and his closest confidante, said of Romney, "He was always for God and always for motherhood and against big government and against big labor."[15]

Romney was not afraid to speak his mind, like Goldwater, sometimes to his own detriment, but he was handsome, dynamic and had a track record of taking on big challenges. If he were the nominee, he would likely welcome the opportunity to go toe-to-toe with the president.

Kennedy had known Goldwater for a long time and knew his weaknesses. He told a friend, "People will start asking him questions and he's so damn quick on the trigger, he'll answer them. And when he does, it will be all over."[16]

Kennedy decided never to mention Romney publicly for fear of building him up. Instead, he wanted to mention Goldwater as often as he could to perhaps help continue the momentum for the man he was sure he could beat.[17]

Romney was having some trouble on his homefront, however. The freshman governor was having some problems getting his legislative program approved but was enjoying his newfound celebrity status in the Republican party.

When he went to Washington to attend a banquet and the next day spoke at the National Press Club, the *Detroit News*, Michigan's largest circulation daily newspaper, sent him a not-so-subtle message in an editorial. "Come home, George, and let's get on with the chores," it said.[18]

Meanwhile, on November 6, Rockefeller, undaunted by public reaction to his marital status, to his Bastille Day declaration of war on fellow Republicans, and his sinking popularity, decided to put his campaign on full throttle.

He became the first Republican to formally announce his candidacy for the presidency. Rockefeller was a man of great ego and great confidence, whose determination and grit sometimes became the victor over caution and reason. He was a man who had received pretty much whatever he wanted in life. And he wanted to be president.

Chapter 8

November 22, 1963

Most of the nation basked under sunny skies on November 22, 1963, and Americans were going about their business. The weekend before Thanksgiving was approaching and grocery stores were preparing for the onslaught of housewives purchasing turkeys and all the trimmings for their upcoming Thanksgiving dinners with their families. Other merchants were stocking up on all forms of merchandise in anticipation of the Friday after Thanksgiving, traditionally the first day of the Christmas season and the busiest shopping day of the year.

In Washington, the Redskins of the National Football League were preparing to go to Philadelphia for a matchup with the Philadelphia Eagles on Sunday. The Redskins were 2–8 for the season and hoped to end a seven-game losing streak. In Chicago, the Bears, the league's hottest team, were to play their archrival, the Green Bay Packers, with the hope of improving their impressive 9–1 record.

In Jacksonville, Florida, LoRaine Leland, 20, and John Davidson, 23, were anxiously awaiting their marriage to take place later that day at the First Baptist Church in Jacksonville.

At Northern Illinois University in DeKalb, Illinois, many students returning to their dorms from morning classes had lunch at around noon and chatted in the student lounge or went to their dorm rooms to relax or prepare to go to their afternoon classes. At about 12:30 p.m., if their radios were tuned to WLS in Chicago, as many of them were, they were hearing one of the popular songs of the day, "Dominique" by the Singing Nuns.[1]

Noted theologian C. S. Lewis, author of *Mere Christianity* and many other thought-provoking Christian works, died in London. Aldous Huxley, an author most famous for his novel, *Brave New World*, also died that day. In Chicago, novelist Saul Bellow was alive and well and was pecking away on his Smith Corona manual typewriter on his latest novel.

On the West Coast, actors Bob Denver and Alan Hale and others were finishing up the pilot episode of *Gilligan's Island*, which would be a long-running television show based on the antics of a group of eccentric people stranded on a desert island.[2]

In Michigan, the *Lansing State Journal* had a big story in its sports section on how Roger Littleton of nearby Williamston went hunting and bagged a 235-pound, nine point buck.[3]

Former Vice President Nixon, now a New York lawyer, had been in Dallas for a meeting of the board of directors of the Pepsi-Cola Corporation, for whom he was legal counsel. Former President Eisenhower was in New York to receive an award that night and had checked in to the Waldorf-Astoria Hotel. At the Waldorf Towers next door, former president Herbert Hoover, 89, was relaxing in his apartment. Former President Harry Truman was at his home in Independence, Missouri.

President Kennedy and Vice President Johnson were in Texas to try to heal some political wounds that had developed between Governor John Connally and Senator Ralph Yarborough, who were hardly speaking to one another. The president placed a call to former Vice President John Nance Garner in Yvalde, Texas, to wish him well on his 95th birthday. Both Kennedy and Johnson surely had seen one of the headlines that morning in the *Dallas Morning News*: "Nixon Predicts JFK May Drop Johnson." Nixon was only repeating what a lot of politicians were thinking because the rumors were rampant.[4]

Senator Goldwater had experienced a personal loss with the death of his mother-in-law and was flying to Indiana for the funeral.

In Dallas, Peter Yarrow, Noel "Paul" Stookey and Mary Travers were resting after performing in a concert in Fort Worth the previous night. Tonight, the singers known as "Peter, Paul and Mary" would be performing their hit songs, "If I Had a Hammer," and "Where Have All the Flowers Gone?" at a concert in Dallas. Almost two years earlier, they had performed for President Kennedy at the White House.[5]

In Washington, the Senate Rules Committee was conducting a hearing that dealt with suspected shady dealings of Vice President Johnson while he was still in the Senate, involving influence peddling and shakedowns. In New York, independent of the Senate investigation, *Life* magazine was preparing a series of articles on Johnson's wealth and some of the questionable ways in which he attained it.

At about 10:30 a.m. in Washington, Donald Reynolds, a Maryland insurance executive, was behind closed doors, telling his story to Burkett VanKirk, a legal counsel to the Senate Rules Committee and Lorin Drennan, who was with the General Accounting Office and who was invited to sit in on the meeting. Their topic was the suspected questionable wheeling and dealing of Lyndon Johnson.

The Senate committee was looking into actions of Robert "Bobby" Baker, secretary to Johnson when he was the Senate majority leader. Baker was well known in Washington as Johnson's errand boy who did nothing without Johnson's knowledge, permission or direct order. Among other things, Baker had helped establish a social club often frequented by members of Congress and their guests where the fun they had was often bawdy and involved women whose job was to entertain their guests.

While the focus of the investigation was on Baker, the testimony of witnesses brought the investigation closer and closer to LBJ. On November 22, Reynolds was telling how he secured a series of life insurance policies for Johnson, who was a poor risk because of heart ailments. The deals were lucrative for Reynolds but they came with a price. He said Johnson had manipulated him to purchase television advertising on television stations owned and operated by the Johnsons in Texas—advertising that would be useless to an insurance man in Maryland.

Reynolds said he also paid for an expensive stereo set for Lady Bird Johnson, a seemingly innocent transaction except it represented an unreported gift to a member of Congress.

He also told of a deal engineered by Johnson in which a contractor was awarded a contract for work on the new D.C. sports stadium in Washington and put up a performance bond of $108,000. The required bond was only $73,000. Reynolds reportedly got a piece of the action for being the middle man, Baker got a cut for arranging it and the remainder reportedly went into the LBJ campaign treasury.

Reynolds was still giving his accounts of alleged LBJ shakedowns when a secretary burst into the committee room weeping as she told the men President Kennedy had been shot and killed in Dallas.[6]

Johnson, the man mired in controversy, was now president of the United States. Because of the tragedy of the assassination and the sudden transition of power that was thrust onto LBJ, he was now looked upon with sympathy and support by much of the American public and by Congress. Nothing ever came of the Senate investigation into his alleged unethical financial deals.

8. November 22, 1963

Lyndon Johnson takes the oath of office aboard Air Force One after the assassination of President John F. Kennedy in Dallas on November 22, 1963 (Lyndon Baines Johnson Presidential Library).

There were many political ramifications to the assassination. Goldwater had been edging closer to finally agreeing to be a candidate. Now, he was the target of abuse by many who believed Kennedy's death was the result of the right-wing extremism that Goldwater symbolized. There were many other assassination theories too—a Mafia hit, a Communist plot, retaliation by Cuba or Russia over JFK's resolve in the Cuban missile crisis of the previous year or the botched Bay of Pigs invasion. But the unsubstantiated claims that right-wingers were involved was a terrific blow to the Goldwater forces.

One of the most extreme right-wing organizations of the day was the John Birch Society, an organization led by zealots who regarded most anything to the left of them as Communist-inspired and whose reputation was such that many Republicans repudiated them or kept a comfortable distance from them. When news of the assassination broke, even Tony Smith, Goldwater's press secretary, told a colleague, "My God, I'll bet one of those Birchers did it."[7]

"If a member of the John Birch Society or any other extremist group had fired the shots, the reaction against respectable conservatism generally and Barry Goldwater specifically would have instantly removed any possibility of him winning the Republican nomination."[8]

The John Birch Society was founded in 1958 in Indianapolis by a group of 12 men with a mission to be God-fearing, to fight Communism, promote small government and adhere to the principles of the Constitution. It published inflammatory, right-wing, anti–Communism literature and soon attracted a national following of admirers as well as detractors who considered the organization too extreme.

Its leader was Robert Welch, a flamboyant businessman who drew national publicity to his organization by some of his outlandish speeches and writings. In one of his more infamous pieces, he accused President Eisenhower of being a Communist sympathizer. The John Birch Society endorsed Goldwater for president.

Goldwater knew Welch's brother who lived in Arizona and met Welch through his friendship with the brother. Goldwater said he believed in Welch's conservative principles but did not approve of his irresponsible statements such as the condemnation of Eisenhower.

Goldwater said he rejected the notion of some John Birchers that people must accept 100 percent of their doctrine or be considered unloyal. In his autobiography, Goldwater wrote, "Most of the John Birchers are patriotic, concerned, law-abiding, hard-working and productive. There are a few whom I call Robert Welchers and these are the fanatics who regard everyone who doesn't totally agree with them as Communist sympathizers."[9]

A maudlin thought circulating around Washington shortly after the Kennedy assassination was that the bullet that killed JFK also "struck" Barry Goldwater.[10]

He had been edging closer to agreeing to be a candidate, albeit a reluctant one, which his supporters and advisers knew was not a good recipe for victory. But he seemed willing to throw his hat in the ring for the good of the cause. The assassination had him backtracking and rethinking what he should do.

Clif White had been criss-crossing the country all year, trying to build up support for Goldwater state by state and lining up delegate support for him that White believed was the key to securing the nomination. And he had watched as Goldwater had progressed from a disinterested noncandidate to someone who remained aloof but did nothing to stop the draft movement; he acted like someone who was about ready to give in and jump in.

Kennedy and Goldwater kidded each other about Goldwater's possible candidacy. "Don't announce too soon, Barry," Kennedy told him early in 1963. "The minute you do, you will be the target. If you give them 18 months to shoot you down, they will probably be able to do it."[11]

The two of them talked about the possibility of having a series of debates throughout the country, appearing together before the same audiences. In good humor, Kennedy reminded Goldwater of an article the Arizona senator had written several years before on how to be a good opponent in an election. There were five key points: Oppose but do not hate; keep a sense of humor; always oppose positively; learn all the tricks of campaigning; and applaud your opponent if he is right.[12]

As he considered his possible candidacy against Kennedy, he thought of the potential for the campaign to be almost a noble venture rather than a vulgar one. "We would lift this presidential campaign above the petty, conniving, scheming which had flawed every political race in my experience. We would present the American voters with an opportunity to make a reasoned decision based on contending political philosophies rather than on personality."[13]

November 22, 1963, changed everything. Goldwater disagreed with Kennedy on most policy issues but liked him personally and the thought of debating him on the campaign trail stirred his political juices. He held no such respect for Johnson whom he considered a faker, a liar and a wheeler-dealer who could not be trusted.

A year later, reflecting on his situation, Goldwater said, "When Kennedy died, I told my wife within a few days that I definitely would not seek the nomination. I didn't feel Johnson could be beaten because Johnson was a Southerner who would or should carry the South. Johnson understood power more than Kennedy did even though Bobby Kennedy understands it very well. Johnson would be more ruthless, which he is."[14]

There were other factors. Goldwater did not believe that the American public, swept up in the grief of the violent death of a vibrant, young president and hoping and praying for the new one, would choose to have three presidents in the space of a year.

From a purely political standpoint, the ascension of Johnson to the presidency changed everything and White recognized the problem almost immediately. He and others had thought that after the nomination was secured and the general election campaign began, Goldwater was in good position to carry most of the south, including Texas, where Johnson's popularity was waning. Indeed, the strategy had been to count on the South and West and Midwest, without ignoring the East, of course, but not counting on that support for victory.

Another problem for Goldwater, and for other Republican contenders for that matter, had been the self-imposed moratorium on political campaigning for one month after the assassination, agreed to by all potential candidates. But Johnson, the new president seeking all the help he could find in keeping the nation on an even keel, was inviting many of the country's most influential leaders to the White House to seek their support.

"The last strains of the bugler's 'Taps' sounding over Kennedy's grave were still echoing ... when Johnson started receiving an unending procession of national leaders—union presidents, businessmen and financiers, civil rights leaders. Everybody came.... And when they left, they almost invariably pledged their whole-hearted support to Lyndon Baines Johnson."[15]

Goldwater had been edging closer and closer to actively pursuing the candidacy but the assassination and the political aftermath had him once again hedging. On December 8, he met with Kitchel, O'Donnell, Senator Tower, Senator Norris Cotton of New Hampshire (home of the nation's first presidential primary), Senator Carl Curtis of Nebraska, Senator William Knowland of California; Congressman John Rhodes of Arizona; Dean Burch of Arizona, a conservative activist and good friend; Karl Hess, a speech writer; Jay Hall, a political philosopher and friend; and Bill Baroody, a wealthy, influential conservative and acquaintance who wanted to be in the inner circle.

Baroody was the head of the American Enterprise Institute, a conservative think tank that was founded in 1943 as a lobbyist for businesses and chambers of commerce. Under Baroody's leadership, it had become an organization filled with scholars, economists and business advocates who smothered Washington with intense lobbying and influence peddling. In Goldwater, Baroody saw the opportunity to be a kingmaker and he relished being part of the inner circle.

"Though he brought some measure of intellectual respectability to the campaign, Baroody was power hungry and jealous, a man Kitchel called 'a real Machiavellian type, a schemer' who had intense feelings of possessiveness about his place in the campaign."[16]

Goldwater reiterated all the reasons he shouldn't run—the odds were stacked against him, he no longer could count on winning the South, the country wasn't ready for yet another change of command and that he didn't want to run against Johnson whom he considered a liar and a hypocrite.

He thought about one of his rules for campaigning that he and Kennedy had talked about—to oppose but to do it without hate. "All my contacts with Lyndon Johnson had instructed me to believe he would be incapable of opposing without hate," Goldwater wrote in his autobiography."[17]

His advisers told him they had done the groundwork, that he had a nationwide brigade of backers who were just waiting to hear the word, that the cause was too great to ignore and that he was the champion of that cause.

Goldwater acquiesced and said he would think about it for a couple of days and get back to them. And there was much to think about. His reasons for not wanting to run had not changed. He didn't think he had much of a chance to win, not only because of his conservative views in a largely liberal world but also because Johnson's ascendency to the presidency had pretty well negated his backers' strategy of winning the south.

He also knew that his personal style would not help him. He didn't mince words when mincing would serve him best politically and he didn't like being shopped around from one state to another, one city to another, one town hall meeting to another, with hardly time to catch a breath.

And there was another personal factor. To some extent, he would have enjoyed running against Kennedy. He abhorred the thought of running against Johnson.

But Goldwater had always thought the principle was more important than the person, the cause more important than the inconvenience. He thought about Clif White and the Draft Goldwater movement and all the people around the country who had rallied to the cause. Their dedication needed a response.

"I think of myself as a pragmatic politician," he said, "one who finds no virtue in leading a lost cause." But he said he felt he was thrust into circumstances "where if I refused to be a candidate, thousands, perhaps millions of dedicated Americans who had responded to my descriptions of the dangers confronting the Republic would have cause to feel betrayed."[18]

So, two days later, he called Kitchel and told him he would run. They decided he should wait until after Christmas to make the formal announcement. Also, Goldwater insisted on not making the announcement in Washington but in Arizona.

Thus, on January 3, 1964, Goldwater emerged from his home in Phoenix, a cast on one foot as a result of recent surgery to remove a calcium deposit, and announced to the press and to the world that he was a candidate for president. "I have decided to do this because of the principles in which I believe," he said, adding he was convinced millions of Americans shared his beliefs. He said he had been expressing the same beliefs for 10 years and would express them even more in the coming months of the campaign.

"I was once asked what kind of Republican I was. I replied that I was not a 'me too' Republican. That still holds. I will not change my beliefs to win votes. I will offer a choice, not an echo," he said, promising a campaign based on principles and not on personalities.

He announced Kitchel would be his campaign chairman. Burch would be his assistant. Richard Kleindienst, another Arizona friend who had served one term in the Arizona Legislature, would be director of field operations; and Ann Eve Johnson of Tucson would head up women's operations.

Conspicuously absent from the campaign team were Clif White or anyone from the Draft Goldwater organization that had been working toward this moment for more than two years. Also missing were Steve Shadegg, who had been with Goldwater ever since he helped direct his 1952 upset victory for the U.S. Senate; Brent Bozell, Goldwater's alter ego and ghost writer of *The Conscience of a Conservative* and many other Goldwater writings; Bill Rusher, one of the founders of the Draft Goldwater movement; and conservative publisher William F. Buckley, an influential and intellectual man whom Baroody, among others, thought would be a liability to the campaign.

The senator had obviously opted for friendship and loyalty and people he knew he could trust as opposed to political operatives whose loyalty he believed was motivated by what they stood to gain personally. Shadegg and Bozell didn't fit into either of these categories and Shadegg later joined the campaign as a coordinator in western states. Except for Baroody, the entire inner circle of the campaign team was from Arizona. They would come to be known by their detractors as "The Arizona Mafia."

8. November 22, 1963

"Other high officials make up their weaknesses by surrounding themselves with advisors who possess the knowledge or judgment that they lack, but Goldwater did not choose his advisors wisely. He surrounded himself instead with incompetent cronies who had no experience in conducting a national political campaign and who reinforced his weaknesses."[19]

At the time Goldwater announced his candidacy, no one could have seen the irony of the man wearing a cast getting off on the wrong foot to start his campaign; that the once-reluctant candidate might find himself in a campaign that would be crippled by conflicts in both personalities and principles.

But now the guessing game was over. He was in it for the long haul.

Chapter 9

The Goldwater Kitchen Cabinet

Clif White and the leadership of the Draft Goldwater movement were surprised and disappointed that they were not invited to Phoenix to be there when Goldwater announced his candidacy. They had worked hard to put together a national organization, and the fact that Goldwater was now a candidate made White and his comrades the most successful draft organization in American history.

Middendorf, the treasurer and fundraiser for Draft Goldwater, said he and others expected Goldwater to announce a campaign staff and team that would include leaders from the Draft movement to work with Kitchel and the Arizona contingent. But it didn't happen.

"Goldwater was uncomfortable with people he didn't know well," said Middendorf. "And perhaps because of the misinformation he had been given about Clif's motives, he was suspicious of some of the Draft Goldwater people."[1]

On January 5, two days after Goldwater announced his candidacy, Kitchel invited White to a meeting at the Mayflower Hotel in Washington so White could brief the campaign team on what had been done so far, what plans had been made, and what to expect.

It was a curious position for White. He had not been told what role he would now have in the campaign, if any, and yet he was being asked to provide lessons to the very people who were apparently replacing him on the team. It was as if a baseball manager or football coach were being given the boot but were being asked to give their successors some lessons on how to manage or coach.

The winter meeting of the Republican National Committee was

to be held the following week in Washington so White spent much of his time discussing the inner workings of the committee and what needed to be done at the meeting to advance the Goldwater candidacy. Kitchel, Burch, Kleindienst and Ann Johnson listened attentively.

At some point, Kitchel brought up the subject of what part White was to play in the campaign and told him he could be an assistant to Kleindienst who was to direct field operations.

White was stunned. He was the only person in the group who had any experience in national political campaigns, dating back to Dewey in 1948 and Eisenhower in 1952. Moreover, it was quite a demotion for the man who spent two years spearheading the Goldwater movement.

White did his best to hide his disappointment but told Kitchel politely that he would not accept the position. He told him he wasn't hung up on titles. It was about the impact his slight role would have on all the people throughout the country who he had recruited and who had a relationship with him. They would be confused and frustrated by White's minor role and that would hurt the campaign. So White said no to Kitchel's offer.

Kleindienst intervened and said he and White could be partners in field operations and that it was important for Clif to have a significant presence and title. They agreed he could be "coordinator of field operations." White agreed to stay on.

That being settled, they all headed for another meeting in the hotel, this one with some members of the Draft Goldwater organization, which was about to be dissolved. Kitchel told the group about the new campaign organization and who would be doing what. He said he was the campaign chairman, Burch was his assistant, Kleindienst was head of field operations and that White would be Kleindienst's assistant. Kleindienst's assistant? It was if the prior conversation about job titles had never taken place.

If there was any thought remaining that the Draft Goldwater and the Kitchel organization would merge or work together in any way, that notion was quashed permanently the next day when Kitchel told O'Donnell, the national chairman of Draft Goldwater, there was no place for him in the national campaign organization. O'Donnell returned to Texas where he worked independently for the Goldwater campaign and resumed his philanthropic efforts.

Kleindienst and White tried their best to work together but did not have a close relationship. It was more of a case in which they tolerated each other and even that situation became strained. A few weeks into the campaign, Arizona Congressman John Rhodes, a friend and supporter of Goldwater's, received an anonymous letter blasting Kleindienst. When Kleindienst learned of the letter, he accused White of writing it or putting someone else up to it, which White denied.

Not long after that, the two men agreed it would be best if their duties were divided so they did not have to work so closely together. White was put in charge of planning and organizing all activities and events related to the national convention—a duty he was superbly qualified for, although in Kleindienst's thinking, his qualifications were secondary to the need for him to have some distance from Kleindienst.

When Kitchel heard about the dispute over the letter, he said White should have been fired. "Not quite two months into the 'marriage' of Draft Goldwater and Goldwater for President, we were ready for a divorce," said Middendorf, who remained as treasurer and was the only Draft Goldwater member who was part of the hierarchy of the new leadership.

"Kitchen cabinets"—teams of advisers whose chief qualification is their friendship and loyalty to their leader—are almost as old as the Republic itself. President Andrew Jackson had an inner circle of advisers who were not part of his official cabinet and had no particular political expertise.

Early in his administration, Jackson discovered that his regular cabinet members were so divided and argumentative that nothing was getting accomplished. So he stopped having cabinet meetings and used his department heads solely to execute the duties of their departments.

He relied on a circle of friends to advise him and help determine policy. Many in this "kitchen cabinet" were newspaper people who not only helped set policies but then promoted them through their publications.

Presidents Theodore Roosevelt and Franklin Roosevelt did not cast their official cabinet members aside but did covet the advice of close friends and cultivated close relationships with the press. And as Goldwater pointed out years after his campaign, President Jimmy Carter brought three Georgia friends to Washington with him: Hamilton Jordan, his chief of staff; Jody Powell, his press secretary; and Bert Lance, his director of finance. None had any national political experience.

The difference with Goldwater's "kitchen cabinet" from those of Jackson, the Roosevelts and Carter, is that in the other cases, the campaigns had been won and the winners were in the White House. Not so with Goldwater.

His campaign organization had some unusual flaws from the beginning. Trust, or lack of it, was a huge issue. Goldwater had enlisted the help of his Arizona friends because he did not have complete trust in the Draft Goldwater crowd. White and others did not trust the new Goldwater for President leadership because of their lack of experience. And, the Goldwater for President newcomers did not trust the Draft Goldwater people as evidenced by the skirmish between White and Kleindienst. Put it all together and there was a situation in which many of the people who should have been singularly focused on getting Barry Goldwater nominated did not trust one another.

Kitchel, 55, lawyer, longtime friend, looked much younger than his years with his blond hair and crew cut. He not only had no experience in Arizona politics, much less national politics, he had little interest in it. He was a friend, a manager, and organizer, not a politician.

Kitchel was born into a well-to-do family in Bronxville, New York, and graduated from Yale and from Harvard Law School. He was often abrupt and direct in his dealings with people, like a prosecutor in a courtroom. Also, he was slightly hard of hearing, an unfortunate quality in a city that often does business in whispers.

Campaign staffers were often taken aback by Kitchel's apparent aloofness. "Denny seemed to listen but without comment," said Middendorf, the Draft Goldwater holdover. "During the campaign I found that his hearing problem caused strangers to perceive him as cold, distant and even disinterested.... He was truly a sweet person albeit somewhat out of his depth in the grinding world of national politics."[2]

He also had disdain for small talk and, showing his lack of background in politics, couldn't understand why so many people in Washington talked in circles instead of just getting to the point. And he was not a conservative scholar or particularly knowledgeable about people who were.

Kitchel's lack of political knowledge made for some classic stories that made their way around the Washington circuit. He was once asked to consult with Arthur Summerfield on a particular matter. Kitchel is said to have responded, "I'll do it if you say so. Who is Arthur Summerfield?" The man whose name he didn't recognize was a former Republican National Chairman and postmaster general in Eisenhower's cabinet.[3]

Kitchel's value to Goldwater was their friendship and loyalty to one another. "He alone could dare talk back to Goldwater, to advise him in the strongest of language without fear of a snappy retort at the time or of being ignored by the senator in the future."[4]

Politicians who wanted to draw near to Goldwater or stay in his good graces soon learned to treat Kitchel with the greatest respect because he held the keys to the kingdom.

Burch was another Washington neophyte who joined the team. He was a 36-year-old lawyer from Tucson who also had the trait Goldwater valued most—loyalty. Whereas Goldwater saw Kitchel as a peer, he regarded young Burch as a protégé, an up-and-comer. He did not have the same influence with Goldwater that Kitchel enjoyed. He was a listener and a learner but not a critic.

Burch was kidded about not having traveled east of the Mississippi River until he was 28 years old when he came to Washington as Goldwater's administrative assistant. He returned to Arizona four years later to continue his law practice. Now he was back in Washington to work with Edward McCabe, a Washington lawyer who had worked in the Eisenhower administration, whom Kitchel hired as director of research for the campaign.

Kleindienst, a Harvard graduate, was the only member of the Arizona team who had any practical political experience. He was a former member of the Arizona House of Representatives and had been Arizona state Republican chairman.

He was born in Winslow, Arizona, in 1923, the son of a railroad man who was also the local postmaster. His mother died when he was a young boy and his father hired a Navajo Indian woman to be a housekeeper. She was a big influence on him and, among other things, taught him the Navajo language, something he never forgot.[5]

He was a brilliant student and was president of his senior class in high school. At the University of Arizona, he was an honor student and an honor cadet in the ROTC. In 1943, in the middle of World War II, he joined the Army and served as a navigator with the Army Air Forces in Italy. After the war, he returned to the United States and enrolled at Harvard where he graduated magna cum laude and was a member of Phi Beta Kappa.

After Harvard, Kleindienst returned to Arizona where he joined a law firm and became friends with Goldwater, who was then a prominent businessman and City Council member. At Goldwater's urging, Kleindienst got involved in politics, became a precinct committeeman and was a delegate to the 1952 Republican National Convention.

9. The Goldwater Kitchen Cabinet

Also in 1952, he ran and won election to the Arizona House of Representatives, becoming its youngest member. His political resume increased as he became president of the Arizona Young Republicans and served on the state central committee.

He had an impressive career in politics, but, like Kitchel and Burch, his background was in Arizona, the land of deserts, dry air, sunny skies, a profound Indian heritage and thousands of miles away—both geographically and culturally—from Washington, D.C., where politics ruled in what was basically a vast, one-industry town.

Kitchel, Burch and Kleindienst had a destination but none of them had experienced the journey they were about to start on behalf of Barry Goldwater.

Chapter 10

The Rocky Road

Barry Goldwater was a reluctant candidate who felt almost forced into a candidacy so he could advance a cause he believed in deeply; but he had an ardent constituency that was growing.

Nelson Rockefeller was an eager candidate in which one of the causes he believed in deeply was his ambition to become president, and if he worked hard enough at it, he would gain the constituency to get it done.

Whereas Goldwater was often victimized by his own words coming back to haunt him, Rockefeller was hurt more by actions he took that had political consequences, such as his divorce and remarriage.

As the campaign season approached, the two chief rivals for the Republican presidential nomination were a study in contrasts. Goldwater was a conservative westerner who was comfortable in jeans and cowboy hat and boots when he was home. He liked to ride horses and fly airplanes and play cards with his friends. Rockefeller was part of the Eastern Establishment liberal wing of the Republican party that had dominated the political scene for years. He was rich, famous and enjoyed the limelight that he inherited at birth.

When Goldwater spoke of offering voters "a choice, not an echo" in announcing his candidacy, he was referring to the choice that the values of conservatism offered voters as opposed to the echo of "me too" politics of the same old Republican dogma that Rockefeller represented and whose roots could be traced back at least as far as Tom Dewey, another New York governor, and a two-time loser for the presidency.

Goldwater had the ability to energize large crowds, to bring them to their feet with cheers and applause with his calls for change, often expressed in brash language. But he was not as good when talking with people individually or in small groups where his impulsive speaking style was sometimes taken as abrasive or offensive. Rockefeller was just the opposite. His speaking style was more stilted and academic and certainly not evangelistic when addressing large audiences. But he loved to go to places where he could shake as many hands as possible, pat people on the back and engage them in conversation.

Both men would have the opportunity to display their strengths and weaknesses as they faced each other in primary elections in several key states. The Draft Goldwater organization had not focused on the upcoming primary elections which they considered "beauty contests" of little value. Instead they wanted their network of supporters throughout the country to concentrate on securing delegates to the national convention.

The Goldwater for President organization, recognizing the backlash against their candidate by opponents who portrayed him as being an extremist and dangerous, saw the need not only to dispel those kinds of notions but to prove to everyone, including his supporters, that he could win. One way of doing that was for him to enter some primaries and prove his ability to win. The first test would be in New Hampshire.

Rockefeller had announced his candidacy on November 7, 1963, on the *Today* television program, a popular NBC early morning show where millions of Americans heard the overnight news as they awoke in the morning, got dressed and prepared to go to work or made breakfast and got the kids off to school.

Rockefeller wanted to get off to an auspicious start and, of course, money was no object. After the *Today* show announcement, he flew to New Hampshire to meet with state leaders and press some flesh. Later that same week, he had lunch in Manhattan with nearly 50 Maryland Republicans who flew to New York on a plane chartered by Rockefeller. Then he flew to Miami to give a speech, then back to New York for another speech and then off to Missouri for a gathering in St. Louis.

The pace was frenetic and seemingly nonstop. Rockefeller was trying to act statesmanlike as opposed to his conservative rival who sometimes seemed almost smart-alecky in the way he reacted to the public pressures of a national campaign. By the beginning of 1964, Rockefeller had paid staffers—not just volunteers—in states from coast to coast. For his television appearances, he had staffers who controlled almost every detail, from how much lighting there should be, to what camera angles were best, what would be the best colored clothing to wear and even how the TelePrompter should be positioned.

Rockefeller had put together an inner circle of polished advisers headed by a Harvard-educated lawyer named George L. Hinman. He was a well-connected New York attorney when he first drew Rockefeller's close attention in 1956. Politicians in New York were contemplating changes to the state's constitution. They created an organization with a typical long-winded bureaucratic title—The Temporary State Commission to Prepare for a Constitutional Convention. In essence, it was a commission charged with the responsibility of making sure everything was constitutional in changing the constitution.

Rockefeller was named chairman of the commission. Hinman was its legal counsel. The two men developed what turned out to be a lifelong professional relationship and friendship. When Rockefeller was elected governor in 1958, he named Hinman his executive assistant, a position Himan held for 12 years. He became a Republican national committeeman in 1959 and was a delegate to the national convention in 1960.

Hinman had a lot of influence with Rockefeller and was a strong advocate of the governor's running for president. He was known in some circles as "Rockefeller's Jim Farley"—a reference to Franklin D. Roosevelt's good friend and adviser who helped convince Roosevelt to seek the presidency in 1932.[1]

When Rockefeller decided to seek the presidency in 1964, Hinman was there to help lead the charge and be what historian Robert Novak called "ambassador at-large."[2]

And there were many others. Dr. William Ronan, a college professor who was on Rockefeller's staff in Albany, had a teacher's ability of not only sharing information but conveying his knowledge in an inoffensive way. He also preferred getting to the point rather than wallowing in small talk. Charles F. Moore, a former vice president of the Ford Motor Co., became a public relations strategist for the campaign. His reason for getting involved was as much his dislike of Goldwater as it was for his passion for Rockefeller. Roswell Perkins was tabbed to head the campaign's research department.

Robert McManus, who had been press secretary for Rockefeller in previous campaigns, would have a similar role this time around because of his familiarity with news organizations and the friends he had made in the media over the years. Harvard Professor Henry Kissinger, later to be a secretary of state and national security advisor in the Nixon presidency, was Rockefeller's advisor on foreign affairs.

The organization was huge. Most of the frontline people had

10. The Rocky Road 91

staffers working under them and the organization itself had a chief of staff, John A. Wells, a partner in a large New York law firm who was known as a fine administrator. "Lavishly funded, high-minded, shrewdly deployed, enthusiastic and tough, this team had been put together over three years of effort."[3]

Seemingly leaving nothing to chance, Rockefeller hired two sets of specialists with specific goals—one was to make him look good, the other to make Goldwater look bad. For the former, he hired the public relations firm of Spencer-Roberts & Associates, who specialized in packaging candidates in the best possible light. Someone with no political experience was portrayed as a model citizen and an up-and-comer, someone to be watched, someone who voters would be smart to get on their bandwagon early. Experienced candidates who might find themselves in a campaign against one of those young up-and-comers were transformed in political ads as elder statesmen, sages, people whose past performance and ideas for the future were worth following. Spencer-Roberts people were image makers.

Graham Thomas Tate Molitor was hired to be an image breaker. His specialty was to work undercover to find out as much dirt as he could about a political opponent or to use techniques to put the opponent in embarrassing positions. Molitor and his people researched past speeches and public appearances by an opponent, situations in which they misspoke, contradicted themselves or looked silly in one form or another, and made sure those instances became public. They would pose as news reporters and infiltrate opponents' press conferences and ask questions to try to catch the opponent off guard. "I can take anybody—I don't care who it is—and develop material that would annihilate them," Molitor bragged.[4]

Early in 1963, Rockefeller was the favorite to win the nomination. The Goldwater forces had mapped out a three-part strategy to overtake him. The first part was to work with state chairmen who supported Goldwater but where his delegate strength was not as good as they would like it to be. The solution was to convince those states to back a "favorite son" candidate—a popular senator or governor in their state who would be the standard bearer long enough to stop Rockefeller from a first-ballot nomination at the convention. Clif White was particularly interested in securing favorite-son candidates in states where Goldwater was likely to lose primary elections.

A second aspect of the strategy was to counter the conception that Goldwater couldn't win the nomination, let alone the general election.

In an effort to prove that Goldwater could win, his strategists had a change of heart about entering primaries. Their thought all along had been not to concentrate on primaries—what Goldwater himself referred to as "beauty contests"—but instead to focus on harnessing delegates. But one way of proving Goldwater could win was for him to run in key primary elections, carefully selected so the outcome would not be in doubt.

The third phase was to convince fellow Republicans that Rockefeller couldn't win. Clif White remembered well how in 1952 the Eisenhower forces did their best to convince delegates that "Taft Can't Win" and, in the end, they succeeded. So the Draft Goldwater organization hired Opinion Research Corp., a highly respected polling agency in New Jersey, to survey voters in New York on their preferences in the 1964 presidential election if the race was between Rockefeller and President Kennedy. The results were even better than expected. The winner would be Kennedy in a landslide. What would Rockefeller's chances be nationally if he couldn't even carry his own state? That was the message Clif White wanted to get out to the voters.

Sometimes the most well-conceived political strategies never get a chance to play out because of unforeseen circumstances that change everything. Sometimes they involve a startling world event or a national disaster that have political consequences. Sometimes a gaffe by a candidate is magnified by the press coverage it receives and causes lethal political damage.[5]

With Rockefeller, it occurred on May 4, 1963, with his marriage to Margaretta "Happy" Murphy. It wasn't just that he had divorced his first wife, although that was a factor for some. And it wasn't that he had remarried, although that was a factor for others. But Happy Murphy divorced her husband and relinquished custody of her four children to marry the governor of New York. And in the moral fiber of the early 1960s, that made Rockefeller a home wrecker.

"Nobody will ever be able to know if this three-part [Goldwater] strategy would have stopped Rockefeller and nominated Goldwater. Rockefeller's unprecedented act of political self-destruction made any Goldwater strategy unnecessary."[6]

Also, there was Rockefeller's "declaration of war" on July 14, 1963, in which he warned that conservative, right-wing extremists were subversives. While it made his position clear, and no doubt had the backing of the "me too" liberals, there was some question as to whether his call to arms put him as far to the left politically as he claimed Goldwater

10. The Rocky Road

was to the right. In other words, had he gone too far? Was he too an extremist? The voters would eventually decide. But it was clear that any hope of party unity was gone.

Sixteen states held primaries in 1964: New Hampshire, Wisconsin, Illinois, New Jersey, Massachusetts, Pennsylvania, Indiana, Ohio, Nebraska, west Virginia, Oregon, Maryland, Florida, California, South Dakota and Texas, as well as the District of Columbia.

On March 10, 1964, New Hampshire voters would go to the polls in the nation's first presidential primary election. The stakes were high. Goldwater needed a victory to prove he could win despite an ideology that many Republicans found extreme. Rockefeller needed to win to prove his political prowess could overcome a personal life that many Republicans found extreme.

And New Hampshire was just the first inning of what would be a long ballgame.

Chapter 11

Lyndon Johnson

Republicans faced an uphill battle in 1964, no matter who they nominated. When Draft Goldwater forces began to organize in 1961, at about the same time Rockefeller was putting together a future campaign organization, they both had similar motives. One was to overcome the mistakes of the 1960 presidential campaign, the errors that many in the GOP felt Nixon made that led to his narrow defeat. The other was to defeat President John Kennedy.

When Kennedy was assassinated in Dallas, the nation was in mourning but the political world, particularly for Republicans, was turned upside down. They were prepared to take on Kennedy, the Roman Catholic, the youngest president ever elected, the man whose cocky brother was now attorney general of the United States and whose father, in his day, was ruthless in getting what he wanted. They were prepared to take on the man who they believed botched the Bay of Pigs invasion, got us involved in the conflict in Southeast Asia and was slow in insisting on strong civil rights legislation moving forward in Congress.

Now, everything changed. The political dominoes had fallen. A new game had to be master-minded. The challenge now was to defeat Lyndon Johnson, the new president who had the sympathy of the country for the position he had suddenly been thrust into and the gratitude of the country for manfully shouldering the burden. And, as Goldwater pointed out many times while he deliberated on his future, the Republican nominee would be asking the American people to accept their third president in little more than a year. It was a tall order.

Lyndon Johnson was the consummate Washington politician. He didn't hide it. He flaunted it. How he became president was tragic. How he put himself in a position to be next in command is intriguing.

11. Lyndon Johnson

One of the challenges for political historians is to sift through facts and try to determine why something happened when all logic and reason would cast doubts on it ever happening.

Such is the case of Lyndon Baines Johnson, the majority leader of the United States Senate, the man who reveled in the power he held over other men and the legislation that didn't get anywhere without his approval. Why would a power-driven man who had reached the pinnacle of his legislative career, give it all up and agree to be second banana on a national ticket? Even if he won, he would be taking on a job that his fellow Texan and former vice president John Nance Garner said was not worth "a bucket of warm [spit]."

Johnson did not want the vice presidency except for the possible political gain he could receive from it, because that is how Johnson approached most any decision he made. In being vice president, he would be in a position to someday be president. And, 1,000 days after the Kennedy election, Johnson did become president of the United States. Thus, as 1964 approached, the two potential candidates, Johnson and Goldwater, pitted the reluctant vice president who was now president against a reluctant candidate who didn't think he could win.

When Johnson became president, or, more to the point, how he became president, was about the only time in his political career where his advancement was not part of a calculated strategy that was based on his ability to somehow always strike when the iron was hot.

He was born eight months after Barry Goldwater in 1908. As a young adult, he was a school teacher but by the age of 23 had already developed the knack of making political connections. He got a job as secretary to Texas Congressman Richard Kleberg in Washington. It wasn't long before he picked up on an important Washington trait—traveling in the right circles and meeting the right people.

He also got a chance to watch a politician he grew to admire—Senator Huey Long of Louisiana. Long, a former Louisiana governor, succeeded in politics by gaining political power and then using that power to help the people he served—by getting them patronage jobs, appointing them to boards and commissions, making sure their streets were paved. In doing these things, he received the adoration of the people. And because they were beholding to him for their jobs and their security, he was re-elected and the cycle of power-service-adoration would start all over again.

It was a formula Johnson used all of his political life—particularly because of his quest for the adoration of the people. That could be done by opening doors for them, providing them with a better life through jobs, appointments, favors and influence peddling—but to do that, the prerequisite was power. Johnson had "both an ego and insecurities as outsized as his extraordinary talent, an intense desire to be loved by everyone and a burning desire to be in control of the action."[1]

In 1935, President Franklin D. Roosevelt signed an executive order creating the National Youth Administration, an agency designed to create jobs for thousands of young Americans out of work because of the Great Depression. It needed directors in each state. Johnson recognized it immediately as an opportunity for him to have influence over people, to help them, and for them to appreciate him. He now had connections with the Texas congressional delegation and he used them to get himself appointed to head the program in Texas.

In 1937, Texas Congressman James Buchanan died and Johnson saw another opportunity to advance his personal agenda. He ran for the open seat and campaigned hard as a champion of FDR's programs. He won and served seven terms in the House, though he tried and failed to win a Senate seat in a special election in 1941.

In 1948, he ran for the Senate again, and this time was elected by the narrowest of margins, defeating Coke Stevenson in a primary runoff by 87 votes out of more than 900,000 cast. Stevenson accused Johnson of vote fraud, of stuffing ballot boxes with phony votes of people who had died or who had moved out of state or who had never lived in Texas. There were claims that in at least one precinct, "voters" had amazingly voted in alphabetical order.

Stevenson filed suit and his claim of vote fraud made it all the way to the Supreme Court. Attorney Abe Fortas defended Johnson and argued the Supreme Court had no jurisdiction over counting or recounting votes in a state election. It was not a constitutional issue, he argued, and the court agreed. It did not hear the case and Johnson took his seat in the Senate. But it earned him the nickname of "Landslide Lyndon," a moniker his political opponents never let him forget.[2]

Johnson was a master of learning the strengths and weaknesses of the people he worked with—knowing the names of their wives and children and remembering their birthdays and anniversaries; knowing their choice of liquor; recognizing what motivated them—and what they feared.

"Conversation for him was always a medium through which he sought to impose his will as well as a source of information that helped him direct his energies toward desired goals.... And such information would serve his compelling inward need to neutralize the possibility of surprise."[3]

Within three years, his colleagues elected him as minority whip, within five years, as minority leader, and within seven years, as majority leader. The majority leader positioned opened up through a set of circumstances that would have repercussions all the way to the 1964 presidential election.

Senator Ernest McFarland of Arizona had been majority leader and had been responsible for pushing through some major legislation during his tenure, including passage of the GI Bill after World War II, providing benefits to veterans returning home from the war. McFarland's Senate seat seemed safe but in 1952, he was defeated by a rising Republican upstart named Barry Goldwater who, by his own admission, was helped by being on the coattails of Dwight Eisenhower's election as president.

So, in a quirk of history, Johnson would probably never have gained the most powerful position in the United States Senate, a position he held until he became vice president, had it not been for the election of Barry Goldwater, the man who would one day run against him for president. By losing an election, McFarland elevated the political fortunes of both Goldwater and Johnson.[4]

Johnson's ability to get things done by manipulating people and circumstances was legendary in Washington. In addition to knowing many details of his colleagues' personal lives and using them to his advantage, he kept careful track of the committee assignments he doled out, using them as both rewards, punishment or incentives, depending on the situation.

He also utilized an almost instinctive sense of entitlement through which he caught companions off guard and yet attentive. Colleagues in the Senate talked of how they would be walking in the Senate parking lot, talking with Johnson, as they all were about to head home, when LBJ would stop, unzip his pants and urinate, all the while not missing a beat in the conversation.

But his domineering spirit was best exemplified by what came to be known as the "Johnson Treatment," a kind of physical engulfment in which he would wrap one arm against a person's shoulder and lean into him to the point where their faces were inches apart or the person was forced to lean backward, still in the grip of Johnson.

If the two were seated, Johnson often would have his guest sit on a couch or comfortable chair with LBJ sitting next to him with his leg stretched out in front of his guest, in effect, caging him in.

Goldwater was familiar with the Johnson Treatment but said it had two separate styles, depending on the situation. "We called the friendly approach, when he just put his hand on your shoulder, the Half-Johnson. When he put his arm clear around you and thrust his face close to yours to make his threats, we called it the Full-Johnson."[5]

Benjamin Bradlee, who worked for *Newsweek* magazine and later became famous as the editor of the *Washington Post*, was often a victim of the Johnson Treatment. "You really felt like a St. Bernard had licked your face for an hour," he said. Bradlee said the Johnson Treatment on women often included close enough physical contact that he would brush up against their breasts or, while gesturing with his hands, actually feel them, but being casual enough to make it seem accidental.[6]

Johnson biographer Doris Kearns Goodwin said, "The intimacy was all the more excusable because it seemed genuine and without menace. Yet it was the product of meticulous calculation. And it worked."[7]

His meticulous calculation was in full gear one night shortly after he became president when he attended the annual Gridiron Dinner in Washington, an event in which politicians and news people, who can be at each other's throats many times during the year, take time out on this night to poke fun at one another.

As Johnson was leaving the dinner, he ran into Senator Harry Byrd, the Virginia Democrat, and invited him over to the White House for a drink. At first Byrd resisted, saying it was late, but then agreed to come over for a short time. Johnson invited Vice President Humphrey to join them—and Humphrey was both witness and participant to what happened next.

When they arrived in LBJ's living quarters at the White House, Johnson and Byrd sat on the comfortable living room furniture. Johnson told Humphrey to fix Byrd's favorite drink—two fingers of bourbon. The three men had a few drinks and a few laughs as they small-talked. LBJ smiled and told Byrd his girlfriend was here. Then the president got up, went to a doorway and called Lady Bird, the first lady to join them. Lady Bird, dressed in a housecoat, came out and sat next to Byrd on the couch and flirted with him a little.

After a few minutes, Johnson got up, said it was getting late and it was time to break up their little gathering. As Lady Bird left the room, LBJ joked that any time he couldn't find his wife, he would go looking

Lyndon Johnson's lawyer and Supreme Court appointee Abe Fortas laughs perhaps because he knows he is getting the "Johnson Treatment," as the president leans into him in a hallway in 1964 (Lyndon Baines Johnson Presidential Library).

for Byrd. They all had a good laugh. Then he went over to where Byrd was sitting and leaned over him, so close that their cheeks practically touched. LBJ whispered to his guest that there was a tax bill tied up in committee and that he would very much like Byrd to use his influence to get it moving. Byrd agreed that he would.

Johnson had gotten what he wanted by inviting a tired old man to his home, softening him up with his favorite liquor and with some carefully staged flirtation and then putting on the full-court press. Humphrey, who witnessed it all, wrote about it in his autobiography and called it "the classic Johnson Treatment."[8]

As Senate Majority Leader, Johnson was in the position of power that he envisioned for himself back in the days when he watched in awe as Huey Long ruled over the people of Louisiana, using his power and influence to get things done and being rewarded by those helped through their votes and admiration for him. So it was a mystery to many observers in 1960 why Johnson agreed to leave the position he coveted to become John Kennedy's running mate and to become second banana in a job that had no power or influence, or for that matter, any clear cut responsibilities.

Kennedy's reasons for asking Johnson to join the ticket were fairly clear. It would probably assure JFK of carrying Texas in the election and help win other Southern states. And his knowledge of the workings of the Senate and his relationship with Senate colleagues would surely be helpful with future Kennedy legislative programs.

Goldwater was his usual blunt self in describing the seemingly unlikely pairing of two such opposite personalities. It was a "shotgun marriage," he said.[9]

But what was Johnson's motivation for seeking a job that he once described as that of becoming a political eunuch? Goldwater speculated that he might have seen it as a stepping stone to the prize he really wanted, the ultimate position of power and influence—the presidency. Of 34 presidents prior to Kennedy, 10 of them—just about one-third—had previously served as vice president. If Kennedy served two full terms, Johnson would be 60 when JFK left office and would have eight years as vice president to add to his resume. He would be in excellent political shape, always a consideration in his mind, unless something got in the way.[10]

Goldwater and other members of Congress had their own ideas on why Johnson agreed to be on the ticket. The word in Washington was that the Kennedy people approached Johnson at the convention in Los

Angeles and made him the offer. It was most likely done in a setting that was perhaps tense and certainly less than hospitable. Kennedy was on a quest to be president and Johnson, who came from a big state and held sway over an even bigger region, was one of the pieces to the puzzle. The offer was not an act of kindness. It was a business deal and refusal came with a price—language Johnson surely understood because he had used it so many times to get his way on the floor of the Senate.

"Lyndon was told that if he refused the number two spot, and Jack Kennedy could win without him, the new president's first act would be to order a full-scale inquiry into the growth of Lyndon Johnson's personal financial empire, including the monopolistic TV license which had helped make him millions."[11]

Senator Huey Long of Louisiana was an early hero of Lyndon Johnson because of his ability to use his power to gain the adulation of the public (U.S. Senate).

It might focus on the alleged kickbacks he received for some of the deals he engineered on the floor of the Senate. It might even reach back to the 1948 alleged vote fraud that got him elected to the Senate and earned him the "Landslide Lyndon" nickname.

For any one of these reasons, and perhaps all of them, Johnson agreed to be Kennedy's running mate. Three years later, he was president.

He was the incumbent, he sought and received the sympathy and support of a grieving nation, he pushed through major legislation emphasizing the memory and legacy of John F. Kennedy—including the Civil Rights bill—and, if past was prologue, he would stop at nothing in order to assure his re-election.

In fact, as Republicans gathered in San Francisco for their convention in July of 1964, Johnson was meeting with his aides and with representatives of the FBI as they mapped out plans for surveillance on people attending the upcoming Democratic convention in Atlantic City—a convention in which Johnson would be unopposed for the nomination. The surveillance would include bugging of hotel rooms, wiretaps and harassment of delegates who might get in the way of how the president wanted the convention to run.

For certain, the political landscape had changed on November 22, 1963, and everyone heavily or remotely involved in national politics knew it.

Chapter 12

New Hampshire

Lyndon Johnson would be a formidable opponent for whoever earned the Republican presidential nomination, and for those who sought it, the journey began in New Hampshire. It is a state as small as a little finger on the body of America but packs a significant political punch because it holds the first presidential primary, the first glimpse for the rest of America of whether a candidate can hold up under the enormous scrutiny that prevails.

New Hampshire has a proud history and a proud populace. It was one of the original 13 colonies and is situated in the heart of New England, bordered partly by the Atlantic Ocean on the east, by the province of Quebec, Canada, to the north, Massachusetts to the south and Vermont, almost like a twin brother in size and shape, to the west.

It is the place that statesman Daniel Webster, writer Horace Greeley, poet Robert Frost, astronaut Alan Shepard and Hall of Fame ballplayer Carlton Fisk all called home at one time or another.

There are a half-dozen cities in the United States that are larger than New Hampshire and it is fifth smallest in land area. But its citizens think of themselves as being rock solid and the state nickname, "the Granite State," comes from the number of granite quarries that exist. The pragmatism and forthrightness of its people and its heritage are embodied in the state slogan, "Live Free or Die."

New Hampshire is picturesque much of the year, with lush green countrysides and snow-capped mountains and an ocean at its side. The winters, though, are cold, damp, snowy and windy, an often uninviting atmosphere for travelers and visitors—and it was this environment that greeted presidential candidates in 1964 as the trudged their way to town hall meetings, Lions Club luncheons, Women's Club teas and stops at coffee shops, barber shops, factories, radio stations, television studios and newspaper offices.

The campaign trail included Nashua, a thriving metropolis, Concord, the state capital, Manchester, home of the state's most influential newspaper and places like Dixie Notch in Coos County. Dixie Notch, population less than 100, had a proud political tradition because of a state law that allowed cities of 100 or less to open their polls at midnight on election day and close after every registered voter had cast their ballot. It was not unusual for people in the rest of the country to wake up, get their morning coffee and turn on the *Today* show to see who "won" in Dixie Notch.

Nelson Rockefeller had announced his candidacy a full two months before Goldwater and had his eye on the presidency long before that. So forays into New Hampshire had become fairly routine to him. He wasn't a New Englander, but as a New Yorker, he was a neighbor. To many in New Hampshire, he was a celebrity, the richest man they were ever likely to meet. And perhaps more important politically, he was an alternative to Barry Goldwater.

A typical campaign day for Rockefeller might start with a reception at a Veterans of Foreign Wars hall outside Manchester, then a meeting with the editorial board of the *Nashua Telegraph*, then a tour of downtown Nashua followed by an opening of a Rockefeller for President headquarters in another nearby town, a dinner and speech at a Chamber of Commerce function in yet another town and then fly home and rest up for another day of campaigning. Each trip involved shaking hundreds of hands and answering dozens of questions, often the same questions over and over again in each town that he hit.

"What was different enough to set the tone for the entire primary round was the nature of the questions—they were flat, serious, drilling and above all, concerned. From beer hall to citizens' receptions to Chamber of Commerce, the same questions came up."[1]

What about Cuba? What about Russia? What about Berlin? What about the bomb? What about the U.N.? These New Hampshire folks were concerned about foreign policy as it related to their security. And the same was true on domestic issues—Social Security, civil rights, taxes.

Rockefeller and Goldwater had widely differing views on the issues, and they also had far different strengths and weaknesses on the campaign trail. Rockefeller enjoyed his celebrity status and loved to mingle with the masses, shaking their hands, patting them on the back, talking to them about their bowling scores and the price of meat at the supermarket. Goldwater was inherently uncomfortable with being treated like a movie star and his penchant for speaking off the cuff hurt him when he talked to individuals who didn't know him or to small groups hoping to get to know him. His gift was speaking to large crowds, energizing them with bold statements that soared across an arena or auditorium and brought applause and adulation and no need for cross-examination.

Moreover, while Rockefeller's campaign was being managed by professionals—professional politicians, professional public relations experts, professional media specialists, professional researchers—Goldwater's was being managed by sincere, loyal, hard-working friends who had never set foot into the thistle-packed terrain of national politics. While Rockefeller's handlers had to ease public concern over the candidate's divorce and remarriage, Goldwater's handlers had to ease public concern over their candidate.

"For mismanagement, blundering and sheer naivety, Goldwater's New Hampshire campaign was unique," wrote historian Theodore White. He had come into the state with the reputation of being the nation's number one conservative; he had the backing of the state's political machine and the support of the state's largest newspaper, the *Manchester Union Leader*. But what he didn't seem to have control over—what nobody who worked with him had control over—was his own candor.

Past comments came back to haunt him. He once had remarked, "Sometimes I think this country would be better off if we could just saw off the eastern seaboard and let it float out to sea"—not a concept endearing to people in the Granite State. He had advocated an overhaul of the Social Security system, suggesting it should be voluntary, which was regarded as a threat to the economic security of senior citizens. Four months before arriving in New Hampshire, he gave a speech in Connecticut in which he gave the impression of favoring use of atomic weapons by NATO commanders. He told another audience "we ought to lob one into the men's room at the Kremlin."

Addressing an economic forum in New York during a break from his New Hampshire campaigning, he gave his frank assessment about unemployment in the United States: "We are told ... that many people lack skills and cannot find jobs because they do not have an education.... The fact is that most people who have no skills have no education for the same reason—low intelligence or ambition."

Those kinds of remarks about atom bombs, Social Security, unemployment and other sensitive issues were regarded as courageous by some, wacky by others. They were good fodder for after-dinner speeches at political events.

"But now he was an avowed candidate for the presidency, followed everywhere by intrusive newspaper and television reporters jostling one another and the candidate to relay whatever unguarded remark might fall at any moment. And his remarks fell, unguarded, one after the other."[2]

In a coffee shop in Hanover, Goldwater seemed perplexed at what he was being asked to do. In a voice easily heard by patrons he was supposed to impress, the senator said, "I'm not one of these baby-kissing, hand-shaking, blintz-eating candidates; I don't like to insult the American intelligence by thinking that slapping people on the back is going to get you votes."[3]

News people whose job it is to follow a political candidate from one state to another and from one town to another, one luncheon or dinner or coffee shop stop to another, have a huge problem in trying to produce fresh copy—something new to report to their readers, viewers or listeners. Candidates develop basic "stump speeches" in which they endorse the same values, emphasize the same points—sometimes using exactly the same words—at each campaign stop. It is up to the reporter to try to find a new angle to the same story where only the setting has changed. Goldwater often provided that new angle by something unscripted that he would say either during his speech or in casual conversation with people before or after his carefully crafted remarks.[4]

The pace of the campaign favored Rockefeller over Goldwater. Rockefeller was much better suited to the daily grind and it was not unusual for him to make appearances in several states, including New Hampshire, in one day. Goldwater grew weary from the intense travel schedule his handlers had arranged, sometimes making it impossible for him to arrive at a scheduled destination on time, and the tardiness and the rush to get from one place to another would occur several times a day, almost every day. Besides that, his foot still hurt. A tired, irritable candidate is not in a good position to put on a happy face.

Such was the case on his first Sunday news show appearance after announcing his candidacy. On January 5, he was a guest on *Meet the Press*, the number one show of its kind, with a huge national audience. He still had a cast on his foot from the recent surgery, but it was a walking cast, allowing him to get around and take short journeys on foot.

On this Sunday morning, the sun was out, the air was cool but not uncomfortable, and Goldwater decided to walk the several blocks from his Washington apartment to the NBC studios.

By the time he arrived, he realized the walking cast was not intended for long jaunts. He was tired, his leg ached and he acted like he just wanted to get it over with. He was given the opportunity to have a briefing before the show and turned it down. He said briefings never helped because questions on the air were never the same as the ones in the briefing.

Then, when the live show was broadcast, the weary candidate misspoke several times, such as referring to political scientist Hans Morgenthau as "one of the greatest physicists in the world." And he couldn't resist giving a sarcastic answer to a reasonable question from moderator Lawrence Spivak about whether he would be willing to negotiate with the Soviet Union on disarmament. He said he would tell Russian Premier Nikita Khrushchev, "If you mean what you say, Mr. Khrushchev, then put up or shut up, as we western poker players say."[5]

When asked what the consequences would be if the U.S. broke off diplomatic relations with the Soviet Union, he said the Soviet Union would do everything they could to prevent that. Then he reminded Spivak (and the television audience) that it would take Senate action to break off relations—which wasn't factual.

Still later in the program when asked what his opinion was of President Kennedy using federal troops to allow black students to enroll at the University of Alabama and University of Mississippi. Goldwater replied that Kennedy hadn't used federal troops; he had used federal marshals, which again was inaccurate.

Goldwater, usually meticulous with his facts, was obviously distracted either by the pain in his leg, his weariness or nervousness. Whatever the cause, it was an awful beginning to what was to be a long campaign.

Goldwater also had a penchant for using salty language when he was upset, a trait political candidates usually guard against and that made some New Hampshire residents shake their heads. It was not unusual for him to bemoan the "damn" cast on his foot or enter a place and ask "where the hell" he was supposed to stand or sit. *Newsweek* magazine quipped it was a good thing Goldwater had a cast on one foot "or he would have that, too, in his mouth."[6]

Rockefeller's handlers did their best to show their candidate in the most positive ways. They left the expensive vehicles at home. They wanted their man to speak profoundly, but not academically or condescendingly on the issues of the day. He was able to do this easily by simply keeping track of what Goldwater had said and then pounce on the Senator's remarks. He did everything he could to counter the image of being the rich boy trying to buy the biggest gift. The image that he had the most difficulty shaking was that of a home wrecker. William Loeb, publisher of the *Manchester Guardian Leader* and an unabashed conservative, referred to Rockefeller in print as a "wife swapper."

So both candidates had image problems that dogged them. And they had other opposition in the primary, although none of the other candidates were considered serious contenders.

Senator Margaret Chase Smith of the neighboring state of Maine became the first woman to be a bona fide presidential candidate when she filed the necessary papers to be on the New Hampshire primary ballot. Mrs. Smith, at 66, the oldest person running, was also the person with the most experience in Washington. She was the widow of Clyde Smith, a congressman who died in 1940. She had been his secretary and won a special election to fill out his term which was to end in several months. She then won the general election and served four terms in the House. In 1948 she ran for the U.S. Senate and won, becoming part of a freshman class that also included Lyndon Johnson, Hubert Humphrey and Russell Long, son of Huey Long, Louisiana's colorful governor and senator. She was the first woman in history to serve in both the House and the Senate.

Senator Margaret Chase Smith, of Maine, was the first woman to have her name placed in nomination president after competing in several primaries in 1964. She is shown here in 1943, three years after succeeding her husband in the House of Representatives (Library of Congress).

Mrs. Smith was best known in the Senate as being the first senator to publicly condemn the actions of Senator Joseph McCarthy, the Republican from Wisconsin who made wild accusations about prominent people who he believed had Communist ties.

Senator Smith was well-respected and considered herself a serious candidate, having filed papers to enter several other primaries. But, traditional New Hampshire, voters were not likely to support the idea of a woman president, but she might gain some momentum for a possible shot at the vice presidency.[7]

Another candidate was Harold Stassen who served three two-year terms as governor of Minnesota in the 1930s and '40s and lost a bid for a fourth term. By 1964, he had also run for president four other times—in 1940, 1944, 1948 and 1952—and had also run for the U.S. Senate, Pennsylvania governorship and Philadelphia mayor. He was a perpetual candidate with no constituency.[8]

A fifth name on the ballot was that of Norman LePage, an accountant from Nashua, for whom there was no accounting for why he was running and would be a no-account on election day.

Governor Scranton in Pennsylvania and Governor Romney in Michigan stayed out of it. Nixon also was not a factor. The race to win over New Hampshire voters appeared to be a slugfest between the two heavyweights, Goldwater and Rockefeller, each representing opposite wings of the Republican party.

Neither one of them could have anticipated what happened in the final weeks of the campaign.

Paul Grindle was a 43-year-old, happy-go-lucky entrepreneur, a Harvard drop-out who had bounced around as a newspaper reporter and then a public relations man in New York who went back to Boston where he developed a unique but successful direct mail business, selling scientific instruments. He had become good friends with a Bostonian, David Goldberg, 34, who was a bored lawyer looking for some excitement. The two of them, and two friends, Sally Saltonstall and Caroline Williams, had gotten involved in the 1962 Senate campaign of George Lodge, son of Henry Cabot Lodge. George Lodge had an uphill and eventually losing battle against Edward "Ted" Kennedy, brother of both the president and attorney general.

The following year, "just for fun" as Grindle later described it, they decided to launch a "Lodge for President" campaign in New Hampshire—not for George Lodge, but for his father—even though their candidate was 10,000 miles away and had no idea what they were undertaking.

Grindle and Goldberg went to Concord on January 10, rented an empty store for $400 for two months, had a telephone put in and got a couch and some folding chairs, most of it donated by the Republican headquarters. They hired a sign painter to paint a "Lodge for President" sign over their doorway, and they were in business.

Their goal was to get 12,000 votes and three or four delegates for Lodge. If they did that, they would try to have the same success in Oregon, site of the next big primary. But they knew, in reality, the goal for New Hampshire was more of a dream, part of the fun for a couple of novices trying to operate a political campaign on a shoestring.

The key to their plan was Grindle's firsthand knowledge of the direct mail business. He and his cohorts got a list of registered Republicans in New Hampshire and sent out 96,000 mailers that included a brochure with photos of Lodge and a summary of his impressive resume. They also included poll results that showed that Lodge had the best chance of defeating Lyndon Johnson—better than Rockefeller or Goldwater.

The mailer included postage-paid postcards with their return address, seeking volunteers who would be willing to work for Lodge's election. In the direct mail business, a 1 percent response is considered very good; companies make a lot of money on a 1 percent response. So the Lodge for President people were astounded when they received 8,600 replies—nearly 10 percent.

Now they were getting the attention of the local and national media, all of whom were desperately looking for a new angle on the New Hampshire primary story. The media attention brought more supporters, more volunteers and some cash to keep this "fun" going.

They had already gotten some help from Robert Mullen, a Washington publicist, who had contacts with key newspaper reporters and columnists. Their working relationship paid off on both ends—Mullen would supply them with tips for good stories. When they were published, Mullen's clients would benefit and his credibility would be enhanced. Grindle talked to Mullen and Mullen talked to Roscoe Drummond of the *New York Herald Tribune*, who told his readers, "My information is that the unresolved question is not whether Mr. Lodge is going to resign his ambassadorship and become an open, active and campaigning candidate—but when."[9]

Also, the same column contained the announcement of a 50-state drive to secure one million signatures in support of Lodge. That was a fabrication—little more than wishful thinking on Grindle's part. He had hardly enough money to pay his rent, let alone finance a nationwide campaign. But he and his friends got nationwide publicity out of it.

They used the names from the response to the first mailing to send out a second one, this one seeking volunteers in every county of the state and asking each recipient to find two friends to join the effort.

The movement to nominate Lodge, still without his consent, had become a factor because some aspect of it was in the news nearly every day. Volunteers were going door to door throughout the state to expand the effort.

A third mailing that went to everyone who expressed an interest contained a sample ballot with specific instructions on the proper way to write in the name of Henry Cabot Lodge.

"The story grew and grew, swelled and swelled. But was the Lodge boom real? Could a write-in candidate, 10,000 miles away, managed by amateurs, beat two such highly organized campaigns so profoundly serious in meaning and in content?"[10]

Could "fun" conquer politics?

On the evening of March 10, after New Hampshire residents had withstood a snowstorm that slowed everyday life and, at the polls, put up with paper ballots for everything from the presidential race to votes on incidental local issues, the final results made national headlines. At about 7:15 p.m., Walter Cronkite was informing his viewers on CBS television that Henry Cabot Lodge had won the New Hampshire primary, amassing 33,007 write-in votes. Goldwater had finished second with 20,692 and Rockefeller third with 19,504. In another quirk, Richard Nixon, with 15,587 write-in votes, had finished fourth, well ahead of Senator Smith who had 2,120.

Goldwater was shocked and disappointed. Rockefeller was livid. Though Lodge was halfway across the world in Saigon, Rockefeller felt he had been double-crossed. Since Lodge worked for the State Department, he could not actively take part in anyone's campaign, let alone his

Henry Cabot Lodge won the New Hampshire primary though he was not on the ballot and was 10,000 miles away (Library of Congress).

own, but before the Kennedy assassination, he had encouraged Rockefeller to run. He convinced Rockefeller he would not only be a strong candidate but a viable alternative for Republicans to Goldwater. Now, Grindle and Goldberg, with support from George Lodge, had upended the Rockefeller express in New Hampshire. Rocky felt the Lodge write-in contingency had siphoned off anti–Goldwater votes from him, and that he would have won the primary had Grindle and Goldberg stayed home and minded their own business.

Rockefeller and his staff began referring to Lodge as "Henry Sabotage."[11]

But the truth was: Lodge got the undecided vote. "While Goldwater and Rockefeller were exhausting themselves trudging up and down the state, the Lodge team quietly completed their political homework for a candidate thousands of miles away. How well their homework paid off became known to the nation within minutes after the polls closed in New Hampshire on March 10."[12]

One other telling factor: Lodge had 35 percent of the vote. Goldwater had 23 percent and Rockefeller just over 20 percent. The two "heavyweights" combined received less than 50 percent of the votes cast.

"By the election's end, the result would prove to be a bitter, exhaustive [sic] and expensive endeavor for nothing, for Goldwater and Rockefeller reaped no delegates, no public relations bonanza and no moral victories of any sort."[13]

When Lodge received the news in Saigon, he said forthrightly that he did not intend to go to the United States, that he intended to continue his work in Saigon and that he was not going to resign from his ambassadorship.

Goldwater summed up the New Hampshire campaign succinctly, saying simply, "I goofed up somewhere." Dating back to his days running for the City Council in Phoenix, this was his first political defeat. Meanwhile, in the White House, President Johnson put out the word to the State Department and Defense Department—keep Lodge happy. LBJ's political instincts, which were part of his DNA, told him it was best to keep a possible political opponent 10,000 miles away.

A joke making the rounds of New Hampshire coffee shops the day after the primary was testimony to the apparent futility of the round-the-clock campaigning of Rockefeller and Goldwater for three months compared to Lodge, who had not set foot on American soil, let alone the streets of New Hampshire. The joke had one townsperson asking another how Lodge could have pulled off a victory. The other man replied, "I dunno. Maybe because he didn't bother us none."[14]

The New Hampshire experience was grueling and the outcome was grim for the "Arizona Mafia" men who were well intentioned but woefully inexperienced. They had been defeated by a bunch of kids "having fun."

The Arizonians had to also realize they were now further behind than when they started, that the senator had lost the primary he had gotten into originally to prove to moderate and liberal Republicans across the country that he could win. And they couldn't say they hadn't been warned.

Peter O'Donnell, the Draft Goldwater chairman who had been thrown overboard by the new regime, advised against Goldwater getting into any primaries. He felt that the senator had enough delegate strength to have locked up the nomination unless something came along to upset the apple cart—and a bad showing in the primaries could do that if some of his delegates were persuaded to back someone else. He also thought a series of bitterly fought primaries would divide the party even more than it already was.

O'Donnell had another novel thought to unite the party. He thought Goldwater should offer the vice presidency to Scranton as another way of unifying the party. Scranton would balance the ticket because of his more moderate views on issues, he came from a large Eastern state and he was well qualified. Also, said O'Donnell, he was likely to accept the offer because of his sense of duty and because of personal ambition.

It was an interesting scenario that O'Donnell proposed but the main point was to skip the primaries. "There's no point in you dissipating your energies by campaigning against other Republicans for the next eight or nine months," said O'Donnell.[15]

At about that same time, the campaign crew received some advice from an old political sage who had been part of several previous successful presidential campaigns.

Raymond Moley had been a speech writer and confidante in the Franklin D. Roosevelt White House in the 1930s who broke ranks with Roosevelt and eventually the Democratic Party. In the strange world of politics, an old New Dealer was now offering help to the man who regarded the New Deal as constitutional blasphemy.

Moley, now a columnist for *Newsweek* magazine, advised Goldwater in person to stay out of the New Hampshire primary, saying it was a no-win situation for him but could elevate some of his opponents.

He told the senator he didn't need the exposure; he and his views were already well known. A win wouldn't be terribly significant but a loss could be devastating. The Arizona Mafia listened to the advice and then ignored it.[16]

Chapter 13

Scranton and Romney

There were many lessons to be learned from the events in New Hampshire, none of them too good for the Republican Party and its candidates. Goldwater's public image had taken a beating at least in part because of his candor—and a lot of his spontaneous combustion was the result of the hectic schedule his inexperienced handlers had set up for him, causing him to be weary and irritable. He did not function well on 18-hour days and campaign stops in which he was forced to chit-chat with small groups and pose for photo ops at supermarkets, barber shops and the openings of campaign headquarters in towns too small to be even seen on state maps.

Rockefeller had a bigger problem. When he walked into a room, many of the undecided voters, the ones he needed to win over, saw him as the man who divorced his wife and married his girlfriend, or that his new wife deserted her husband and children to marry him, or, worse yet, that he was a "wife swapper," as Manchester publisher William Loeb had portrayed him.

The election results showed there was still a political vacuum in the Republican Party, just as there had been when Nixon lost the presidential race to Kennedy in 1960. A political vacuum has two distinct byproducts: It forces the question of "where do we go from here?"—and someone always emerges to fill the vacuum. Rockefeller had believed for four years that he was the person to do it. Clif White believed for almost that long that Goldwater was the right man at the right time but it took a couple of years to convince Goldwater.

Rockefeller, the early front runner until his remarriage but now consistently behind in most polls, thought New Hampshire would help turn the tide and be the first step in his march toward the nomination and eventually the presidency. Goldwater thought New Hampshire would be the place where he could prove to doubting Republicans—and to a skeptical nation—that he could win.

But when the two of them failed to get even half the vote between them, despite this very small sampling of public opinion, one inevitable conclusion was that rank-and-file Republicans were looking for an alternative. In New Hampshire, that turned out to be Henry Cabot Lodge—the voters' choice perhaps, but someone who was not highly regarded within the party as a strong candidate.

Goldwater considered him to be politically lazy, someone whose best days were behind him. In Goldwater's estimation, Lodge didn't do much as Nixon's vice presidential candidate to help win the election. And most recently, by accepting President Kennedy's appointment as ambassador in Saigon, he not only had compromised his loyalty to the Republican Party, he had also damaged his credibility concerning the merits of the war in Southeast Asia.

For Rockefeller, the assessment of Lodge was much simpler. He had betrayed him in New Hampshire. He had stabbed him in the back. He had deprived Rockefeller of the win he needed to shift the momentum. He was Henry Sabotage.

"There were no winners out of New Hampshire and only two non-losers, Nixon and Scranton. Nixon's fourth place finish in New Hampshire was lackluster, but nothing much had been expected of his listless write-in campaign anyway. Scranton collected only 77 [repeat, 77] write-in votes but he had no campaign at all."[1]

Nixon always seemed to have a way of rising from the ashes. Like Lyndon Johnson, he thought of most everything in terms of its political ramifications and lacked warmth in his personal relationships. He overcame a possible scandal as Eisenhower's running mate in 1952 with his famous "Checkers" speech and had survived a disastrous televised debate with John Kennedy in 1960 to almost win the presidency. He seemed to have written his own political obituary in 1962 when he lost the governor's race in California and held the news conference in which he declared the press wouldn't have him to "kick around" any more. But Nixon had a way of hanging around and got 15,000 write-in votes in New Hampshire from people who seemed to be saying they preferred someone else—even Nixon—to Goldwater or Rockefeller. That was not a rousing endorsement, and nationally, he was thought of by many Republicans as damaged goods. He had "the odor of a loser," as historian Theodore White put it.[2]

13. Scranton and Romney

The Rockefeller advertising team had been busy trying to shape their candidate's image in a way that would make voters forget about his divorce and remarriage. Later, they produced an ad that showed, in one part of it, Rockefeller surrounded by Scranton and Romney and other possible contenders. Nearby in the same ad was a photo of Goldwater with no one around him. The caption, in headline type beneath the photos, asked: "Which do you want—a leader or a loner?" Though the ad was produced after the New Hampshire primary, voters of New Hampshire had seemed to answer the question: "Neither."[3]

The *New York Herald Tribune* editorialized on the dilemma of the GOP three months before the New Hampshire primary. It pointed to the motivation and ambition of Goldwater, Rockefeller, Romney and Scranton but warned, "none of these men will have a chance and all their preparations will be purely academic if every faction pursues its own fractious way and the main goal of a party victory is submerged by the lesser goals of personal victory."[4]

Scranton, serving his first term as governor of Pennsylvania after serving a term in the U.S. House, had said repeatedly he was not a candidate for president but he had a way of couching his words as if to leave the door open a crack. In his home state of Pennsylvania, where he had agreed to be a favorite son candidate, he sometimes corrected newsmen, saying he was simply a "favorite son," apparently reminding them of his popularity but still keeping his distance from the race.

But unlike Goldwater, Rockefeller and Nixon, he came out of New Hampshire unscathed despite his paltry 77 votes and he was considered a moderate within the party rather than a "me too liberal" or a wild, extremist conservative. And he represented a large state in the Northeast, a factor that wouldn't hurt Republicans on election day—and neutralized the geographic element that Rockefeller represented.

Scranton also had a boyish charm that reminded some observers of Kennedy and he had a pedigree, like Kennedy, of wealth and influence. His ancestors had founded the city of Scranton. His wife, Mary, was attractive, intelligent and energetic. She was a devoted wife and a political asset to her husband. Scranton's brother-in-law, James Linen, was president of the corporation that published *Time* and *Life* magazines, two of the most popular periodicals of the era.

The noncandidate had a way of showing up in Washington at opportune times, such as when the Republican National Committee was holding its annual meeting. Scranton said the timing was purely coincidental.

And he did not stop people like Thomas McCabe of Philadelphia, the wealthy head of the Scott Paper Company, who arranged luncheons with politicians and business leaders in the company's board room and would invite the governor to come and speak about his programs and political philosophies.

One such luncheon included the likes of William Paley, head of the Columbia Broadcasting System (CBS); Walter Thayer, publisher of the *New York Herald Tribune*; Herbert Brownell, former chief of staff for New York Governor Thomas Dewey; George Humphrey, secretary of the treasury for President Eisenhower; and Thomas Gates, secretary of Defense under Eisenhower and now president of Morgan Guaranty Trust Company.[5]

Scranton had a lot to talk about in his first year as governor. He oversaw reforms and expansion of the state's civil service system, improved medical care for senior citizens, strengthened professional licensing processes, stiffened controls over strip mines and convinced the legislature to increase state spending on a number of issues.

While Scranton may have talked about his legislative program over soup and sandwiches, it was not lost on those attending as to McCabe's real purpose of the luncheon. He enjoyed his role of being a kingmaker and the potential king did not resist while publicly appearing aloof.

The *New York Herald Tribune* was not as subtle. Never a big fan of Rockefeller, the newspaper editorialized on December 23, 1963, that "Pennsylvania's governor, William Scranton is a man with a weakness for one temptation—the call to duty." It mentioned his service in the House of Representatives and as governor and concluded, "It seems clear to us that duty again calls William Scranton, this time the highest political duty of all: to place himself open in the running for the Republican presidential nomination."[6]

Scranton and Goldwater had enjoyed a professional relationship that had nothing to do with politics. "It might seem surprising, given the ideological differences between the two, that Scranton and Goldwater earlier in their careers had been good friends. Goldwater had been Scranton's officer in a Capitol Hill Air Force Reserve unit. They corresponded frequently. They even shipped out together in NATO exercises in 1959."[7]

The Scranton forces did their best to keep things low key outside of Pennsylvania but were sometimes ruthless inside the state to prevent the party faithful from submitting to the bidding of Clif White's delegate hunt for Goldwater. One of White's early zealots was Paul Hugus,

Republican County chairman in Allegheny County, which included Pittsburgh.

Despite overtures from Scranton and company for Hugus to change his loyalty, he remained steadfast in his support for Goldwater. He paid the political price for his Goldwater allegiance when many state patronage jobs were eliminated in Allegheny County, Hugus' pay as county chairman was shut off and he was prevented from being a delegate to the Republican National Convention, replaced by someone handpicked by Scranton. It was, as historian White called it, "political judo."[8]

Meanwhile, McCabe continued to have his luncheons and the national press was paying ever more attention to the rookie governor in Pennsylvania who appeared to have star qualities. A January luncheon in McCabe's board room at Scott Paper included some recent political heavyweights—James Hagerty, former press secretary to President Eisenhower and now an ABC television executive; Neil McElroy, one of Eisenhower's secretaries of defense who now headed Proctor & Gamble; and Chrysler executive David Kendall. Significantly, three other luncheon guests were Congressman Bill Miller of New York, who was chairman of the Republican National Committee; and veteran political operatives Len Hall, whom the Goldwater forces lobbied hard to join their campaign, and Meade Alcorn, a longtime Republican strategist.

The luncheons did not go unnoticed by the press. Scranton remained a noncandidate—but he was beginning to hedge. "Only if faced with a series of highly unlikely circumstances would I feel it my duty to become a candidate for the presidency," he said.[9]

Governor Romney was noticed by the Kennedys as a possible formidable opponent for JFK in 1964—and he enjoyed his political status. He showed up in Washington to address the National Press Club the week after Goldwater announced his candidacy. The timing of his visit was not lost on the Washington press corps. Asked if he was going to run for president, Romney replied, "I am not an active candidate seeking the nomination, but if it should come to me, I'd have a duty to accept it."[10]

Romney and Scranton had many things in common. They were both handsome, first term governors with business backgrounds who supported programs appealing to the more moderate and liberal wings of the Republican Party. Both had said on numerous occasions that they weren't candidates—but historically, that is what all candidates say 18 months before an election. What each of them had going for them after the New Hampshire primary is that neither one of them was named Goldwater or Rockefeller.

Romney had been touted in some circles as a possible presidential candidate even before he was elected governor because of his success in running American Motors. A year after he was elected, the *New York Times* reported that former President Eisenhower and Richard Nixon both favored Romney for the Republican nomination.[11]

Both men denied making any endorsement. Nixon wanted to be an interested observer who offended no one in case the Republicans became deadlocked and needed a compromise candidate who knew what a presidential campaign was all about. Eisenhower wanted to remain neutral because he favored a wide open convention. He would discover that his encouraging words to some candidates to get into the race were misinterpreted by them as an endorsement which caused some embarrassing backtracking by Ike.

Romney's speech at the National Press Club was well received and got a lot of press coverage because Washington news people know that speaking to the National Press Club is a prerequisite for anyone thinking about running for president.

While in Washington, J. Willard Marriott, the millionaire founder of the hotel chain, threw a party in his honor, attended by 300 Republican businessmen. Romney, the noncandidate, held two press conferences while he was there.

In May, shortly after Rockefeller's remarriage, Romney returned to Washington to attend a fund-raiser for Goldwater. Though appearing at a testimonial for the conservative icon might have seemed unusual on the face of it, Romney used the occasion to his advantage. Robert Novak reported, "His speech was short, punchy, and—unusual for Romney—partisan. There was some thought that he had stolen the show from Goldwater."[12]

Pennsylvania Governor William Scranton made a last-ditch effort to wrest the nomination away from Goldwater and in so doing, eliminated a chance to be the vice presidential nominee (Library of Congress).

13. Scranton and Romney

It did not resonate well with Goldwater or his backers, who had put together this $1,000-a-plate dinner, that Romney grabbed the attention of many of the reporters and photographers on hand when he entered the banquet hall.

And prior to flying to Washington for the dinner, Romney had telephoned Goldwater's office requesting a meeting with the Senator. Goldwater granted the request, assuming Romney wanted to have a private conversation with him. So he was mad when the Governor arrived with an entourage of reporters with him.

Characteristically, Goldwater didn't mince words when he talked publicly about Romney. He referred to him as just another Wendell Wilkie—he might as well have said lovable loser—and said the Republican Party couldn't afford another Eisenhower. In insulting Romney, Goldwater also treated Eisenhower with disrespect—one reason the former president probably advocated a wide open run for the nomination.

Romney began having problems at home getting some of his programs through which prompted the *Detroit News* editorial chiding him to "Come home."

The editorial went on to say, "We are proud as always to have a native son talked about for the Presidency. But there can't be a future for Governor Romney without a present. For the present, we think he'd be better off avoiding political jamborees in the big time and stick to his homework."[13]

The political implications of the editorial were not lost on Romney. If he had any future presidential ambitions—and as it turned out, he did—he needed to take care of business in Michigan lest he lose the support of his home state. He had little choice but to lay low for a while.

Meanwhile, the primary election season was just getting under way and the Republicans, as was their nature in recent years, had a vacuum to fill.

Chapter 14

The Eisenhower Factor

General Dwight David Eisenhower was an American war hero after serving as supreme commander of Allied Forces during World War II. When he returned to the United States after the war, he became president of Columbia University and was wooed by both political parties as a potential presidential candidate. "Ike" as he was called, was not driven by political aspirations. From the time he entered West Point as a young man, he was motivated by a sense of duty, a trait that he recognized and respected in people he came in contact with all of his life.

It was this sense of duty, rather than ambition, that allowed him to accept the Republican presidential nomination in 1952 and to be elected to two terms as president, breaking a 20-year lock on the presidency by the Democrats. Eisenhower said his political career was different from almost anyone else's—he was never trained in politics—and he entered at the top.

The years of his presidency are generally regarded as a time of peace and prosperity, free of major scandals, but also a time when the "Cold War"—the relationship between the United States and Russia, the dominant Communist nation, was constant.

"Eisenhower was a great peacekeeper in a dangerous era when rival superpowers were developing ways of war that could end civilization itself," wrote one Eisenhower biographer, Evan Thomas. "The United States was blessed to be led by a man who understood the nature of war better than anyone else, who had the patience and wisdom, as well as the cunning and guile to keep the peace.[1]

Not all historians have been as kind. Theodore H. White wrote that Eisenhower tried to reorganize the U.S. Postal Service and improve mail delivery but succeeded only in changing the colors of mailboxes and trucks from a drab olive green to red, white and blue. White said he signed a civil rights bill that set up commissions but the changes, like the changes in the postal system, were "almost completely ornamental." He also created a new federal agency, the cabinet-level Department of Health, Education and Welfare, a huge bureaucracy that, in principle, was counter to Republican mantra of downsizing government. White did concede that, with a few exceptions, Eisenhower's foreign policy was superb.

Eisenhower's legacy, much like Ronald Reagan's a generation later, is the public persona that he was able to create with his spirit, his optimism and his smile. White wrote, "When he was president, the American people were never happier, or at least, never more convinced of the opportunity to be happy."[2]

One of his biographers, Stephen Ambrose, who was not always complimentary about his subject, wrote, "Eisenhower gave the nation eight years of peace and prosperity. No other president of the 20th century could make that claim. No wonder that millions of Americans felt the country was damned glad to have him."[3]

When Eisenhower left office and retired to his home in Gettysburg, Pennsylvania, his counsel was sought by the next two Democratic presidents, Kennedy and Johnson, both of whom talked to him about use of the armed forces. Kennedy summoned him to give him a critique on what he had done wrong in the failed Bay of Pigs mission in Cuba. Johnson talked to him about the war in Vietnam. Eisenhower's message to Kennedy was what he should have done and to Johnson, what he should do. And the message was the same: Play to win. In military action, there is no other goal.

Though Eisenhower and Johnson were miles apart politically, Johnson had huge respect for the former president's honesty. In a telephone conversation with former Treasury Secretary Robert Anderson on January 30, 1964, LBJ said, "I served under this man eight years and all the goddamn gold in Fort Knox wouldn't cause him to move one inch if he didn't think it was right."[4]

Eisenhower was never the politician's politician. He had never run for public office of any kind before he ran for the presidency. Now, in his 70s, he was one of the elder statesmen of the Republican Party, a status he enjoyed but sometimes allowed him to get into awkward situations.[5]

He had his own ideas on who he thought would make a good president. High on his list was Robert Anderson, his secretary of the treasury; General Lucius Clay and General Alfred Gruenther, with whom he served in the military; and his brother, Milton. Eisenhower admired each of these men who had displayed over the years qualities that Ike valued in a person more than others—trust, loyalty and a sense of duty.

Anderson was a Texas businessman and politician and a Democrat when he supported Eisenhower for president in 1952. He served as secretary of the Navy and deputy secretary of defense before serving as Eisenhower's treasury secretary from 1957 to 1961. In that role he became one of the president's most trusted advisers.[6]

Clay had a distinguished record in World War II and received the Legion of Merit Award, the Distinguished Service Medal and the Bronze Star without ever having served in combat. The awards were in recognition of his skills as a planner, organizer and logistics specialist that were important traits in the war effort. In 1945 he served as deputy to General Eisenhower and the following year was named deputy governor of Germany, guiding the economic reconstruction of the war-torn country. He was the mastermind behind the Berlin Airlift which began in 1948 and lasted nearly a year, demonstrating American support for citizens of Berlin. It started two days after the Soviet Union had imposed a blockade on Berlin. Historians regard the airlift as a telling moment in the Cold War that had developed between the United States and the Soviets.

Gruenther was a key officer under Eisenhower during the war and served as supreme military commander of NATO forces from 1953 to 1956. After retiring from government service, Gruenther made a name for himself in civilian life as head of the American Red Cross from 1957 to 1964. Eisenhower said Gruenther was "one of the ablest, all-around officers, civilian or military, I have ever encountered."[7]

Milton Eisenhower, the younger brother of the president, was a distinguished educator who had served as president of Kansas State University, his alma mater, Penn State University and Johns Hopkins University. He was one of his brother's most trusted confidantes and advisers and later served in advisory roles to presidents Kennedy and Johnson.

Ike thought any of these men would have made great presidents. But Anderson was not interested and in fact supported Lyndon Johnson in the upcoming presidential campaign. Gens. Clay and Gruenther were flattered by their old boss's assessment of them but neither man was interested or thought they had any chance of getting the nomination.

14. The Eisenhower Factor

Milton Eisenhower was doomed by his genes. Even if he had expressed interest in the presidency, which he didn't, he would have had trouble getting support from fellow Republicans because of the "brother factor." As one Republican put it, "How could we hammer Jack and Bobby Kennedy if Ike was running his brother for the presidency? It would have destroyed the brother issue."[8]

Dwight Eisenhower had said repeatedly that he would endorse no Republican candidate, that he favored a wide open convention and let the chips fall where they may. Yet he was continually being linked to supporting one candidate or another, some by way of wild speculation, some by his own doing.

In May of 1963, the *New York Times* published an article reporting that Eisenhower and Nixon were impressed with Governor Romney in Michigan and favored him for the Republican nomination. The article was purely speculative but it brought Romney's name into the national conversation.[9]

Not long after Johnson took office, the *New York Times* reported that Eisenhower endorsed Lodge, who had been his U.N. ambassador, for president. The same article mentioned that Lodge, contacted in Vietnam, dismissed the notion that he was a candidate and that Eisenhower, contacted for confirmation, denied ever saying it. The newspaper had either published a rumor that wasn't true or Lodge and Eisenhower were denying something that was true. Either way, the word was out that Ike backed Lodge.[10]

Eisenhower and Scranton had known each other for years and enjoyed a warm professional relationship. When Scranton was in Congress, representing the state where Eisenhower now lived, the former president encouraged him to run for governor. In 1963, when Scranton barely had his feet wet in the governor's office, Eisenhower ventured to Harrisburg where he told Scranton he needed to run for president to save the Republican party from the radical right. It wasn't an endorsement but Scranton certainly could have taken it that way. After the meeting, he told reporters, "I probably will give even deeper thought to this matter than I had expected."[11]

A year later, when Scranton thought Eisenhower's continued encouragement was indeed an endorsement, he was about to go on television to announce it when he received a phone call in which Eisenhower said he was sticking to his policy of endorsing no one and that his words of encouragement should not be misconstrued. It was a severe blow to Scranton, killing what he thought would be a momentum builder.

Eisenhower was asked to write an op-ed for the *New York Herald Tribune* on the traits he'd like to see in a presidential candidate. He wrote, among other things, that the candidate should embody "responsible, forward-looking Republicanism." Whether he meant it or not, the language was construed as a slap in the face to Goldwater, not a good thing considering Eisenhower had steadfastly determined to be neutral. When reporters asked Ike if his newspaper column was meant to be anti–Goldwater, he replied in a typical Eisenhower colloquialism: "Try to put that shoe on that foot."[12]

Naturally, Goldwater was asked his reaction to the Eisenhower column. He said he agreed with it. Privately, however he thought it was a subtle endorsement of Rockefeller. On the same day the column was published, Goldwater spoke at Shasta College, and of course, the national media was there. When he got up to speak, he turned his back to the audience and they saw what looked like an arrow that had been shot into his back. The crowd loved it. Photographers took many pictures.[13]

Dwight D. Eisenhower was the elder statesman of the Republican Party who wanted a wide open convention in 1964. But some of his private talks and public statements misled candidates into thinking he was endorsing them (White House photograph).

By now, Eisenhower, the senior statesman of the Republican Party who did not want to throw his support to any candidate, had seemingly endorsed, at one time or another, Lodge, Romney, Scranton and Rockefeller. Some of it was by his own doing. Some was by people manipulating his comments for their own political purposes or by publishing speculation that had no foundation but did have influence. And all of it created the "anybody but Goldwater" impression.

Eisenhower bristled. Reacting to how his newspaper column had been perceived, he told the press, "You people tried to read Goldwater out of the party; I didn't."[14]

Eisenhower's comments, and public and media reaction to them, had muddied the waters a bit but one of the things he wanted most was seemingly coming to pass, particularly with the results of the New Hampshire primary. It was anybody's ballgame, but there were a lot innings left to play and, in politics as in baseball, anything could happen.[15]

Chapter 15

The Battlefields

The Gallup Poll numbers told a somber story for the two leading candidates for the Republican presidential nomination. From the time of the Kennedy assassination up through the New Hampshire primary, their popularity among voters nationwide was plummeting.

From December through April, Goldwater's approval percentages were 27, 23, 20, 17 and 14. Rockefeller's were worse: 13, 12, 16, 13 and 6. Whereas Rockefeller's numbers were lower, Goldwater's had taken a much deeper dive since the assassination. That was attributed at least in part to wild speculation and theories, in the hysteria after the Kennedy death, that right wing extremists might have had something to do with the assassination.

More alarming to followers of the frontrunners during this same period was the fact that Lodge and Nixon, who had done no campaigning, were held in higher regard than the candidates who had been out in the hustings, making speeches, shaking hands, attending breakfasts, lunches and dinners in an effort to demonstrate their mass appeal.

The April Gallup Poll showed Lodge, who was 10,000 miles away, leading the pack:

Lodge	42%	Rockefeller	6%
Nixon	26%	Romney	4%
Goldwater	14%	Scranton	4%

The numbers were revealing in terms of public support for Lodge and Nixon and bleak for Goldwater and Rockefeller but they were also misleading in their impact on the nomination process. Polls show popularity but they can be swayed quickly by current events, such as the results of the New Hampshire primary and they don't reflect the strength of the candidates in the only factor that matters—delegate strength. And Clif White had been working on that for three years on behalf of Senator Goldwater.

In the carnival of nominating a candidate, primaries and public opinion polls are the roller coasters that capture "oohs and ahs" of the public and the news media with their dramatic ups and downs but it is the unexciting, hardly noticed locomotives of state conventions and delegate selections that, in the end, are the telling factor.

"Clif White had to laugh. The New Hampshire primary ... scrambling—this obsession with Mr. Gallup—it didn't matter if 98 percent of Republicans loved Lodge if none of their numbers were convention delegates. The battle for the nomination was fought in hotel ballrooms. Only greenhorns and TV anchormen thought it was fought at the ballot box."[1]

The *New York Herald Tribune* reported in May, "Both polls and primaries have indicated that Goldwater is far from being first choice of the party's rank and file, i.e., the people who vote in November. But he's been steadily gathering in the delegates, i.e., the people who will vote in July in San Francisco."[2]

The Goldwater forces made some strategic changes after the debacle in New Hampshire. Never again would his campaign be dominated by hustling from one town to another, making small talk with one small group after another, all of which catered to his weaknesses as a candidate. Coupled with that, he would no longer put up with a back-breaking schedule that made him weary when he wanted to be strong, and agitated when he should have been cheerful.

Also, the campaign would play to his strengths, allowing him to evangelize the conservative message to large crowds. He would limit himself to two or three "stump speeches" with specific themes for specific audiences instead of trying to think of something new to say at every stop.

To facilitate this, the campaign hired Karl Hess, a veteran journalist and author, as his speech writer. Hess, 41, was an eccentric, accomplished wordsmith whose anti–Communist views were well known. He had done some work for Baroody at the American Enterprise Institute and Baroody, one of the few non–Arizona advisers in Goldwater's inner circle, had recommended him as a speech writer.

Hess and Goldwater clicked right away. For one thing, the two men saw eye to eye on most of the major issues of the day and they spoke the same language; Hess was able to put Goldwater's thoughts into sharp words and catchy phrases. Hess had a way of phrasing things that sounded like Barry Goldwater and rolled out of Goldwater's mouth naturally and easily. One line that made its way into several of the senator's speeches was meant to counter the fears that some people had that he would lead us into war. "Why, I'm the biggest peace monger you ever saw," Goldwater would say.[3]

Perhaps the biggest change in the Goldwater campaign, and the most significant, was to elevate Clif White's status in two key areas—recruiting delegates, which he had been doing for three years anyway, and putting him in charge of operations for the convention and at the convention. White would never be part of the social circle of the Arizona Mafia—he didn't have cocktails with them every night—but his roles in the campaign were a perfect match for his talents.

The Rockefeller strategy hadn't changed much after New Hampshire. He would continue to hit as many places, shake as many hands, make as many speeches as his schedule and stamina would allow, and for his public relations people to put on a full-court press of image-building advertising. While the Goldwater people perceived the primary elections as "a necessary nuisance," as historian Robert Novak called them, Rockefeller saw them as a way of drawing public support and capturing at least enough delegates to put on a good fight in San Francisco.

The Lodge juggernaut was particularly misleading. He was held in high regard by the American people and his standing in the polls jumped considerably after his surprise write-in victory in New Hampshire engineered by a group of young people who wanted to have a little fun. Those voters had basically said "none of the above" with respect to names on the ballot and were not likely to show up en masse at county conventions where the delegate selections were made.

Nixon had to be thrilled with his standing in New Hampshire and in the polls because he had not campaigned and had no intention of actively campaigning in other states. He was in a position of being the ideal person to be called upon at a deadlocked convention and, for now, that was enough to satisfy his political appetite.

Scranton's status was puzzling. He had not declared himself a candidate, yet he frequently postured himself as one. He could conceivably muster an Eastern bloc of voters that could hurt Rockefeller and, if it grew, could be a threat to Goldwater as well. Of all the potential candidacies, his was the most difficult for other Republicans, the press and the pundits to figure out. Romney was not a factor so far but he had

15. The Battlefields

no objections to his names being included in the same conversation with the others. One difference between Scranton and Romney is that Romney had difficulty getting his legislative programs through the Michigan legislature while Scranton was able to achieve major reforms in Pennsylvania.

The Goldwater delegate train was chugging along. Clif White's strategy that started in a Chicago hotel room three years ago was paying off. Thousands of volunteers had schooled themselves on the laws and guidelines pertaining to delegate selection in their respective states. They had gone to the precinct meetings. They had gone to the town hall meetings. They had gone to the district conventions. They were finding that Bill Middendorf's theory on local government was right.

Middendorf called it his "stoplight theory." At the local level, he said, politicians have a tendency of glossing over the big-picture issues but could argue for hours on the pros and cons of putting up a stoplight at an intersection. To win over delegates, it was important to be able to relate to them on the stoplight issues in order to draw them into the bigger picture. And it was working.

On February 29, 25 of 26 delegates at the North Carolina state convention pledged their support to Goldwater. This was 10 days before the New Hampshire primary and hardly got a mention in the national press.

The first test of delegate strength after New Hampshire came five days later in the Virgin Islands whose convention elected three delegates for Rockefeller.

On March 21, Goldwater received support of all 16 delegates at the South Carolina state convention. On April 18, not surprisingly, all 16 delegates in Goldwater's home state of Arizona pledged their votes to their senator. On April 25 in Nevada, it was another Goldwater sweep with all six delegates supporting him.

These victories were important because they all put points on the board but they also came in states Goldwater was expected to win. His strategy from the beginning was to carry the South and the West and, so far, it was happening.

In between these state conventions, Wisconsin held its primary election and it caused some key strategy moves for Rockefeller and Goldwater. Wisconsin was one of the few states that allowed crossover voting in primary elections—registered voters of either party could "cross over" and vote in the primary of the other party. And in Wisconsin in 1964, Democrats did not have a primary, opening the door for mass crossovers to the Republican side.

It was conceivable that Democrats could determine the outcome of the Republican primary if they organized and supported one candidate over another. In the wily ways of politics, the goal would be to try to engineer a victory for the weakest candidate.

Clif White recognized the landmine in Wisconsin and thought it best for Goldwater to skip that primary. But that could lead the way to a possible Rockefeller victory. There had to be a way of keeping Goldwater out of the fray, neutralizing Democrat interference and at the same time preventing Rockefeller from chalking up a win—i.e.—gaining delegates.

The answer was to have Governor John Byrne, a Goldwater supporter, run as a favorite son candidate. He would easily have the support of fellow Republicans from his state. Not only did Goldwater stay out of the primary—so did Rockefeller, who saw it as a no-win situation for him. Barring a miracle, he would lose to Byrne, and even if he should happen to do well or win, it would be looked on as small potatoes because none of the other major potential candidates were on the ballot. Byrne won. Delegates were pledged to him on the first ballot in San Francisco and then would support Goldwater.

The Wisconsin experience was a good example of how favorite-son candidacies work in political campaigns. Seen by the casual observer as a measure of a politician's strength in his home state—a point of pride for him or her—the favorite-son candidacy is often a political ploy in which the candidate willingly serves as a means of stopping a political opponent from advancing. That is exactly how it worked in Wisconsin.

In Oklahoma, the result did not come as easily as it had in some of the other states because Governor Henry Bellmon wanted to lead an uncommitted delegation to the national convention to avoid any infighting until the chips were down. But Clif White's people made the rounds at the state convention and, in the end, after much wrangling, Belmon relented, deciding the infighting was already happening in his own backyard. Goldwater came away with the support of all 22 delegates.

Georgia was an important state because it was in the heart of the South—Goldwater territory. Bob Snodgrass, a national committeeman, was a friend of Rockefeller's and supported him for president. He hoped to sway others in the delegation to follow his lead, but only one other person did. The tally was 22–2 for Goldwater.

The Illinois and Kansas primaries, similar to Wisconsin, had their own sets of peculiarities. Goldwater entered the Illinois primary because he thought it was one he could win and it would demonstrate his strength in the Midwest, a crucial element for him, not only in winning the nomination but the election as well.

"He might run badly in a vest-pocket, backwoods state like New Hampshire, but Illinois was where the electoral votes were [26 compared to New Hampshire's 4]. A smashing victory in the primary in this big, industrial state could well extend Goldwater's prestige beyond the devoted ranks of the Goldwater movement."[4]

Rockefeller chose not to run in Illinois. Goldwater's only opponent on the ballot was Margaret Chase Smith who hadn't fared well in New Hampshire, which was pretty close to her home territory. Just as Wisconsin had a quirk in its election laws that allowed for crossover votes, Illinois also had an unusual feature in its laws. By Illinois state code, county officials were not required to count write-in votes. That snuffed out the chances of any of the "noncandidates"—Scranton, Lodge and Nixon—to have any impact on the outcome. Illinois was Goldwater's to win and win big and grab the headlines in the next morning's newspapers.

Illinois had a hotly-contested race going on in the Republican primary race for governor. Secretary of State Charles Carpentier, a friend of Senator Everett Dirksen and a longtime Republican of good standing, was running against Charles Percy, president of the Bell & Howell camera company who was thought to be in the liberal wing of the party, and Cook County Republican Chairman Hayes Robertson, who was one of the charter members of the Draft Goldwater Movement three years earlier.

In January, Carpentier held a commanding lead over the others, according to the polls, with Percy second but well behind and Robertson even further back. Clif White was concerned for two reasons. The obvious one was that Robertson was running so poorly. But also, Carpentier had a lot of political sway in the state and he detested Goldwater. He liked Nixon. White's concern was that Illinois law also allowed the candidate for governor to personally pick 10 at-large delegates to the national convention. The nominee would also have great influence on who else would be selected.[5]

The political climate changed dramatically in January when Carpentier suffered the first of two heart attacks. After the first one, he dropped out of the race for governor. He later died from a second heart attack. A rising young star in the Illinois Republican Party was William

J. Scott, 37, the state treasurer. Early on, he was urged to get into the governor's race but he resisted. He had a good job with no immediate political risks. The only way he would get in, he said, was if the ranks were fewer, increasing his chances for victory.

With Carpentier ailing and Robertson trailing so badly, Robertson agreed to drop out of the race and Scott, who, like Robertson, was a Goldwater supporter, agreed to get into it. His only opponent was Percy who at that point could best be described as a non–Goldwater Republican.

Clif White liked the prospects of the two-man race. If Scott could win convincingly, he would control delegate selection and Goldwater would benefit. Also, a big Scott win would show the Republican Party that Goldwater had coattails—a reassuring concept to politicians in other states whose names would be on the ballot in November below Goldwater's.

Goldwater won convincingly as expected. He received 512,840 votes to Mrs. Smith's 209,521. But Percy crushed Scott in the gubernatorial race, 626,111 to 388,903. So much for the coattails. As it turned out, most county election officials did count write-in votes and Lodge and Nixon received 68,122 and 30,313 respectively. Rockefeller and Scranton had about 4,000 votes between them.

The Goldwater supporters were elated with their candidate's receiving 62 percent of the vote in the presidential primary—but that was misleading. The official canvass showed more than 200,000 Illinois Republicans who voted in the primary skipped the presidential preference race and voted only in the gubernatorial and other races on the ballot. That was as if they were saying "none of the above" to the presidential candidates. It also changed Goldwater's winning margin from 62 percent to 49 percent. But he did get 33 out of 48 delegates elected that day.

Clif White and other Goldwater stalwarts criticized the press for not giving Goldwater the credit they thought he deserved in Illinois. Percy's big win was perceived as a negative reflection on Goldwater as was the lack of participation in the presidential primary by those who voted that day. There was also the fact that Margaret Chase Smith got over 200,000 votes—the most she would receive in any primary. White said it was the only election he had ever been involved in where the winner was declared the loser by the press.[6]

Two days later, *Washington Star* columnist David Lawrence wrote, "Judging by some TV and radio broadcasts Tuesday night and subsequent comments in the press, Senator Goldwater got the highest number of votes in the presidential preference primary in Illinois but nevertheless suffered a 'setback.' Such commentaries serve only to mislead many people ... and take away some of the prestige he deserves."[7]

Kansas was Republican country and had been for a long time. It was also the most Republican state in the nation. It had been the home of the late journalist William Allen White, editor of the *Emporia Gazette*, who was a personal friend of presidents William McKinley and Theodore Roosevelt, and whose editorial, "What's the Matter with Kansas?" helped shape the Republican Party platform at the start of the 20th century.

It was also the home of Alf Landon, the 1936 Republican presidential candidate who lost unceremoniously to Franklin D. Roosevelt but whose Republican legacy was to live on through his daughter, Nancy Kasselbaum, who would one day be elected to the United States Senate. And in 1964, it was the home of up-and-coming politician and war hero Robert Dole, who would one day be a leader in the Senate and would run for both vice president and president.

In 1964, Republican stock in Kansas was still booming. It was the only state in the nation that had a Republican governor, two Republican senators, an all–Republican congressional delegation and Republican majorities in both houses of the state legislature.

Rockefeller had a good campaign organization in Kansas with the solid backing of Governor John Anderson. Rockefeller hoped Kansas would be an example for the rest of the nation to see that he had support beyond the Eastern seaboard. Winning in a state like Kansas would also cut into the territory that the Goldwater forces had staked out for themselves.

There were only 20 delegates to be elected from Kansas but Clif White saw the outcome as a possible harbinger for future trouble if Rockefeller won. It would be an indication of the influence of Governor Anderson and might set an example for other states to follow.

White was confident that Goldwater had the support of 10 delegates who had been elected at district conventions—but that could change if enough pressure was put on at the state level. Ten delegates were to be elected at-large. Rockefeller had the support of at least five, and maybe more. If elected, Anderson as governor would be allowed to name the other four (in addition to himself). It was possible that Rockefeller would have a majority of the delegates and perhaps as many as 16 out of the 20.

White decided the only way to insure a Goldwater victory was to find someone to challenge Anderson's election as a delegate. He and Goldwater leaders from Kansas met in his hotel room into the wee hours of the morning on the day of the convention to come up with someone who could defeat Anderson.

It was a delicate situation because Anderson was also the chairman of the Republican Governor's Conference, an organization whose support would be vital later on. The challenge then, was to defeat Anderson at the state convention without embarrassing him—without destroying unity within the party.

Those meeting in the hotel room decided to ask Effie Semple, a 75-year-old retiring national committeewoman, well respected in Republican circles throughout the state, and a Goldwater supporter, to challenge Anderson. Mrs. Semple was not interested in causing disharmony. But she was an ardent supporter of Goldwater and thought it would be a fitting end to her political career to be a delegate to the convention in San Francisco.

Later that day, she was nominated to run against Governor Anderson. But so was a third person, Lahoma Dennis, president of the Kansas Republican Women's Federation, who was also a Goldwater supporter.

Clif White understood immediately what was happening. Anderson, like White, was no stranger to hardball politics. He and his people recruited Miss Dennis to run and she accepted because she thought it would help the Goldwater cause and besides, she too, like Effie Semple, would enjoy the honor of being a delegate.

White realized that Dennis and Semple would probably split the Goldwater vote and provide a victory for Anderson. By the time the nominations were over, it was too late to do anything about it. A Rockefeller victory seemed imminent. But the ploy did not work. Mrs. Semple had a strong following as was evidenced when the voting began. Midway through it, Anderson went to a microphone and withdrew, asking for a unanimous vote for Effie Semple. The Goldwater team had prevailed. The result was 11 delegates for Goldwater, 9 for Rockefeller.

White had projected that Goldwater could probably count on 400 delegates from state caucuses and conventions, a remarkable feat from something that started as a grass-roots draft movement for someone who did not want to run.

But a delegate count of 400, as impressive as it was, fell well short of the 655 needed to win the nomination in San Francisco in July. Rockefeller was undaunted and was in it for the long haul. Lodge and Nixon

15. The Battlefields

had supporters all over the country, even though one of them wasn't even in the country and neither of them had launched campaigns on their own. Scranton and Romney were like handsome but shy teenagers, trying to decide if they wanted to go to the prom. And Margaret Chase Smith, the only other declared candidate, did not intend to be a wallflower. Though she had no chance of winning the nomination, she could siphon support from other candidates and cause them problems. All of that was the backdrop of this primary election season, the "necessary nuisance" of the political game.

And two crucial primaries were coming up—Oregon on May 15 and California on June 2. Rockefeller, hanging on because of his ambition, his courage and his money, needed to win both primaries. The Goldwater team had set its sights on California even as they were trudging through the snow in New Hampshire in January and February.

Just as Wisconsin allowed crossover voting and Illinois didn't have to count write-in votes, Oregon offered yet another twist in the labyrinth of presidential preference primaries. It had a strange law that required Howell Appling, the secretary of state, to contact all potential candidates and have them sign an unusual pledge. The statement they were asked to sign read: "I am not and do not intend to be a candidate in the November election."

The intent was that anyone who signed the statement would not be on the primary ballot. But of course the reverse was true. Anyone who didn't sign it would be on the ballot—and "anyone" was defined as those people whom the secretary of state deemed worthy of receiving the statement in the mail.

For such an important matter, the selection process was fairly subjective. Long before the days of the Internet and Google, the secretary of state had to depend on newspaper and magazine clippings and radio and television reports to determine who should receive the pledge statement.

There were potential legal issues too. If a candidate signed the Oregon pledge that they wouldn't be a candidate in November and then, later on, changed their mind, what would the recourse be for Oregon voters? And what impact would it have on the credibility of the candidate in future primaries?

The law presented some other challenges. Goldwater hadn't planned on campaigning much in Oregon but he was definitely a candidate so he couldn't sign the pledge. This put him in a position of being forced to run in a state where he was likely not to do well on election day—never a good position for a candidate to be in and yet he had no choice. There was no dilemma for Rockefeller. He didn't sign it. He had to be in it and he had to win.

Lodge, Nixon, Scranton and Romney were all sent the pledge. Only Romney signed it. The others considered the political consequences and came to remarkably different conclusions. Scranton sought legal advice from Pennsylvania Attorney General Walter Alessandroni who advised him not to sign it. Alessandroni reminded Scranton that he had publicly stated that he would be open to running if he felt duty-bound to do so. Scranton agreed.

Nixon did not sign the pledge. He had built a strong campaign organization in Oregon during his 1960 presidential run and his confidence and ego were boosted by the number of write-in votes he had received in earlier primaries. In Oregon, he had the opportunity to put his popularity out front. People could see his name on the ballot and cast their vote for him instead of writing it in.

The situation with Lodge was strangest of all. As a member of the diplomatic corps, he was prevented from actively taking part in politics. He had lived up to the letter of the law. In the past three months he had received tens of thousands of write-in votes without soliciting the first one. He was not a declared candidate because, so far, he didn't have to be. But now he was being asked to formally say he was not a candidate. That would keep his integrity intact but it would also snuff out the grassroots campaign for him which he was reluctant to do.

Politicians are adept at finding ways of skirting around laws without violating them. Lodge found a way of doing that by what historian Robert Novak later called "an elaborate charade." Secretary of State Appling sent him the disavowal of candidacy form on February 27 with a deadline of March 9 for returning it. The deadline was that early to allow time for the ballots to be printed.

On March 11, Appling received a cable from Lodge which stated, "Have just now seen your letter. In reply, wish to state I am not a candidate and I am precluded by foreign service from engaging in any political activity." The cable was sent two days after the deadline—and one day after Lodge had won the New Hampshire primary. Lodge had managed to uphold the law of refraining from politics and yet still get his name on the ballot in Oregon because he allegedly had missed the deadline for sending the notice of non-candidacy.[8]

The team of Paul Grindle and David Goldberg, who had engineered Lodge's write-in victory in New Hampshire, professing to do it

15. The Battlefields

"just for fun," were now on the other side of the country, trying once again to put their man on top—only this time they didn't have to educate the public on how to cast a write-in vote. Just as they had done in New Hampshire, Grindle and Goldberg implemented a mass mailing blitz.

One ploy they used successfully in New Hampshire was shot down in Oregon. They had taken an old film clip from 1960 of Eisenhower endorsing Lodge for vice president and doctored it to make it look like it was current and that Ike was supporting Lodge for president. When Eisenhower learned of it, he issued a statement repeating what he had said so often, that he was not endorsing anyone.

The Goldwater campaign stumbled in Oregon. Its state leaders were well meaning but not adept at participating in national campaigns, something they had in common with Kitchel, Burch and Kleindienst. They were meandering and spending a lot of time trying to fix things instead of forging ahead.

Help arrived from a surprising source—Stephen Shadegg, who had been Goldwater's campaign manager when he ran for the Senate in 1952 as well as a speech writer, articulate conservative spokesman and trusted adviser. But he and Goldwater had a falling out in 1961 when the Senator thought Shadegg was telling people he was Goldwater's speech writer. The following year, Shadegg ran for Arizona's other U.S. Senate seat against Goldwater's wishes (and lost in the primary). So instead of being part of the "Arizona Mafia," Shadegg was tossed to the sidelines.

But now the campaign needed a seasoned veteran, an organizer, and, in the spirit of "politics makes strange bedfellows," the outcast became the man of the hour. Shadegg was named West Coast regional director with the mission of righting a sinking ship in Oregon.

He soon discovered the problems went well beyond lack of organization. Goldwater's erratic personality was on display and it did not set well with the public or the press. Columnist Mervin Shoemaker observed in the *Portland Oregonian* that Goldwater seemed surprised when he got off a plane at the Portland airport and was greeted by throngs of supporters who were cheering, waving banners and were excited to see him.

"He smiled and paused briefly to shake hands here and there but strode almost directly to his car. It occasioned some grumbling in the crowd. Many of the welcomers had waited more than two hours."[9]

When they arrived at his hotel, Goldwater informed his campaign team that he had decided to no longer campaign in Oregon. He was convinced that Lodge would win, just as he had in New Hampshire, and that he wanted to concentrate on winning California and to save his stamina and energy for that crucial primary which was to take place on June 2. It was a startling decision. A campaign team had been in place and working and Shadegg had been recruited to help, and now the candidate was not going to even appear in the state for the last six weeks before the primary.

Meanwhile, the Rockefeller forces were rolling. He was spending big money on direct mail and radio, television and newspaper advertising and his public relations team was redoubling its efforts to polish his image. And everywhere he took advantage of Goldwater's decision. The Rockefeller slogan in Oregon became "He Cared Enough to Come" and he reminded his audiences of that by shouting it at the end of most of his speeches.

On election day, the voters responded—Rockefeller, 94,000 votes, 33 percent; Lodge 78,000 votes, 27 percent; Goldwater, 50,000 votes, 18 percent; Nixon, 48,000 votes, 17 percent; Smith, 7,000 votes, 3 percent; and Scranton, 4,000 votes, 2 percent. The big winner was obviously Rockefeller and it gave him momentum going into the do-or-die primary in California. Goldwater knew he would lose but was caught by surprise that Rockefeller had done so well.

Cliff White said the Oregon primary had three results. Lodge had to win to remain a viable candidate. Nixon, who, like Lodge, had never declared a candidacy, was also pretty much eliminated from serious contention. The question now was whether their backers would pack up and go home or throw their support to Rockefeller.

A second effect, said White, was the Don Quixote candidacy of Scranton, getting only 2 percent in the only primary in which his name was on the ballot.

The third outcome, according to White, was the most disturbing. It had given a flicker of hope to Rockefeller going into the California primary, the same hope a football or basketball team has when it is losing badly but rallies at the end of the third quarter to gain a little momentum. Almost overnight, Rockefeller shot ahead of Goldwater in the polls in California.

For almost four years, Republicans found themselves creating vacuums and working to fill them. It happened after Nixon lost to Kennedy in 1960. It happened after Lodge, a write-in, won in New Hampshire—the "anybody but..." voter response; and it seemed to be happening again, what with Goldwater's retreat in Oregon. The beneficiary of all of this was obvious.

Shadegg summed it up in his post mortem of the Oregon experience: "With Lodge in Saigon, Goldwater in Washington and Nixon diffident and aloof, Rockefeller had a political vacuum to huff and puff in."[10]

Chapter 16

California

In a way, California was a nation unto itself. With a population of 18 million, it had 30 times the number of people in New Hampshire, where the presidential sweepstakes had started just three months earlier. The state stretched along 1,200 miles from Oregon to the Mexican border, inhabited by ranchers, farmers, minorities, business tycoons, union members, movie stars.

More than 120 years earlier, hopeful citizens migrated to California panning for gold. The same was true in the 1960s only the "gold" was in many different forms. About 7½ million people—more than 40 percent of the residents—lived in southern California, in and around Los Angeles. Many had migrated there from the Midwest, the South and the East Coast, looking for fame and fortune that had eluded them back home. Some were in the aeronautics and electronic industries. Others had wineries. Some had rich farmland. Others were poor farm workers and people who had to settle for menial jobs to make ends meet while they awaited their big break. The maids and gardeners and dish washers worked for folks who had air conditioners in their homes and swimming pools in their yards.

The television and motion picture industries provided entertainment for the rest of the nation and employment for thousands who acted, produced, directed and worked on the sets of television shows like *Car 54, Where Are You?* and *Dr. Kildare* and movies such as *The Hustler* and *Breakfast at Tiffany's*.

California was a sports mecca. A decade earlier, there were hardly any professional teams west of the Mississippi River. In 1958, the Brooklyn Dodgers and New York Giants moved their franchises to Los Angeles and San Francisco respectively and enjoyed almost immediate success. The Dodgers won the World Series in 1959 and were back in the World Series in 1963, a year after the Giants had been there. In 1961, when baseball expanded its operations, one of the new teams was the Los Angeles Angels. In football, the San Francisco 49ers and Los Angeles Rams were immensely popular. The UCLA college basketball team was on the brink of becoming a dynasty under the guidance of coach John Wooden.

California was a fertile area for ambitious politicians where Democrats outnumbered Republicans in voter registrations by a 3–2 margin. It was a difficult place for politicians to establish a foothold and build organizations from the local levels on up because of the mobility of the people. One out of every four people moved every year.

In recent Republican politics, there had been many heavyweights. Earl Warren had been governor and had been considered a possible presidential or vice presidential candidate a decade before. But in 1953, he was appointed chief justice of the United States where he presided over many historic cases, including Brown versus the Board of Education that prohibited segregation in the nation's public schools.

Goodwin Knight, considered a liberal like Warren, succeeded him as governor. Senator William Knowland and Vice President Nixon were the conservative torch bearers from the state. In 1958, Knight and Knowland tried to switch jobs, Knight running for the Senate and Knowland for governor. Both lost. Then Nixon lost the presidential election in 1960 and the governor's race in 1962, defeated by Pat Brown who had defeated Knowland four years earlier.

So the Republican Party, like its national counterpart, was in a state of flux, trying to redefine itself. "The California situation was a bigger-than-life replica of the Republican turmoil nationally, with conservative and moderate factions at each other's throats for party control primarily and the presidential nomination only incidentally."[1]

There were 86 delegates at stake for the GOP presidential candidates in 1964. California was not a winner-take-all state in the primary. But Knowland, who was state Republican chairman, drew up a slate of delegates of Goldwater supporters and had them sign a pledge that they would support the senator at the convention in San Francisco. The Rockefeller supporters did the same thing, essentially setting up a winner-take-all competition.

"It was a struggle not merely for votes but for the minds of men and women and it was being waged in thousands of neighborhoods and communities strung out along the freeways and clustered in the majestic hills, fertile valleys and air-conditioned desert oasis of this great nation-state."[2]

It was liberal versus conservative, east versus west, Goldwater volunteers versus Rockefeller professionals. It was a political prize fight.

As with so many other states, California had its own set of peculiarities in presidential primaries. A total of 13,400 signatures were required for a candidate's name to be on the ballot—but the candidate who collected the required number the fastest would be listed first on the ballot—a distinct advantage that some experts speculated might provide as much as a 5 percent boost.

The Arizona Mafia recruited Robert Gaston, 34, a native of New York, an arch conservative and a Young Republican activist, to round up signatures for Goldwater. He mobilized volunteers throughout the state and within days had 85,000 signatures. Rockefeller also had an ardent team of volunteers—and they offered an incentive. The volunteers were paid 50 cents for every signature they procured. They came up with about 44,000. When Gaston realized what Rockefeller was doing, Goldwater was so far ahead in signatures that the outcome was not in doubt. So Gaston had some of his people infiltrate the Rockefeller volunteer organization. They gathered what they knew would be meaningless signatures, got paid 50 cents for each one they received—and donated the money to the Goldwater campaign.

George Hinman, Rockefeller's right-hand man, had been in California for months, trying as best he could, as a native New Yorker, to identify California's DNA. His purpose was to put together a delegate slate that would be appealing and represent all walks of life, California style, and yet be people of influence. He got Senator Thomas Kuchel and former governor Knight and former San Francisco Mayor George Christopher. He got Jack Warner, head of the Warner Bros. movie empire and recruited bankers, scientists, business executives and a representative of the Chandler family which owned the *Los Angeles Times*—an honor roll of achievement as historian Theodore White referred to it.[3]

The Rockefeller people were great at putting on galas, showcasing their candidate in a "Madison Avenue comes to Hollywood Boulevard" fashion and raising lots of money. They were not the type of people who were going to go door to door, ringing doorbells, passing out brochures and talking about their candidate over the fence post. Rockefeller hired public relations firms to help his campaign get the Negro and Mexican vote.

By contrast, Goldwater's corps of ardent supporters were in neigh-

16. California

borhoods all over the state, spreading the conservative message in a much more grassroots fashion, void of glitz and fanfare. But there were clashes within the organization. Knowland was a veteran old-school politician, who believed in maximizing contact with the public, going to as many gatherings as possible, big or small, shaking thousands of hands, making speech after speech after speech, and holding press conferences at just about every stop.

Goldwater wanted none of that. He had fears of New Hampshire happening all over again with back-breaking daily schedules that would wear him out and make him prone to expose his weaknesses such as irritability and a loose tongue. He set the ground rules: no more than three or four appearances a day; few press conferences; appearances before large, friendly crowds; and having the appearances televised, whenever possible, to maximize the number of people reached.

The campaigns were filled with a constant drumbeat of propaganda for one candidate or the other. Goldwater was characterized as an extremist who would end Social Security, fight against helping the poor and get the country into war. Rockefeller was seen as a rich, ambitious, Eastern Establishment snob who sought the presidency as something he was entitled to and someone whose personal life was questionable.

The win in the Oregon primary had given the Rockefeller campaign new life—and some new supporters. Grindle and Goldberg, the gurus of the now defunct Lodge campaign had come to California. Their mission was more of a "stop Goldwater" effort so it took the form of supporting Rockefeller. But Nixon, Scranton and Romney did not get onboard for anyone and Eisenhower was still walking the tightrope of encouraging candidates without endorsing them.

Rockefeller resisted courting support from Lodge because he still held a grudge from how he felt Lodge deserted him in New Hampshire.

With the two candidates running close in the polls, Rockefeller got an unexpected boost when the Eisenhower column appeared in the *New York Herald Tribune* and was distributed nationally. Ike had been persuaded to write a piece on the qualities he'd like to see in a Republican candidate and, without naming names, it appeared that he was belittling Goldwater. The former president realized the misconception and did what he could to clarify what he had written. It was on that day, in the evening, that Goldwater went on stage to give a speech and turned around to show what appeared to be an arrow in his back.

Louis Harris, like George Gallup, a highly respected pollster, was keeping tabs on California voters. In his last poll before the Oregon primary, the results were:

> Goldwater 48 percent
> Rockefeller 39 percent
> Undecided 13 percent

Five days after the Oregon primary, there was a dramatic shift:

> Rockefeller 47 percent
> Goldwater 36 percent
> Undecided 17 percent

Ten days after the primary:

> Rockefeller 48 percent
> Goldwater 39 percent
> Undecided 13 percent

Then on Saturday, May 30, 1964, three days before the California primary election, Nelson Aldrich Rockefeller, Jr., was born in New York. Rockefeller had flown home on his private jet the night before so he could be there with his wife. The news of the birth, of course, made nationwide headlines and served as a reminder of what many considered Rockefeller's sordid recent past—divorcing his wife, marrying a younger woman who deserted her family—and now this.

The Harris poll of Monday, June 1, two days after the birth of the Rockefeller baby and one day before the primary:

> Rockefeller 44 percent
> Goldwater 44 percent
> Undecided 12 percent

On Tuesday, June 2, Californians poured into the polls—men, women, disheveled young people, immaculately groomed senior citizens, bankers, lawyers, farmers and farmhands, white, black, Hispanic—a microcosm of a state that was a microcosm of a nation. And when the votes were counted that night, Goldwater won by 68,350 votes out of 2.1 million votes cast—a remarkable turnout.

Naturally, there were many opinions as to what was the deciding factor.

Was it the incessant ground war of the Goldwater forces, convincing voters to go to the polls and keep the conservative movement alive?

16. California

Was it Goldwater remembering his New Hampshire debacle and adjusting his campaign style to meet his comfort level?

Was the Rockefeller approach just too Brooks Brothers starchy in a land whose populace ranged from scientists to movie stars to scuba divers to migrant workers?

And finally, and perhaps obviously, was it the birth of the Rockefeller baby to the governor's second wife three days before the election?

In some ways, California was the poster child for divorces where, seemingly every week, one movie star or another was divorcing one partner to hook up with another.

Goldwater, looking back on it years later, said the Rockefeller divorce and remarriage was no secret but it wasn't part of the political debate. A situation occurred in California, however, that raised public attention to it in a way the Rockefeller people should have anticipated but didn't.

During the final week of the campaign, Rockefeller was scheduled to speak at Loyola University, a Catholic University in Los Angeles. The Catholic Church frowned on divorce but absolutely frowned on a divorced person remarrying. James Francis Cardinal McIntyre, bishop of the diocese of Los Angeles, had approved the Rockefeller appearance on campus but had not considered the implied endorsement of him that the appearance would bring. So, a few days before Rockefeller was to speak, the bishop pulled the plug on it and cancelled his appearance. He told the press he did not want to give the impression that the church condoned the divorce and remarriage.

The same day the bishop acted, a group of 16 Protestant ministers issued a joint statement saying Rockefeller should withdraw from the presidential race altogether because of his inability to manage his home life. Whether those two actions were planned to be simultaneous or whether they just happened that way is not known. But two days later, on Saturday, May 30, the Rockefellers' baby was born. Goldwater speculated the whole chain of events involving the bishop, the ministers and the birth of the baby made for interesting conversation the next day in churches throughout California and may have impacted the vote on the following Tuesday.[4]

Clif White, ever loyal to the cause he championed three years earlier and to the effort of his volunteers in California, thought Goldwater would win regardless of the timing of the birth of Nelson Aldrich Rockefeller, Jr., and how the public felt about it.

"Many political observers claim the birth of the Rockefeller child reversed a tide of victory for the governor," he wrote. "Actually, the day before the baby's birth, which I had no way of knowing was imminent, I confided to reporters that Goldwater would win the primary by 50,000 votes."[5]

Nobody could doubt White's expertise at vote counting prior to election day or the faith he had in his troops getting out the vote. But it was hard for others to ignore the timing of the arrival of the newest Rockefeller and seeing what happened to his poll numbers after that happy day for Rocky and Happy.

As one of Goldwater's original backers, publisher Bill Rusher put it, "Only Rockefeller could turn motherhood into a liability."[6]

Chapter 17

Cleveland

In politics as in sports, "it ain't over till it's over" and moderate Republicans still wanted to find a way of overturning the Goldwater bandwagon. That was on the minds of some Republican governors as they attended the annual National Governors Conference in Cleveland on the weekend after the California primary election.[1]

These are meetings in which all 50 governors have a chance to get together under one roof and talk about problems they encounter in their states and how they're handling them and get some ideas from their counterparts. There is a business meeting they all attend where they hear speakers drone on about the relationship of the state and federal government and things of that nature.

But frequently, the most useful discussions are the ones they have with their eggs and English muffins in the morning, the soup-and-salad-and-sandwich lunches at noontime or the cocktail hour and steak dinners in the evening. The Republicans and Democrats also hold what amount to caucuses while they are there to discuss problems within their own parties.

The national conferences had been fairly low key for many years with one notable exception. In 1952, Governor Thomas Dewey of New York, a liberal Republican and twice-failed presidential candidate, rallied a majority of governors to fight for a "fair play" plank in the party platform to be ratified at the upcoming Republican convention. The effect of the change Dewey advocated was to change the delegate count in some states to tip the balance from the leading candidate, Senator Robert Taft of Ohio, to General Dwight Eisenhower. The tactic worked, delegate counts were changed and Eisenhower won the nomination.

One difference between 1952 and 1964 was that in 1952 there were

36 Republican governors, enough to exert a lot of influence. In 1964, there were only 16 and there was no organized effort to unite them on any cause.

Any effort to stop Goldwater from getting the Republican nomination was considered by most of them as too little, too late. General Lucius Clay, who years earlier Eisenhower thought would make an excellent president, expressed the dilemma of moderate Republicans as the primaries were winding down. "Nobody made a move," he said. Not Bill (Scranton) or the others or Eisenhower," referring to Eisenhower's decision not to endorse any candidate. "The sheer lack of anybody doing anything has got us where we are. It's a good lesson in how not to select a president."[2]

Of the Republican governors gathered in Cleveland, three were staunch Goldwater supporters—Tim Babcock of Montana, Paul Fannin of Arizona and Henry Belmon of Oklahoma. Four were definitely anti–Goldwater—John Love of Colorado, John Chafee of Rhode Island, John Reed of Maine and John Anderson of Kansas. Three were anti but were in a class by themselves—Rockefeller, the defeated candidate and Scranton and Romney, the potential candidates. A fourth group—James Rhodes of Ohio, Robert Smylie of Idaho, Mark Hatfield of Oregon, Archie Gubbrud of South Dakota, George Clyde of Utah and Clifford Hansen of Wyoming—felt the die had been cast, that the game was over and it was time to support Goldwater and move on.

Rockefeller, representing the largest state among those present, was not there to discuss or get involved with presidential politics. In a few days, he would formally drop out of the race. Romney was a maverick, a first term governor and a former business executive but had not achieved the level of respect among other governors that he had with the public at large. Scranton seemed to have all the attributes a candidate should have except the most important one—an appetite for it.

The Democrats already had their candidate and, typically, the party with the incumbent president does not have as much pressing business or press coverage at the party out of office. But the Democrats did have a wild card in their midst, Alabama Governor George Wallace, an avowed segregationist who had stood at the door at the University of Alabama to block black students from enrolling. Wallace had entered some Democratic primaries which he knew going in that he had no chance of winning. But he received enough support to draw attention to himself which was his intention at the governors conference.

On the Republican side, as if they had been struck with a cattle prod, the stop Goldwater forces suddenly sprung into action. At Eisenhower's invitation, Scranton went to meet with the former president in Gettysburg on Saturday, June 6, a day before conference in Cleveland was to begin. Scranton planned to be in Cleveland Sunday morning for a closed-door breakfast with Republican governors. After the breakfast, he was scheduled to appear on the CBS program *Face the Nation*.

Eisenhower and Scranton had a genial conversation in which Ike once again told Scranton he should make himself more available for the presidential nomination. Scranton came away from the meeting thinking he finally had the backing of the former president. He would let the governors know at the breakfast in Cleveland the following morning and tell the rest of the nation on his appearance on *Face the Nation*.

Meanwhile, Romney, not knowing anything about Scranton's latest plan, decided it was time to break his silence about what he considered the disaster a Goldwater candidacy would be. Some of his concern was personal. Goldwater was not especially popular in Michigan and Romney was up for re-election in November. The former head of American

Michigan Governor George Romney tried and failed to start an anti–Goldwater movement at the June National Governors Conference in Cleveland. Here, in July, he addresses the delegates of the Republican National Convention (Library of Congress).

Motors knew a good deal from a bad one and decided it was time to cut any ties that might link him to Goldwater.

"Ordinarily I undertake nothing of a political character on Sunday," Romney, a devout Mormon, told his colleagues. "I do it now because of what I consider the importance of the situation." He then lashed out at Goldwater, saying the Senator's views varied greatly from the heritage of the Republican Party. "I will do everything within my power to keep him from becoming the party's presidential candidate and I fully realize what the odds are on that score," he said.[3]

Romney's pleas did not get the reception he had hoped for. Many remembered how he had not attended two Republican conferences in 1963, giving excuses that left the impression he had more important things to do. Also, his timing was questionable. Hatfield of Oregon, not a strong Goldwater supporter but who, in the interest of unity, had agreed to give the keynote speech at the convention, told him he was too late. Hatfield asked Romney where he was when Rockefeller was doing exactly what Romney was trying to do now.

Romney held his press conference where he once again lacerated Goldwater but there were two things he didn't do. He didn't announce his own candidacy and he didn't endorse Scranton, who was the most likely person to climb the political Mount Everest that the anti–Goldwater faction faced. In effect, he just vented.[4]

Scranton arrived in Cleveland Sunday morning and checked into his hotel before going to the breakfast. He had a bounce in his step for now he felt he was in a position to make a move. Having received the blessing of President Eisenhower and feeling assured of his support, Scranton had in his coat pocket a statement announcing his availability to be a candidate for president. It was late in the game, he knew, but he had something going for him that no other moderate had, not Rockefeller, not Lodge, not Romney, not Nixon. He had President Eisenhower on his side, perhaps the most influential and certainly the most beloved Republican.

There was a message for him in his hotel room that morning to call Eisenhower. He was running late for the breakfast but he knew he must return the call immediately. When he did, Ike told him he didn't want their conversation of Saturday to be misinterpreted. He was sticking to his long-held position of not endorsing any candidate. He was just encouraging Scranton to let it be known that he was available.

Scranton was crestfallen. He went to the breakfast in time to hear part of Romney's verbal assault on Goldwater. He supported Romney in asking Goldwater to clarify his views on many major issues—but he never took his prepared statement out of his coat pocket. It remained there later that morning when he went to the CBS television studio in Cleveland to appear on *Face the Nation*.

Scranton had intended to use the nationally-televised program to offer himself as an alternative to Goldwater, a candidate representing the best traditions of the Republican Party. But the phone call with Eisenhower had deflated him and he came off as bland and indecisive. At one point, Paul Niven, a CBS correspondent, asked him what his position was with regard to the Republican presidential nomination.

This was his opportunity to use the statement still in his suitcoat pocket. Instead he replied, "I feel very strongly that we should have the type of reaction in the country to the Republican Party that we have had under Lincoln and under Theodore Roosevelt and under Dwight David Eisenhower.... And I am concerned about the next six weeks because I want to make sure that we do that."[5]

Later in the same broadcast, Alan Otten of the *Wall Street Journal* asked him if he was, for all practical purposes, saying Goldwater was not the type of Republican that Scranton wanted to lead the party. The governor replied, "No, I am not saying that. And I think you are putting words in my mouth, sir."[6]

Scranton's aides had carefully scripted the governor's activities Sunday after his visit with Eisenhower on Saturday. There would be the breakfast, then the appearance on *Face the Nation* and the day would be capped off with a press conference late in the afternoon—but in time for the evening newscasts—in which Scranton would lay out his ideas in detail on how he would snare the nomination from Goldwater.

All of that was hastily planned after what they thought was an endorsement from Eisenhower. Scranton had not told them about the Sunday morning phone call from Ike so his staffers were perplexed at watching the governor meander through the television interview and press conference.

Clif White was amused rather than frustrated at Romney and Scranton's comments in Cleveland in which they called for Goldwater to clarify his views on major issues. White thought, for better or for worse, no candidate had ever been more specific on where he stood, dating back to the publication of *The Conscience of a Conservative*. In fact, it was the clarity of Goldwater's views, not the lack of it, that had created the friction now represented by Scranton and Romney.

On Monday, two Republican heavyweights arrived at the conference. Eisenhower was the keynote banquet speaker Monday night and gave a pep talk on Republican values, still being careful not to support any one candidate.

Goldwater made an appearance but did not speak. The Senator was not about to take the podium and give the impression he was clarifying his views on anything. Instead, he chatted amiably with Eisenhower and others while partaking in the banquet food—and while his aides were going table to table passing out copies of *The Conscience of a Conservative* and other Goldwater writings—a way of underscoring that his views were well known.

The next day, Nixon arrived from Michigan, where he had spent the weekend as part of a nationwide tour to keep him in the public eye prior to the convention. Romney had returned to Michigan so he could accompany the former vice president to Cleveland.

Nixon had spent the past three years positioning himself to be available if needed. He knew his best chance at being nominated once again was if there was a deadlocked convention and he could offer himself as a compromise candidate. But in Cleveland, he changed his tactics. He attacked Goldwater on his stands on many of the issues that Romney and Scranton had said needed clarification. And he said Goldwater's views needed to be rejected for the good of the future of the party.

He allowed time for questions from the governors if they had any, perhaps hoping for the obvious one—would he be willing to challenge Goldwater for the nomination. But the question was never asked.

By now, most of the governors agreed with Hatfield who had asked Romney "where were you?" when the primaries and caucuses were taking place. The same could have been asked of Scranton and Nixon.

Chapter 18

The Civil Rights Bill

Goldwater returned to Washington to take part in the Senate debate and vote on President Johnson's landmark Civil Rights bill which was being hotly contested in the Senate.

President Kennedy had proposed the legislation five months before his assassination. In a year filled with racial strife marked by mass demonstrations, sit-ins, marches and, in many cases, violence, public officials in the South were contributing to the problem because of their inherent belief in segregation. In early June, Alabama Governor George Wallace stood in the way of black students trying to enroll at the University of Alabama.

On June 11, 1963, in a televised address to the nation, Kennedy said, "This nation was founded by men of many nations and backgrounds. It was founded on the principle that all men are created equal and that the rights of every man are diminished when the rights of one man are threatened.

"It ought to be possible for every American to enjoy the privileges of being an American without regard to his race or color.... Every American ought to have the right to be treated as he would wish to be treated, as one would wish his children to be treated. But this is not the case.... It is better to settle these matters in the courts than on the streets, and new laws are needed at every level....

"The old code of equity law under which we live commands for every wrong a remedy, but in too many parts of the country, wrongs are inflicted on Negro citizens and there are no remedies at law. Unless Congress acts, their only remedy is in the street...."[1]

Eight days later, he presented Congress with his remedy, a civil rights bill requiring equal rights and opportunities for black Americans.

President John F. Kennedy addressed the nation in June of 1963 urging an end to segregation and racial discrimination in America (John F. Kennedy Presidential Library).

The bill languished in Congress because of strong Southern opposition.

After the Kennedy assassination, President Johnson, a native Texan and thus somewhat a Southerner, made it a priority to pass civil rights legislation as a tribute to his fallen predecessor. Addressing a joint ses-

18. The Civil Rights Bill

sion of Congress, he urged passage of a bill to end racial discrimination and segregation in public accommodations, public education and federally assisted programs. "We have talked long enough in this country about equal rights. We have talked for one hundred years or more. It is time now to write the next chapter, and to write it in the books of law," he said.[2]

Sixteen years earlier, campaigning for a U.S. Senate seat in Texas, Johnson had a far different attitude. In one of his campaign speeches, he told his audience, "This civil rights program, of which you have heard so much, is a farce and a sham—an effort to set up a police state in the guise of liberty. I am opposed to the anti-lynching bill because the federal government has no more business enacting a law against one kind of murder than another. I am against the FEPC [Fair Employment Practices Commission] because if a man can tell you whom you must hire, he can tell you whom you cannot employ. I have met this head-on."[3]

On February 10, 1964, the House of Representatives passed HR 7152, the civil rights bill, and passed it on to the Senate. In an unusual move, Senate Majority Leader Mike Mansfield placed the bill directly on the Senate calendar rather than referring it to the Judiciary Committee, for two reasons—one, to speed up the deliberations so the bill would become law sooner; and two, to avoid inevitable controversy since the Judiciary Committee was headed by Senator James Eastland of Mississippi, a staunch, proud segregationist.

In 1956, after the Supreme Court had issued rulings in two consecutive years, outlawing segregation of public schools (the Brown v. the Board of Education decision) in one decision, and prohibiting local ordinances mandating segregation in the other (the Rosa Parks decision), Eastland was one of many Southern senators who signed a document that came to be known as the Southern manifesto.

Senator James Eastland of Mississippi was a staunch segregationist and one of many Southerners who opposed the civil rights bill (U.S. Senate Historical Office).

In it, the document, which became part of the Congressional Record of the 84th Congress, said, in part, "This unwarranted exercise of power by the court, contrary to the Constitution, is creating chaos and confusion in the states principally affected. It is destroying the amicable relations between the white and Negro races that have been created through 90 years of patient effort by the good people of both races. It has planted hatred and suspicion where there has been heretofore friendship and understanding.... We commend the motives of those states which have declared the intention to resist forced integration by any lawful means."[4]

But Mansfield's efforts for smooth sailing of the legislation did not materialize. Southern senators led what became the longest filibuster in U.S. history in an attempt to prevent the bill from coming to a vote on the Senate floor.

The filibuster began on March 9 and carried on through the end of March and all of April and May. The rest of the nation's business came to a standstill in the Senate.

The Senate has a parliamentary procedure called cloture which is a way of ending a filibuster if two-thirds of its members—67 of the 100— vote to stop it. Senator Hubert Humphrey of Minnesota, manager of the bill on the Senate floor and a man known for his gregarious and persuasive personality, worked frantically to round up enough votes to invoke cloture. It was Humphrey who, in 1948 when he was mayor of Minneapolis, gave a stirring speech at the Democratic National Convention urging support for civil rights legislation—the same type of legislation that Senate candidate Lyndon Johnson opposed the same year.

Humphrey needed support from northern Republicans to offset the opposition of Southern Democrats. He enlisted the help of one of the most powerful and influential Republicans, Senator Everett McKinley Dirksen of Illinois. Dirksen was a longtime supporter of civil rights but opposed the bill because of certain provisions he found objectionable. Humphrey worked to get some of the language changed and Dirksen gave a powerful speech on the Senate floor, concluding that racial integration was "an idea whose time has come."

On June 10, a coalition of 44 Democrats and 27 Republicans voted to invoke cloture and limit debate on the bill. Barry Goldwater voted against it. On June 19, the Senate passed the most sweeping civil rights bill in American history by a voted of 73 to 27. Again, Goldwater voted against it.

He had long been a champion of civil rights from as far back as

18. The Civil Rights Bill

his days heading the department store in Phoenix and he approved of most of Johnson's bill. But there were two sections of it, dealing with fair employment and public accommodations, that he believed were unconstitutional. Goldwater said any rights that were not specifically given to the federal government in the Constitution became rights of individual states—and there was no mention of employment or public accommodations in the constitution.

Beyond that, the proposed civil rights bill stipulated that no one could be denied housing at the whim of a bank or a landlord or anyone else. The intent was to assure fair housing opportunities for black Americans but Goldwater argued the language of the bill meant that drunks and prostitutes and drug dealers could not be denied.

So Goldwater voted against the civil rights bill, starting with his vote against cloture. So did Democrats Albert Gore, Sr., of Tennessee, Sam Irvin of North Carolina and J. William Fulbright of Arkansas as well as Republicans Norris Cotton of New Hampshire, Bourke Hickenlooper of Iowa, Edwin Mecham of New Mexico, Millard Simpson of Wyoming and John Tower of Texas.[5]

Each of the other senators who opposed the bill had their own individual constituencies to deal with back home, which no doubt influenced their votes. Goldwater's situation was different. He was running for president of all the states. His reasons for voting against it—sections he believed were unconstitutional—became a footnote. What would be remembered is that he had voted against the civil rights bill.

"It made no political sense for him to vote against a controversial but popular social issue on the very eve of a national campaign," wrote his finance director, J. William Middendorf. "Barry did a lot of things that made no political sense, though, because he believed they were right. His vote laid down one more roadblock to his election."[6]

Walter Lippman, one of the nation's leading columnists, wrote, "In his extreme views of state's rights, Goldwater is in fact one who would dissolve the federal union into a mere confederation of states.... He would nullify the central purpose of the Civil War amendments, and would take from the children of the emancipated slaves the protection of a national union."[7]

Lippman was one of the most widely read and respected columnists in the country. Known for his intellect and his probing of the intricacies and fallacies of democracy, he founded the *New Republic*, a decidedly liberal magazine at a young age, wrote several books and was a syndicated columnist for nearly 50 years with the *New York World* and *New York Herald Tribune*. Lippman graduated from Harvard University in three years, embraced socialism as a young adult and later rejected it, and was a champion of democracy though was never shy about pointing out its shortcomings. It is said that in his career he endorsed seven Democrats and six Republicans for president.

Two people in Pennsylvania were infuriated by Goldwater's vote on cloture. One was President Eisenhower who had signed a civil rights bill in 1957 that did little more than set up commissions to study and investigate discrimination but was nonetheless a progressive step applauded by civil rights activists. The other was Governor Scranton, back home and licking his wounds from his embarrassing performance in Cleveland.

Though he had stumbled through press conferences, television appearances and the governors conference in recent days, Scranton's principles had not changed. He was a loyal Republican, devoted to the party of Lincoln and he had a quality that had inhabited his soul from as far back as when he was capable of thinking for himself, a quality that Eisenhower had and thought all men should have—a sense of duty.

And because of that, after consulting with his wife and his staff, and despite all odds, Scranton decided on Thursday, June 11, that he would do more than make himself "available," that duty compelled him to take on Goldwater head-on. So he decided to declare his candidacy for the Republican presidential nomination.

"Several factors pushed Scranton. He had been hearing from fellow Republicans that Goldwater would lead scores of them to defeat. Personally he was appalled at Goldwater's hostility to the federal government poverty programs, but the final straw was Goldwater's vote against the Civil Rights bill."[8]

Scranton's wife Mary played a big part in his decision as well. She had been reluctant to have her husband to get into the race but as events evolved and she saw his frustration and determination, she changed her mind. According to one newspaper account, the two of them talked in their hotel room in Cleveland and he said, almost flippantly, "I have an idea. Why don't I run?" And she replied, "Bill, I think you better run."

The next day, in Harrisburg, as Scranton was planning his strategy, she reportedly came into his office and told him she wanted to make sure his decision was based on something more than wishful thinking. "It appeared to me he had done a great deal of thinking and was ready to move," she said.[9]

A sense of duty is an honorable thing but it sometimes can end

18. The Civil Rights Bill

up in a head-on crash with reality. And the reality was Scranton had little chance of overtaking Goldwater. The Goldwater forces had been working for three years; Scranton had about a month before the convention to mount a charge. Goldwater had about 600 delegates committed to him and needed only about 50 more to secure the nomination; Scranton had fewer than 100. Scranton needed the support of all the "favorite son" candidates—from Michigan, Wisconsin and Ohio and elsewhere—to have a chance and yet many of the "favorite sons" had been arranged by Goldwater people as an attempt to block Rockefeller early on. Scranton needed the whole-hearted, vocal support of President Eisenhower who still felt the need to remain neutral, though he was infuriated with Goldwater over his vote on the civil rights bill. He needed the support of both Rockefeller and Lodge. And perhaps most important, Scranton needed to convince fellow Republicans that the soul of the Republican Party was at stake, and that he was the man that could save it.

If any one of those many factors did not materialize, the Scranton candidacy was doomed. The reality was, as many historians have noted, it was doomed from the start. Two rays of hope were that Lodge resigned his ambassador position and returned home to campaign for Scranton, and Rockefeller turned over his staff and contributed financially to the fledgling, johnny-come-lately Scranton campaign.

Both Lodge and Rockefeller called Eisenhower and pleaded with him to get actively involved but the former president said he needed to preserve his influence. "For what?" Rockefeller reportedly asked him.

Meanwhile, the Scranton campaign was reminiscent of the early Goldwater efforts—a dedicated, energetic staff that had zero political experience outside of Pennsylvania; an exhaustive schedule that had the candidate speaking in 25 states in 32 days, spending nearly $1 million in the process. It was a formula that failed Goldwater in New Hampshire but he had time to recover. The one thing Scranton didn't have was time.

Another parallel to the early Goldwater campaign was Scranton's standing in public opinion polls. He was drawing big crowds and good press coverage wherever he went as he crisscrossed the country and his popularity was steadily increasing in the polls. But just as Clif White had no fear of what the Gallup and Harris polls were showing for Goldwater earlier in the year, he was not disturbed by Scranton's surge in late June. White was steadfast in his conviction that polls don't vote at conventions; delegates do and Goldwater had the delegates.

White, who had been involved in politics long enough to recognize a shrewd politician when he saw one, had never considered Scranton to be a reluctant candidate. He was an honorable but ambitious politician who had served one term in the U.S. House and was serving his first term as governor and enjoyed the power, privilege and prestige that higher office afforded. And there was another higher office within his sights, White believed, and to White's way of thinking, Scranton's eye on the presidency had been there for quite a while.

He traced Scranton's presidential aspirations back to a day when few people in the nation were thinking about politics—November 22, 1963. According to White, a few hours after Kennedy was assassinated, Scranton called Paul Hugus, the Pittsburgh businessman who headed the Draft Goldwater efforts in Pennsylvania, and set up a meeting with him a few days later.

In the immediate aftermath of the assassination, conspiracy theorists were emerging from many different directions. Some claimed the killing was a Communist plot inspired by Cuban dictator Fidel Castro in retribution for the Bay of Pigs operation and the standoff over Russian missiles in Cuba. Others were certain it was a mob hit because of the Kennedys' involvement in the U.S. Senate probes of racketeering. Some believed it was the act of a lone gunman, Lee Harvey Oswald, while others thought a second assailant was involved.

But still others believed right-wing fanatics were the perpetrators and somehow linked Goldwater because, after all, he was one of them. As bizarre as that thinking might have been, it affected Goldwater's popularity among likely voters.

When Scranton met with Hugus, he asked that Hugus work to have Pennsylvania's delegation support him as a favorite-son candidate at the Republican convention. Hugus, who was not going to drop his allegiance to Goldwater, refused but suggested a meeting among leading Republicans in the state to come up with what Hugus referred to as a "harmony" slate of delegates. Scranton rejected the idea, holding fast to his plan for a favorite-son candidacy.

By this time Scranton had been attending Tom McCabe's luncheon meetings at the Scott Paper Company offices in which the stated purpose was to bring business leaders up to date on his legislative agenda. But it also provided the governor with political friendships that would be helpful in the future.

The favorite-son plan died without the backing of Hugus, who was a powerful politician in his own right as chairman of Allegheny County

18. The Civil Rights Bill

Republicans. Within a short time after his meeting with Hugus, the governor initiated budget cuts that eliminated all nonessential state jobs in Allegheny County. Under the threat of more layoffs, Republicans at the state convention backed a Scranton delegate from Hugus' district, preventing Hugus from being a delegate to the national convention. He was also forced out of his position as county chairman.

"It is a question of loyalty to the governor," a Scranton aide told a reporter for the *Pittsburgh Post Gazette*. "The governor is a national figure at this time and deserves a loyal delegation to the San Francisco convention in July."[10]

So while Scranton was publicly displaying humility about being mentioned as a possible candidate and maintaining the image of a reluctant candidate, White wasn't buying it. He believed Scranton saw himself as what the *Saturday Evening Post* described in a headline as "The Logical Candidate." Stewart Alsop, author of the article on Scranton for the magazine, described him as "a reflective man, oddly reserved, highly intelligent but seemingly without ambition or deep political passion."[11]

White paid close attention to Scranton because he believed this man "without ambition" had a strategy worked out behind the scenes while Goldwater opponents like Rockefeller were front and center in the headlines every day. By staying out of the primaries, he avoided the intense press scrutiny that comes with them and also avoided unnecessary losses at the polls.

Historians differ on the motivation and timing of the Scranton decision to run. While Clif White believes it was carefully thought out and calculated months in advance, Theodore White and others believe he remained reluctant until Goldwater voted against the civil rights bill and his wife encouraged him to get in the race.

While those circumstances are unclear, one fact is indisputable. Scranton needed to get the support of a lot of delegates in a short period of time and his search for them throughout the country after his candidacy announcement proved to be pretty much fruitless.

Politics is a strange business. The ends justify the means. Power is the goal, for without power, even the noblest of goals falls short of the mark. Achieving power creates strange political relationships. In 1960, John F. Kennedy chose Senator Lyndon Johnson as his running mate, not because he liked him—he didn't—but because Johnson could help Kennedy carry the Lone Star state and much of the South in the election.

And in 1964, as the time of the Republican National Convention drew near and Goldwater seemingly had the nomination wrapped up, he was thinking about having William Warren Scranton, the man who was clamoring now to beat him, join him on the ticket as his vice presidential running mate. Scranton was from a large, industrial state in the Eastern U.S., an area where Goldwater was politically weak, and his moderate views would help balance the ticket philosophically.

The next stop for everyone involved was San Francisco.

Chapter 19

San Francisco

San Francisco had an identity all its own in 1964. It was urban, it was congested, it was majestic, it was multiethnic, it had sports, it had entertainment, it had tradition, it had vision. It was a place in which, in the same year, *Life* magazine devoted its cover story to the growing gay community in the city—a startling revelation for its time—and was the host city for the conservative takeover of a national political convention a few months later and, a month after that, played host to the Beatles, a quartet of British singers who were taking America by storm with one number one hit after another.

Republicans started pouring into San Francisco in late June and early July for their convention that began on Monday, July 13. Clif White arrived two weeks in advance to oversee the set-up of a massive communications network that operated from a trailer outside the Cow Palace and connected him with his operatives inside the convention hall as well as with Senator Goldwater and his staff on the 17th floor of the Mark Hopkins Hotel a few miles away.

Hundreds of journalists were there. Many of them stayed at the San Francisco Hilton, which had the aroma of newness about it; it had opened for business only three weeks earlier. Three blocks from the Hilton was the St. Francis, the site of the Platform Committee hearings which took place a week before the convention began. It was also where Eisenhower, Nixon and Lodge "and others of yesterday's heroes," stayed, as historian Theodore White referred to them. A few blocks up, on Nob Hill were the Fairmont Hotel and the Mark Hopkins Hotel, directly across the street from one another. Somehow over the years, the Fairmont had become the Democrats' hotel while the Mark Hopkins, owned by cowboy legend Gene Autry, was the bastion of the Republicans.

By virtue of some innocent planning months ahead of the convention, the Goldwater and Scranton teams had both been assigned to the Mark Hopkins. The Scranton command center was set up on the 12th floor. Goldwater's operatives occupied the 14th and 15th floors (there was no 13th). Scranton and family and friends were on the 16th floor while Goldwater's suite was on the 17th.

There were few signs of Republican Party unity as Pinkerton guards and other security stood watch by stairways and elevators on the 12th through 17th floors to make sure none of the opponents infiltrated the others' ranks. Goldwater sometimes took a service elevator up to his suite to avoid having to mingle with others on any of the three public elevators available. The probable presidential candidate sometimes emerged from the elevator in the company of kitchen staff hauling dirty dishes retrieved from room-service guests or housekeepers carting their linens.

While supporters of Goldwater and Scranton were cold-shouldering one another at the Mark Hopkins, and the Platform Committee hearings, under the direction of Congressman Mel Laird of Wisconsin, a Goldwater man, were taking place at the San Francisco Hilton, Clif White was at the Cow Palace, checking every detail of the plan he had been designing in his mind for three years.

The Cow Palace was the scene of hundreds of diverse and unique events since it opened in 1941. Actually located in Daly City, adjacent to San Francisco, it was built originally as a setting for large agricultural shows and was under the auspices of 1-A District Agricultural Association, the fairs and exposition component of the California Department of Food and Agriculture.

The need for a big arena was first discussed after the Pan-Pacific livestock exhibition in 1915 drew huge crowds. By 1925, the San Francisco Exposition Company was formed to finance the project with private funds. Nearly 20 individuals and businesses contributed $20,000 each to get it kickstarted.

In 1931, the California Legislature allocated $250,000 to purchase land for a suitable site for the exhibition center. That drew considerable public criticism because the Great Depression had begun, leaving thousands of people homeless or starving or both. A San Francisco newspaper editorial posed the question, "Why, when people are starving, should money be spent on a palace for cows?" A headline writer took the cue from the story and shortened it to "Cow Palace." That name was retained thenceforth.[1]

19. San Francisco

It opened in April of 1941 as the setting for the Western Classic Holstein Show. Later that year, the Grand National Livestock Expo, Horse Show and Rodeo was held there. After the Japanese bombed Pearl Harbor and America entered World War II, the giant facility was used as a staging area for soldiers headed overseas and as a repair facility for military vehicles.

After the war, the Cow Palace once again became the venue for large livestock and horse shows but gradually its uses increased. In 1947, college basketball was played there for the first time and, the following year, the Ringling Brothers Barnum & Bailey Circus entertained thousands of people.

The Cow Palace became the center for sports events, concerts, business and industry expos, trade shows and major political events, including the Republican National Convention.

As Clif White sauntered inside the place in the last week of June of 1964, his eyes focused on the ceiling high above the six acres of enclosed space all around him. There, at the top, hardly noticeable unless someone was looking for it, was an antenna that he arranged to have put up there. It was the pulse of a massive communications system that White would operate from a 55-foot trailer in the parking lot outside.

From this command post, he could keep in contact with all delegations on the convention floor via an elaborate walkie-talkie and phone system, and with Senator Goldwater on the 17th floor of the Mark Hopkins and with the Goldwater staff on the 15th through two direct telephone lines. There was also communication to the fleet of vehicles, including chartered buses for each delegation, that would transport delegates and staff back and forth in case there were any urgent messages in transit.

One other novel communications ploy: White purchased several time slots for advertising on a local radio station. Everyone connected with the campaign was instructed to carry a transistor radio with them and to tune in at specific times in case White wanted to use the advertising time to deliver a message to his troops.

Security was another matter. White had worked enough campaigns to know the lengths the opposition goes to in order to learn the other guy's secrets or to persuade delegates to back another candidate. Prior to the convention, and with the help of state chairmen, the Goldwater people organized delegates in pairs, even those who didn't know each other. Starting in June, they were asked to call each other at least once a week and then stay together when they were in San Francisco. The goal of this "buddy system," as it was called, was to help prevent a delegate from falling victim to skullduggery from the opponent. White thought this plan was particularly effective in pairing a strong delegate with one who might be prone to weakening. Also, it was more likely for someone who was alone to be approached.

On Saturday, July 11, two days before the convention started, White staged a dress rehearsal to make sure his communications system worked. While he sat in his trailer with a console in front of him, looking like a pilot in a large cockpit, he made contact with operatives all over the convention floor as well as with Goldwater and his staff on two floors of the Mark Hopkins and with drivers in vehicles making test runs on the streets of San Francisco. All systems were go. The technical part of the plan was in place.

The policy part of the Goldwater plan began on Monday, July 6, when the Platform Committee convened at the St. Francis Hotel. It consisted of 100 delegates—a man and a woman from each state—who sat on red cushioned chairs in 10 rows of 10 and listened to one speaker after another bloviate for or against one proposal or another. The duty of the committee every four years is to come up with a platform its candidate can run on. Typically, the daily sessions are long, the process is tedious and the outcome is never in doubt because the final document contains the basic doctrine of the political party, spelled out in specific sections or "planks" of the platform.

Scranton had to work to find any chinks in the Goldwater armor and the Platform Committee offered an opportunity. If he could successfully challenge a plank offered or supported by Goldwater or at least bring the attention of the American people to it, it might provide an opening for him. But it did not happen.

Romney addressed the committee on Monday, Rockefeller on Tuesday and Scranton on Wednesday. They each had about 15 minutes. Romney and Rockefeller focused on the dangers of the direction the Republican Party was headed. Scranton stuck to his usual theme of being the party of Lincoln. Observers said Scranton's speech was the best but it didn't matter. They were speaking to an audience that was lockstep in favor of Goldwater. Their words "fell on the ears of the composed ladies and gentlemen with the near soundless thud of a cracked egg dropping in sawdust."[2]

When Goldwater spoke to the committee on Friday, delegates shouted "We want Barry" when he entered the room as well as several times during his short message to them and again when he left. It is doubtful many of them even heard what he said because of the din. But they would have had the same raucous reaction had he been reading the phone book to them.

Goldwater told them, "I shall not presume for a moment to tell you what should go into this platform. You are Republicans. You know our Republican record. You know where we stand in Congress. You know the programs we've created and fought for. Let those meaningful principles guide your minds and hearts...."[3]

The committee made some minor changes. Instead of advocating strong "enforcement" of the recently-passed Civil Rights Act, the language was changed to "faithful execution"—a concession to members from the South who bristled at the word "enforcement." The new language also conformed to what every president pledges to do when he takes the oath of office.

Scranton had no choice but to go along with the finished platform when it was approved by the committee but planned to challenge some of its planks when it came up for a vote by the full convention on Tuesday, July 14. But he knew that was a longshot, a very long one, and even if it worked, it would be the night before the voting for the presidential nomination—in other words almost certainly too little, too late.

The final document produced by the committee began with, "Humanity is tormented once again by an age-old issue—is man to live in dignity and freedom under God or be enslaved? Are men in government to serve , or are they to master their fellow men? It befalls on us now to resolve this issue anew...."

Several thousand words later, it promised that "we will reconsecrate this nation to human liberty, assuring the freedom of our people and rallying mankind to a new crusade for freedom all around the world."

Scranton had a national following but it did not make its way into the tightly woven web spun by Clif White and the rest of the Goldwater forces at the Cow Palace. His campaign had been hopeless from the start but it did not suffer from lack of effort. He had traveled to 25 states trying to shake loose some Goldwater delegates or convince the undecided. When his trips concluded, he could count the number of delegates he had gained on his fingers. In San Francisco, he was making the rounds, speaking to any of them that agreed to hear him.

In addition, Scranton's staff produced a "newspaper" called *Convention News* and distributed to all delegates. It purported to provide general information useful to everyone attending the convention. In truth, it was a Scranton propaganda piece—one more effort to try to sway some votes. The issue of July 12 carried stories under headlines such as "Vicious Drive for Goldwater Opened by Radical Backers" and "Goldwater's Post Convention Plans Raise Questions of Nuclear Sanity."[4]

Newsweek columnist Raymond Moley, whose political background dated back to the days when he was a speechwriter for Franklin Roosevelt, berated the clumsy Scranton campaign, saying the moderates were immoderate "who never learn and never forget."[5]

Nothing in the plan to try to snatch the nomination from Goldwater was working. Scranton had not picked up the delegates he had hoped to get; he had not received an endorsement from Eisenhower; and he had not made much of an impression with the Platform Committee. Clif White believed Scranton was smart enough to realize all of this and wily enough to use the 1964 convention to start building a base for a 1968 presidential run. Also, though he probably did not know it at the time, he was still at the top of Goldwater's list for vice president because of the strength he would bring to the ticket in areas where Goldwater was weak.

Scranton's strategists, who now included Rockefeller, Lodge, Senator Hugh Scott of Pennsylvania, Senator Jacob Javits of New York and former Republican National Chairman Meade Alcorn, a Connecticut lawyer, met on the weekend before the convention to determine if there was any one issue Scranton could raise that would resonate with the delegates; they decided there wasn't.

Alcorn suggested, and the others agreed, that a way of confronting Goldwater that would be hard for him to ignore would be to write a letter to him, challenging him to a debate on the convention floor prior to the nominating speeches on Wednesday night. The letter would be made available to the press. In whatever way Goldwater responded, it would bring attention to the issues and the beliefs that Scranton held so dearly and had resonated well with the American people—and might sway some delegates.

Meanwhile, the Goldwater forces, though virtually assured of a first ballot nomination, were dodging arrows being shot from a number of different directions which was not an unusual position for a front-runner to be in. That same weekend, Daniel Schorr, a correspondent for CBS News, had reported on an interview Goldwater had given to a German newspaper, *Der Spiegel*, in which he told of an upcoming trip to Germany after the convention. Schorr reported Goldwater was planning to meet with right-wing elements there; in truth, he was planning to go there for a short vacation. Schorr retracted his story but the incident furthered Goldwater's distrust for the media and especially CBS.[6]

The letter written by the Scranton staff was delivered to Goldwater Sunday night and was released to the press. It was much more than a request or a challenge to debate. It was a scathing rebuke of Goldwater and the conservative movement.

"Will the convention choose a candidate overwhelmingly favored by the Republican voters or will it choose you?" the letter asked. "Your organization does not even argue the merits of the question. They feel they have bought, beaten and compromised enough delegate support to make the outcome a foregone conclusion."

The letter went on to say that the Goldwater organization had contempt for the dignity and integrity of the delegates and had treated them like a flock of chickens who were about to have their necks wrung.

"We're not counting noses, we're counting hearts," the letter said. It then lashed out at Goldwater himself: "You have too often casually prescribed nuclear war as a solution to a troubled world. You have too often allowed the radical extremists to use you. You have too often stood for irresponsibility in the serious question of radical holocaust. You have too often read Taft and Lincoln and Eisenhower out of the Republican Party....

"In short, Goldwaterism has come to stand for a whole crazy-quilt collection of absurd and dangerous positions that would be soundly repudiated by the American people in November."

The letter concluded with Scranton's request to debate Goldwater at the convention prior to the nominating speeches on Wednesday night. It was signed "William W. Scranton."

Goldwater was infuriated with the viciousness of the letter. He also suspected that Scranton authorized the letter but did not write it and perhaps had not even seen it before it was delivered. He and Scranton had known each other for many years and had served in the Air Force Reserve together. As politicians, they had corresponded many times. And every time, Scranton signed his letters, "Bill." This letter, Goldwater surmised, just did not fit Bill Scranton's style. One certain result of it: Scranton was no longer the Senator's choice for vice president.

While the Scranton people were distributing the letter to the press, Clif White made sure copies of it were slipped under the hotel room doors of every Goldwater delegate and alternate so they could read firsthand what was being said about them and their candidate.

How the two candidates handled distribution of the letter is an instructive example of the difference between the two campaigns. Scranton sought public support whereas Goldwater worked to solidify delegate support.

As historian Theodore White wrote in his book chronicling the 1964 election, "Where the Scranton leaders confused the applause and the press and the reading of the polls with the will of the Republican party, the Goldwater leaders confused the applause and the praise of the San Francisco convention with the will of the nation."[7]

The convention opened at 10:20 a.m. Monday as delegates, many of whom were bused to the Cow Palace from their hotels, made their way through or around throngs of anti–Goldwater protesters, peaceful but vocal, and most of them independently organized. They held placards and signs, some of them clever—"Goldwater '64," "Hot Water '65," "Bread and Water '66"—and others unimaginative but pointed—"Goldwater Must Go."

The morning and afternoon sessions were filled with parliamentary procedures and speeches by minor political figures who competed with the din of delegates socializing with one another and finding their seats. The main attraction Monday was the keynote address by Senator Mark Hatfield of Oregon, a Rockefeller supporter who switched allegiances to Goldwater for the sake of party unity when he saw a Goldwater nomination was inevitable. It was Hatfield who chastised Governor Romney in Cleveland a month earlier when Romney tried to rally GOP governors to try to stop Goldwater.

Keynote speeches are a time-honored tradition at political conventions, an effort to put some focus to the political pep rally by espousing the party principles, its platform and a reminder of the work to be done if the party's nominee, and the state and local candidates below him on the ballot, are to be elected in November. For the party not in office, the keynote is also a chance to issue a blistering attack on the party in office that will provide cheers from the audience and a standing ovation for the speaker. National Public Radio once referred to keynote speeches as a "tribal harangue."

Hatfield did not disappoint. He said the Republican Party's commitment was "an act of unwavering faith in the American people, in the cause of freedom, in the eternal principles of morality."

The Johnson administration, he said, offered a stark contrast. "In

19. San Francisco

place of faith, we find fear. Anxieties and tensions infect and corrupt our country. At least three fears have typified this administration—fear of the facts, fear of the future and fear of the people," said Hatfield.

The crowd was revved up now. Delegates were no longer mingling in the aisles and talking among themselves. Their eyes were riveted on the speaker and their hands were poised to clap. Hatfield said President Johnson, from the time he was in the Senate, "was standing with one foot on the banks of the Rio Grande and the other foot on the banks of the Potomac.

"And in these two postures, we find that his national foot pointed towards school integration; his state foot pointed toward school segregation. His national foot pointed toward repeal of state right-to-work laws; his state foot endorsed a right-to-work law. I say to you that one cannot dance for long on two platforms without stubbing his toe."

At the time of Hatfield's speech, the Johnson administration was working on getting his domestic program through Congress, a program the administration called the "War on Poverty." Hatfield told the Republican convention delegates "the current administration should wage a war on the poverty of its own ideas."

At the conclusion of his speech, the crowd roared, a band played and delegates filed out of the Cow Palace, their hopes high, their voices hoarse and their emotions not unlike those of people who had just been to a religious revival.

On Tuesday, President Eisenhower took the podium, a man who had earned the reverence he was treated with by his fellow Republicans. Not only was he a war hero, but he was the only Republican to occupy the White House in 32 years. He had steadfastly tried to play the role of the elder statesman, encouraging candidates without endorsing them, although he inadvertently had given the wrong impression from time to time.

He was not a Barry Goldwater fan but on this day, he attacked those he felt unfairly attacked Goldwater. Without mentioning the Senator by name, Eisenhower told the delegates, "Let us particularly scorn the divisive efforts of those outside our family, including sensation-seeking columnists and commentators, because, my friends, I assure you these are people who couldn't care less about the good of our party."

Eisenhower's pep talk was followed by the reading of the entire Republican platform, a tedious exercise that provided an aura of boredom to most of the delegates. But it was a calculated move by the Goldwater forces who controlled most of the proceedings of the convention through surrogates, in this case, Congressman Laird, the Platform Committee chairman.

He insisted on the reading of the document, which took close to two hours, because by the time amendments were offered and voted on, it would be past prime time in the Midwest and close to midnight in the East. So when Goldwater opponents such as Nelson Rockefeller and others got their chance to speak, much of the nation would have gone to bed, lulled to sleepiness by the reading of the platform—and the East Coast morning papers would be past their deadlines.

The Scranton campaign team, still scratching to find some chink in the Goldwater armor, chose to challenge three planks in the platform—on extremism, civil rights and nuclear weapons.

When Rockefeller took the podium to offer an amendment denouncing extremism, he was met with a chorus of boos, something he expected but was nonetheless an extraordinary reaction from members of his own party at a national convention. Historians have compared it with the convention of 1912 when ex–President Theodore Roosevelt's supporters clashed with those of President William Howard Taft in nasty confrontations that split the Republican Party and caused Roosevelt to run independently on the Bull Moose ticket. He didn't win but he took enough votes away from Taft to help Democrat Woodrow Wilson win the general election.

In 1964, the party was divided again and the unity that President Eisenhower talked about two hours earlier was drowned out by the boos as Rockefeller prepared to speak. Senator Thruston Morton of Kentucky, the permanent chairman, banged his gavel and called for order. The boos continued. Rockefeller smiled. He was rather enjoying the disrespect. It was showing an element of the Goldwater campaign that opponents wanted the nation to see. Clif White, in his trailer outside the Cow Palace, frantically pushed a button that allowed him to talk to his state chairmen simultaneously. His message was simple: "Stop it." But they couldn't stop it. Most of the commotion was coming from the galleries of spectators and guests, not from the delegates.

When Rockefeller finally got a chance to speak—five minutes, by the rules of the convention—he purposely used language that he knew would incite the crowd time and again.

He talked about the tactics of extremist elements in the country using smear campaigns, hate literature, harassing late night phone calls, bomb threats. "Some of you might not like to hear it, ladies and gentlemen, but it's the truth," he said. The jeering grew louder. Rockefeller tapped his foot almost as if keeping time to the beat of boos.

"Here is the incident that Goldwater's opponents have tried all week to provoke. It comes far too late to prevent the senator's nomination. But it pins the extremist label on Goldwater and his movement more effectively than Lyndon Johnson ever could. As the minutes crawl by, the Cow Palace becomes a political slaughterhouse...."[8]

"This is still a free country," Rockefeller declared. Over the din of the crowd, he said, "I'm going to finish this last line. I move the adoption of this resolution." It failed, of course, but the larger objective was met.

As he left the podium, Rockefeller gave a wave to the crowd, a sarcastic gesture, to be sure, and then exited, as Governor Hatfield later observed, "looking for all the world like he had been given a standing ovation. He couldn't have had a happier look on his face."[9]

The Rockefeller amendment was defeated on a voice vote as was a similar amendment offered by Romney. But the open sores of the Republican Party were clearly visible. Cecil Holland, reporting for the *Washington Star*, wrote, "There was no sign of party unity that President Eisenhower earnestly advised."[10]

The proposed amendment on nuclear responsibility was also cast aside easily by the delegates. That left only the civil rights amendment, the last bullet in the Scranton gun. Congressman John Lindsay of New York was the spokesman for a proposal to reduce a state's congressional representation if it denied anyone the right to vote. The pros and cons of the amendment were incidental. A roll call vote would determine the strength of the Scranton challenge to Goldwater. The amendment was defeated, 847–409, closing the lid on a Scranton candidacy.

On Wednesday, traditionally a festive day in American political history—the day a candidate for president is nominated—turned out to be a tedious one for Republicans as eight names were placed in nomination. That meant eight nominating speeches, each one followed by seconding speeches, resulting in a parade of speakers to the podium, a process that went on for hours.

Senator Everett Dirksen of Illinois, he of the curly mop of hair and a mellow voice whose oratory often had the tone and cadence of a church sermon, nominated Goldwater. A month earlier, Dirksen was instrumental in helping President Johnson get the civil rights bill passed in the Senate—the bill that Goldwater had voted against.

Without mentioning the civil rights bill specifically, Dirksen called

Goldwater "a man of blazing courage" who was not afraid to vote his conscience, even if it hurt him politically. When Dirksen concluded, Clif White gave the signal for the Goldwater delegates to let loose with their enthusiasm. As balloons and confetti descended on to them, they cheered, yelled and waved signs and banners. It was a moment they would never forget and wanted to be part of. A band played "When the Saints Come Marching In."

While Clif White, not surprisingly, loved the speech, historian Theodore White called it "one of the most tasteless nominating speeches ever made," in which Dirksen, among other things, referred to Goldwater as a "Jewish peddler's grandson."

Seconding speeches were delivered by Senator William Knowland of California, Senator John Tower of Texas, Congressman Charles Halleck of Indiana, and former congresswoman and Ambassador to Italy Clare Booth Luce, among others.

The enthusiasm of delegates bordered on rowdy behavior in some cases on the convention floor. In one area, where a disturbance seemed likely to break out, NBC television correspondent John Chancellor, who headed over to report on the trouble, was literally picked up and carried out of the convention hall by security people. In another incident, Jackie Robinson, the first black man to play major league baseball, who was at the convention as an ardent Rockefeller supporter, was confronted by an Alabama delegate for Goldwater who acted like he wanted to fight but the man's wife intervened to halt any trouble.

The other potential or former candidates all got some attention. Senator Kenneth Keating of New York nominated Rockefeller. Milton Eisenhower nominated Scranton. Congressman Gerald Ford of Michigan nominated Romney. Senator George Aiken of Vermont nominated Margaret Chase Smith, who had not waged a headline-hunting campaign and had not received much delegate support but who nonetheless had persevered long enough to have her name placed in nomination.

Robert Forsythe, Minnesota Republican chairman, nominated fellow Minnesotan Dr. Walter Judd, a favorite son candidate who had been the keynote speaker at the 1960 convention. Senator Hiram Fong of Hawaii, another favorite son, was nominated but asked his supporters not to put on a celebratory demonstration, perhaps because he was not a viable candidate or perhaps he knew the hour was drawing late and the delegates were getting restless.

Lodge, who was upset with the conduct of the Goldwaterites, left the convention before the nominations were complete and asked that his name not be placed in nomination. The New Hampshire delegation ignored his wishes and a spokesman nominated him anyway.

After seven hours of pompous, predictable oratory, the roll call of the states began. It was 1 a.m. on the East Coast, 10 p.m. in the West. As the delegations from each state cast their votes, it was an event in which the outcome was already known. The only detail left was the final score, which was:

Goldwater	883	Smith	27
Scranton	214	Fong	5
Rockefeller	114	Lodge	2
Romney	41		

When the results were in, and the obvious had become official, Scranton made his way to the podium and, in the traditional call for unity, asked that the nomination be made unanimous.

Some of the weary delegates exited the Cow Palace before South Carolina cast the votes that put Goldwater over the top. As delegates, candidates, staff and news people headed back to their hotels, there was a stark contrast to the mood of the citizenry around them. Historian Theodore White reported seeing groups of black people near the Cow Palace singing "We Shall Overcome" in soft, mellow, reverent cadence. In his hotel room later, he was awakened by boisterous revelers singing "Dixie."

In his hotel room, Goldwater had watched the proceedings sitting on a couch, occasionally propping one leg up and stretching it out. He thanked the people around him for their support and called White and a few others to express his gratitude. He too was weary and in a mood reminiscent of his demeanor after a long day on the campaign trail. Someone told him a Gallup poll showed President Johnson beating him 80 to 20 percent. "Christ," he said, "we ought to be writing a speech telling them [the delegates] to go to hell and turn it down."

He refused to take a call from Rockefeller who wanted to offer his congratulations, a traditional gesture toward party unity. "Hell, I don't want to talk to that son of a bitch," he said.[11]

There were two more important orders of business at the convention, both of which would take place Thursday. The delegates would nominate Goldwater's running mate and they would hear his acceptance speech.

The naming of a running mate was most often the decision of the presidential candidate and the person selected earned the honor by virtue of the fact he plugged a gap in the resume of the top man on the ticket. Four years earlier, John Kennedy tabbed Johnson, a man he did not like personally, to be on the ticket with him because Johnson, a Texan, would help Kennedy carry the South. And he did.

The most recent contested candidacy for the vice presidential nomination occurred in 1956 when the Democrats nominated Governor Adlai Stevenson of Illinois for a second time as their candidate for president. Senator Estes Kefauver of Tennessee and Senator John F. Kennedy of Massachusetts were nominated for vice president. Kefauver, a gregarious, popular, longtime senator won the nomination but Kennedy acquired national name recognition that was the unofficial start of his 1960 presidential campaign.

Scranton was Goldwater's choice to be his running mate until he authorized the letter with his signature delivered to Goldwater the night before the convention opened. It was too vicious and hurtful and Goldwater was not of a mind to forgive and forget even if it would help him politically.

Instead, the Senator picked seven-term Congressman William

Barry Goldwater's supporters celebrate after their candidate wins the Republican nomination for president at the Cow Palace in San Francisco in July of 1964 (author's personal collection).

Miller of New York, who had been Republican Party chairman and who was smart and witty but unknown to most Americans. Goldwater had not conferred with anyone before making the decision. From a political standpoint, Miller was a Roman Catholic from a large Eastern state who was well known in Republican circles because of his party chairmanship. Goldwater knew him to be a hard-working, dedicated conservative who was energetic, witty and often sarcastic for the good of the cause. Because of that, Goldwater was certain he would drive Johnson nuts.[12]

Chapter 20

The Acceptance Speech

Goldwater had many opportunities during convention week to start to mend fences with other factions of the Republican Party. He could have ordered his delegates on the Platform Committee to allow minority reports to prevail on issues that were basically meaningless to the overall conservative cause. He could have chosen a moderate to be the next Republican national chairman, replacing Miller, but instead chose Dean Burch, one of the Arizona Mafia who had no experience in national politics beyond working in the Goldwater campaign. And he could have balanced his ticket by picking someone to run for vice president who was palatable to other wings of the party. But in choosing Burch and Miller, Goldwater fell victim to one of his political weaknesses, choosing loyalty over expertise or political advantage.[1]

Another avenue toward reconciliation is one used so often by presidential candidates that it is almost considered one of the traditions of political conventions. It is when the nominee spices his acceptance speech with soothing words to bring everyone together in a spirit of unity—the same unity President Eisenhower had urged Tuesday night, tarnished a couple of hours later when the Goldwater loyalists unleashed their chorus of boos on fellow Republican Nelson Rockefeller.

But Goldwater felt that he had been tarred and feathered unfairly, not only by the press but by members of his own party and he was not in a conciliatory mood when he took the podium Thursday night. Rather, he was the conqueror with little sympathy for the vanquished.

Looking back on the experience years later, Goldwater said, "By the time the convention opened, I had been branded as a fascist, a racist, a trigger-happy war monger, a nuclear madman and a candidate who couldn't win."[2]

20. The Acceptance Speech

The Senator said the tone of comments by his opponents had an effect on how he handled himself, perhaps adding to the damage of his public image. He was accused of being brusque and unfriendly. He said perhaps the criticism was accurate. "It isn't easy to be cheerful, charitable and forgiving when comrades from your earlier battles are thrusting their bayonets into your back."[3]

Goldwater met with his speech writers and his top campaign officials on the Saturday night before the convention in his suite on the 17th floor of the Mark Hopkins. At about the same time they were discussing ideas and themes for his acceptance speech, Scranton operatives, two floors below, were talking about the letter they would send to the Senator the next day, the one that knocked Scranton out of any consideration to be the vice presidential candidate.

Karl Hess had prepared a first draft of the Goldwater acceptance speech. It contained the usual, almost ceremonial call to cast all differences aside, to let bygones be bygones in what had been a campaign full of sniping and to move forward in unity.

The draft was summarily rejected. There would be no words of endearment, stated or implied, for Rockefeller or Scranton. Harry Jaffa was assigned the task of coming up with a new draft. Goldwater thought Jaffa had a way with words and was particularly impressed with a presentation he wrote for the Platform Committee in which he tried to defuse the connotation of "extremism," a word that was often used to tie a noose around Goldwater's neck. Jaffa argued that extremism was little more than a synonym for "principle."

Baroody, always cherishing his role backstage as an advisor—influential but out of the limelight—was now heavily involved in the writing of the speech. Meetings were held in his suite at the Mark Hopkins. Goldwater had the final say, of course, and he sometimes would read sentences from the draft aloud, perhaps to hear for himself how they sounded or to make sure they weren't words he would stumble over when he addressed the convention.

The writing, the rewriting, the editing, the back-and-forth of Baroody, Jaffa and others discussing the contents—everything from general themes to specific phrases and words—went on for five days. The challenge was to get the message across, to get everyone on board with the message and to not provoke anyone who wasn't already provoked.

Clif White could have helped but he wasn't with them. He had been outside the inner circle for weeks, sticking to his role of managing delegate counts and coordinating the convention logistics. He had seen rival factions within the Republican party in the past. As recently as 1952, Robert Taft, affectionately called "Mr. Republican" by his admirers, thought Eisenhower had stolen the nomination from him at the convention. But he understood that was how politics worked.

Taft worked hard for Ike in the fall to help elect him. It was in that election that Eisenhower's long coattails helped Barry Goldwater get elected to the Senate for the first time. White had been around national politics longer than Baroody or any other of the Goldwater advisers planning the acceptance speech. But he was not in the room.

As the speech was taking shape, the men in the room disagreed on whether to include two lines Jaffa had put in—30 words that paraphrased eloquent pronouncements other statesmen had used in the past but could possibly ignite some embers that the Goldwater team had been stomping on for months to put the fire out.

But Goldwater had the final say. So the words remained in the speech, underlined twice. The final version of the speech was approved as the sun came up Thursday morning and was guarded as if it was the original draft of the Constitution. No one outside the room saw it except the workers who prepared it for the Teleprompter and they did their work in a locked room.

On Thursday night, delegates were in a celebratory mood. Their heavy lifting was over for the week. No more platform fights. No more drama on the convention floor. They cheerfully nominated William Miller for vice president and awaited the call to action from the man they chose to be their leader.

Richard Nixon, the party's most recent nominee, introduced Goldwater. Those who knew Nixon knew he never did anything without thinking about the

This campaign button capsulized the phrase from Barry Goldwater's acceptance speech that helped his opponents brand him as an extremist (author's personal collection).

20. The Acceptance Speech

political ramifications. He had been through national political campaigns three times in the past, twice as a winning candidate for vice president and his failed attempt for the presidency in 1960. He never declared his candidacy in 1964 but neither did he discourage his supporters. He was like an understudy in a huge production, always being ready in case the leading man stumbled. And as he introduced the guest of honor on July 16, 1964, before a packed convention and a national television audience, he likely could have had flashbacks to four years ago and what might have been, or perhaps he saw it as a way of reminding people he was still around in case things didn't go well this year; after all, there would be 1968 to think about.

Richard Nixon narrowly lost his race for the presidency in 1960 and then lost his bid to be governor of California in 1962. By 1964, he was viewed by many as "damaged goods" but, after making himself available as a compromise candidate, introduced the winning candidate at the convention (Library of Congress).

Nixon was eloquent in his introduction, telling delegates it was time not for the New Deal or the Fair Deal "or the Fast Deal of Lyndon Johnson but for the Honest Deal of Barry Goldwater." He concluded by turning to the walkway leading to the podium, decked out in red, white and blue, and said, "Down this corridor will walk a man into the pages of history."

With that, the band played "The Battle Hymn of the Republic" and Goldwater made his way down the catwalk, hearing the cheers of "We want Barry, we want Barry, we want Barry," the same loud refrain where, early in his campaign, he had stepped to the microphone and said, "Well, if you shut up, you'll have him." That was back in the days when he was a challenger. Tonight he was the victor and he stood before the delegates as a proud, passionate man. The Cow Palace became a bastion of competing noise, as the band played, the people shouted and hundreds of balloons descended from the ceiling, accompanied by the sound of pop, pop, pop as delegates stabbed them with their lit cigarettes.

As the bedlam subsided, as the band members lowered their instruments, as those who were singing along concluded with "as truth goes marching on," Goldwater prepared to lead the march.

His speech was remarkable in many ways. Of the 3,186 words he spoke, not one of them was "conservative" or any derivative of it. Four years earlier, at the Republican convention that nominated Nixon, Goldwater spoke and chided Republicans with the very word he avoided on this night. "Let's grow up, conservatives," he had said.

Without mentioning it by name, he gave the delegates at the Cow Palace an eloquent description of conservatism. "We do not seek to lead anyone's life for him," Goldwater said, "we seek only to secure his rights and to guarantee him opportunity to strive, with government performing only those needed and constitutionally-sanctioned services which cannot otherwise be performed."

Goldwater began his speech by acknowledging Nixon, former President Eisenhower and former President Hoover, who was ill and unable to attend. He attacked the Johnson administration as being "false prophets" and he warned that U.S. involvement in Vietnam could turn out to be another Korea.

He warned of the threat of Communism and the importance of assuring and preserving freedom. "Those who seek absolute power," he said, "even though they seek it to do what they regard as good, are simply demanding to enforce their own version of heaven on earth. And let me remind you, they are always the ones who create the most hellish tyrannies.

"Equality, rightly understood, as our founding fathers understood it, leads to liberty and the emancipation of creative differences. Wrongly understood, as it has been so tragically in our time, it leads first to conformity and then to despotism."

Soon he came to words in his text that he had underlined twice, the lines that his speech writers couldn't agree on but that Goldwater insisted be included. "I would remind you that extremism in the defense of liberty is no vice. And let me remind you also that moderation in the pursuit of justice is no virtue."

The Goldwater crowd rose to its feet, almost as one and cheered wildly. Scranton, Nixon and Romney remained in their seats. Clif White, who had orchestrated the rise of Barry Goldwater for three years, sat in his trailer outside the Cow Palace, shaking his head in disbelief.

Goldwater, ever the headstrong orator, had taken a big bite out of the forbidden fruit of his campaign. He said the word "extremism"—

20. The Acceptance Speech

blatantly and purposely extolling the label that had haunted his campaign, that his political opponents had used to try to tie a noose around his neck—as recently as two nights earlier when Rockefeller was booed vociferously by Goldwater supporters during the platform speeches.

With those 30 words, he shined a spotlight on an image his handlers had worked for months to try to eliminate. It was at that moment that a reporter in the gallery said, "My God, he's running as Barry Goldwater."[4]

Prior to his speech, a Rockefeller aide approached Clif White to talk about ways in which the different factions of the Republican Party could work together to unite. After the speech, in which Goldwater had in effect said, "In your face, Nelson Rockefeller," there was no chance for unity talks.

At the White House, President Johnson kept up with what was happening in San Francisco. On Thursday, the morning after Goldwater was nominated, the *New York Times* reported that when a reporter asked the Senator if he thought his vote against the civil rights bill might help the Democrats in the coming campaign, Goldwater replied, "After Lyndon Johnson, the biggest faker in the United States? He opposed civil rights until this year. He's the biggest phony who ever came around."[5]

Upon winning the nomination Wednesday night, he pledged not to get personal in the campaign.

"Someone got a hold of him," Johnson told his press secretary George Reedy. "He said I was terrible yesterday morning. Last night he said I'm fine.... We spent a hundred years building the presidency up ... and here's a wild man—mad dog that's going to tear it down in 15 minutes and then want to succeed to the job."[6]

The convention was a fiasco for Republicans. The split in the party, no secret to insiders for years, was put on public display on national television. Reporters didn't have to hunt for juicy stories; they were hand delivered.

"The Goldwater convention gave most of us our first taste of the right rank and file," wrote Ben Bradlee, publisher of the *Washington Post*. Referring to the reception Rockefeller received, he wrote, "No one in the Cow Palace that night will ever forget the booing thousands. You could feel the hostility of the delegates. The liberal wing of the GOP was dying before our eyes."[7]

Historian Doris Kearns Goodwin, who later worked for Johnson, wrote, "In the months before the convention, it seemed almost inconceivable that Lyndon Johnson's shining political prospects could be improved—until the Republicans nominated Barry Goldwater.... For John Kennedy's successor in 1964, Goldwater's nomination made a Johnson landslide inevitable."[8]

On November 3, the landslide occurred. Lyndon Johnson carried 44 of the 50 states. Goldwater won only Alabama, Arizona, Louisiana, Georgia, Mississippi and South Carolina—his home state and five states in the Deep South, the ones Clif White figured he'd win as far back as 1961. Johnson received about 42 million votes, 15 million more than Goldwater—64 percent to 36 percent.

Reflecting on it years later, Goldwater said the election was lost in July, at the convention. "Lyndon Johnson grabbed the big brass ring in November but it was my fellow Republicans, Nelson Rockefeller, Henry Cabot Lodge, William Scranton, George Romney and the other members of the 'Stop Goldwater' cabal who made Lyndon Johnson's victory such a runaway."[9]

Politics is a bruising business. Scranton said he would never run for public office again after his term as governor was up, and he never did. Romney looked at a possible presidential bid in 1968 but lost credibility when after a trip to Vietnam, told the press he had been "brainwashed" concerning his views on the war. Rockefeller still had hopes of being president but never again made a serious run for it. When Gerald Ford became president in 1974 after Nixon's resignation, he named Rockefeller as his vice president but he was not on the ticket when Ford ran in 1976. Lodge, who had never officially been a candidate in 1964 except for the Oregon primary in which he missed the deadline to withdraw, never sought public office again.

Nixon, who waited in the wings in 1964, made a remarkable political comeback when he was elected president in 1968, re-elected in 1972 and then was forced to resign when he faced certain impeachment in 1974. One of the senators who went to the White House to inform him of his impending doom was Barry Goldwater, who regained his Senate seat in 1968 and served there until his retirement in 1987.

Chapter 21

Convention Myths

The tumultuous 1964 Republican campaign and convention were filled with moments that are now footprints in history—the Rockefeller "Bastille Day" declaration of war against conservative extremists; the Scranton last minute challenge and his incendiary letter to Goldwater; the booing of Rockefeller as he attempted to speak to the delegates; and the Goldwater acceptance speech with his 30-word defense of extremism. Many of those moments are not only included in the many written histories of the convention but are preserved on film and video for all to see and validate.

But the convention has also produced some myths or perhaps, more charitably put, some confusion of facts that persist today, more than 50 years after the convention.

In Mitt Romney's campaign for the U.S. Senate in 1994 and for the presidency in 2008 and 2012, he made reference to the admiration he had for his father, Governor George Romney. He said his father stuck to his principles and walked out of the 1964 convention when Goldwater defended extremism as being no vice.

The incident has become part of the 1964 convention folklore, mentioned as recently as in *The Real Romney*, a 2012 biography of Mitt Romney, and repeated in stories in the *New York Times* and in *New Republic* magazine. A PBS documentary on the Mitt Romney campaign, "The Choice 2012," broadcast on the *Frontline* program, reports, "when Goldwater received the nomination, Mitt saw his father angrily walk out."[1]

Walt DeVries, a Goldwater aide who was at the convention, said Romney did not walk out. "I don't remember him walking out, no. Every time I see that quote from Mitt—I just don't remember. I've searched my mind and I think I would have [remembered]."[2]

Goldwater himself may have contributed to the confusion. In a 1966 interview, he was asked about George Romney's chances of winning the Republican nomination in 1968. He said, "Republicans wouldn't nominate someone in 1968 who took a walk-out in 1964."[3]

It is not clear whether Goldwater was speaking about a walk-out literally or whether he was speaking figuratively about Romney's lack of support for him. Goldwater makes no mention of it in his autobiography.

The most ludicrous myth about the convention that has been accepted as fact involves someone who was not a candidate and an event that occurred three months after the convention.

One week before the election, Goldwater got a boost from an unexpected source, a Hollywood actor who had been the host of a television show called "GE Theater"—the GE standing for General Electric, the show's sponsor. The actor was Ronald Reagan, whose movie career included roles such as the portrayal of George Gipp—"the Gipper"—in *Knute Rockne, All American*, heralding the famed Notre Dame football coach, to forgettable films such as *Bedtime for Bonzo* in which one of his co-stars was a chimpanzee. Reagan was now making a good living as a spokesman for General Electric.

He had been a liberal Democrat for most of his adult life and was a supporter of Franklin D. Roosevelt's New Deal policies. He dabbled in politics but his first elective office was as president of the Screen Actors Guild, the union for performers of stage and screen, in 1947. In 1952, he was active in the Democrats for Eisenhower movement.

In his work with the Screen Actors Guild, he became incensed with what he believed were pro–Communist elements within the film industry community. He also became more familiar with the entrepreneurial side of the business, understanding the free enterprise system from the standpoint of those running the companies.

In 1954, General Electric was looking for someone who could be their spokesman not only to consumers but to their thousands of employees. GE wanted someone handsome and personable and who could deliver their message with flair. They chose Reagan.

"The image GE hoped to convey was of a company that was an indispensable cog in America's well-being." The company believed a key to its success was putting as much emphasis on job marketing as in product marketing. "A crucial part of the task was explaining how free enterprise created a virtuous circle harmoniously joining labor, management, customer and community."[4]

Reagan's good looks, amiability and his ease in delivering a message made him a natural for the job. He had appeared as the host of GE Theater every Sunday night, seen by millions of Americans. (The show went off the air in 1962 but the Reagan image remained intact.) He had traveled the country giving pep talks at General Electric plants and making public appearances spreading the GE message. In doing all of this, he became an example of what he was talking about. He was an individual gaining tremendous success espousing free enterprise as the American way. And he became a Republican.

He was a popular speaker at California political events and was courted by Republicans who urged him to seek public office himself. He resisted that—for the time being—but began to speak out on national issues and became a spokesman for conservative values. One of his stump speeches, "A Time for Choosing," drew rave reviews on the banquet circuit and became known as "The Speech." Goldwater's people heard about it and Goldwater himself asked for a tape of it and loved it. The decision was made for Reagan to deliver it one more time and prevailed upon his acting skills to carry out the mission.

On October 27, 1964, a week before the election, Reagan gave the speech to a national television audience as a paid political endorsement of Goldwater. He spoke from a podium in a setting draped in red, white and blue in front of a captive audience of people impersonating Goldwater supporters for the sake of the cameras. And Reagan, the actor, performed well, at this fake political rally.[5]

"This is the issue of this election—whether we believe in our capacity for self-government," said Reagan, "or whether we abandon the American revolution and confess that a little intellectual elite in a far distant capital can plan our lives for us better than we can plan them ourselves."

He went on, "No government ever voluntarily reduces itself in size. So government programs, once launched, never disappear. Actually a government bureau is the nearest thing to eternal life we'll ever see on this earth.

"The trouble with our liberal friends is not that they're ignorant; it's just that they know so much that isn't so."[6]

The speech was inspiring and motivating to the Republicans who were already going to vote for Goldwater. The big questions were whether anyone else was moved by it and, if so, was it too little too late? The answer to the latter turned out to be yes.

The speech was so well received that it has become part of Repub-

Ronald Reagan gave a speech on behalf of Goldwater in October of 1964 that has repeatedly been mistaken as the keynote speech at the Republican convention, which took place three months earlier. Here he speaks in support of Goldwater at the Americanism Education League's 38th anniversary dinner, also in October (Ronald Reagan Presidential Library).

lican folklore and, ironically has been identified by many as the keynote speech of the convention, including by Wikipedia, Fox News host Greta Van Susteren and conservative commentator Glenn Beck on his website.[7]

The legend of the Reagan speech has even affected the memories of people who were at the convention and witnessed Mark Hatfield deliver the keynote address. Jerry Blizen, who covered the convention for the *St. Petersburg Times*, wrote a guest column about it 48 years later for the *Tampa Bay Times* in which he states Reagan was the keynote speaker.[8]

Chapter 22

The Lion and the Lamb

Phyllis Schlafly, a conservative writer and activist, wrote a book in 1964 espousing the principles of Barry Goldwater and titled it, *A Choice, Not an Echo*, the phrase Goldwater used to describe himself when he announced his candidacy on January 3, 1964.

In 1998, Schlafly wrote, "It is unlikely that any nominee for president who was not elected ever had the lasting influence on American politics that Barry Goldwater did. Unlike other defeated presidential candidates, he will never be just a footnote in the history books."[1]

Lee Edwards, who was Goldwater's director of information in the 1964 campaign, said Goldwater "was the most consequential loser in modern presidential politics."[2]

Barry Goldwater, Jr., who followed his father into public office when he served as a congressman from California from 1969 to 1983, described his father's plight in 1964 by sharing a story Winston Churchill liked to tell. It was about a zoo that had a lion and a lamb living together in peace and harmony. A tourist asked the zookeeper how he trained the lion to be so peaceful and loving. The zookeeper replied the problem was not with the lion; it was trying to find a new lamb every morning.[3]

The younger Goldwater said the mission of conservatives was to constantly find new recruits, people willing to step up, like his father had, because they believed so much in the principles of conservatism that they were not willing to give up the fight.

The 1964 Republican convention is compared by many historians to the convention of 1912 when Theodore Roosevelt, who left the presidency in 1908, tried to grab the nomination from William Howard Taft, his onetime good friend and his hand-picked successor. Roosevelt, unhappy with some of Taft's policies and some of his political appointments, went to the 1912 convention intent on getting the nomination and getting his old job back. But Taft had developed some political clout of his own by that time and his supporters beat back every Roosevelt challenge.

Roosevelt bolted the party and ran as an independent on the Progressive ticket. He didn't win, but he took enough votes away from Taft to assure the victory for Democrat Woodrow Wilson. Goldwater's situation was different because unlike Taft, he was not the incumbent president and Taft's political philosophy, while different from Roosevelt's, was not considered as radical or "extreme" as Goldwater's. But one thing they had in common was the discord within their own political party that manifested itself at their respective national nominating conventions. Goldwater believed he lost the election in July, not November, and Taft could have reached a similar conclusion.

Sixteen years before the Roosevelt-Taft debacle, at the Democratic convention of 1896, William Jennings Bryan gave a rousing speech in which he urged Democrats not to support gold as the only standard for America's monetary system. The gold standard, which had been the cornerstone of the monetary system for about 20 years, limited the money supply but helped in trade with other nations such as Great Britain, which also had the gold standard.

Many Americans, including Bryan, believed in "bimetallism," making both gold and silver legal tender because they believed it would open up new avenues for prosperity and economic growth in the U.S.

President Grover Cleveland supported the gold standard. Bryan, a congressman from Nebraska, took to the podium at the convention, and exhorted delegates to support bimetallism. At the conclusion of his speech, he said, "Having behind us the producing masses of this nation and the world, supported by the commercial interests, the laboring interests and the toilers everywhere, we will answer their demand for a gold standard by saying to them, "You shall not press down on the brow of labor this crown of thorns; you shall not crucify mankind upon a cross of gold."

With that, he spread his arms out as if to emulate Jesus Christ on the cross. What came to be known as the "Cross of Gold" speech catapulted Bryan into the "headlines of American history," as his biographer put it.[4]

His admonition, "you shall not crucify mankind upon a cross of gold" was thought to be the most quoted line from a political convention speech until Goldwater's 30-word pronouncement on extremism 68 years later.

As was the case with Goldwater, some in the press did not look kindly on Bryan's speech. The *New York World* reported, "Lunacy having dictated the platform, it was perhaps natural that hysteria should evolve the candidate."[5] The *New York Times* dismissed Bryan as "the gifted blatherskite from Nebraska."[6]

Bryan, like Goldwater, won his party's nomination but lost the election.

As is often the case, history has been kinder to Goldwater in retrospect than his peers were when he was making his mark on that very history. He thought the character assassination of him by members of his own party, particularly Rockefeller and Scranton, and the unfair treatment he thought he received from the press cost him any chance of winning the election. He said if he had to cast his vote based on all the things said about him, "I'd have voted against the son of a bitch too."[7]

After his humbling defeat for the White House in 1964, Goldwater won election again to the Senate in 1968 and remained there until his retirement in 1987 (U.S. Senate).

Eugene McCarthy, a Democratic senator from Minnesota at the time, observed the folly of Scranton, Rockefeller, Romney and Lodge sniping at Goldwater when his nomination was well in hand. He said the Republicans seemed to "shoot the wounded after the battle was over."[8]

But some of Goldwater's actions as a candidate were hard for the press or the public to ignore, and there is no better example than those 30 fateful words in his acceptance speech in which he extolled the virtues of extremism with the same fervor as Bryan had warned about the "cross of gold" generations earlier.

"For a candidate whose chief vulnerability was his supposed extremism, embracing extremism seemed the height of, well, extremism, not to mention imprudence," wrote history professor Steven F. Hayward.[9]

22. The Lion and the Lamb

Conservative writer and commentator Ed Hubbard wrote, "The words we choose to express our ideals matter as much—and often more—than the ideals themselves."[10]

Lee Edwards wrote, "Regardless of the provocation, Goldwater's words divided the Republican Party and gave the Democratic opposition a word—extremism—that they would affix to Goldwater and every other Republican candidate in the fall. Any chance of Goldwater winning the general election, already slim because of Kennedy's assassination, was rendered nil."[11]

J. William Middendorf, Goldwater's campaign finance guru, aptly named his book about the campaign *A Glorious Disaster*—a disaster because of the embarrassing slaughter on election day but glorious because of the awakening and mobilization of the conservative wing of the Republican Party.

Sixteen years later, Ronald Reagan, carrying the torch of conservatism, was elected president and re-elected in 1984. Ten years after that, Republicans won big in mid-term elections and House Speaker Newt Gingrich had many takers on his "Contract with America," a conservative manifesto that outlined principles that were, at their core, a rebirth of *The Conscience of a Conservative*. About 20 years later, the Tea Party movement emerged with yet another rebirth of conservative principles.

The conservative movement has had its ups and downs, its peaks and valleys over the past 50 years like blips on the political radar screen. But it has never died and owes its life to the "glorious disaster" of Barry Goldwater's presidential campaign of 1964.

Middendorf claims the Goldwater campaign was the political birthplace for the next generation of conservatives who scoff at the "me too" philosophy of the liberal Republicans of the Northeast and believe instead that "government does not have an unlimited claim on the earnings of individuals."

He also says history refutes the press reports of how badly the Goldwater movement hurt the Republican Party as a whole, pointing out Republicans won five out of the next six presidential elections (Nixon twice, Reagan twice and George W. Bush once).[12]

Reagan, the onetime actor and pitchman for General Electric, got his first widespread notice from Republicans when he delivered the televised speech for Goldwater one week before the 1964 election. Two years later he was elected governor of California and his political career was off and running. He was re-elected governor, then challenged President Ford for the Republican presidential nomination in 1976 before winning the presidency four years later. But it all started with the speech on behalf of Goldwater.[13]

From Goldwater in 1964 to Reagan in 1980 to Newt Gingrich and the "Contract with America" in 1994 to the rise of the Tea Party movement in the 21st century—all within about the same time span of one another, the strength and durability of the conservative movement was launched in a landslide by the opposition.

It was durable but it was not immediate and it was not inevitable. Goldwater's opposition to the civil rights bill is often cited as one of the reasons voters turned against him. Voters demonstrated the same view in congressional elections across the nation. No Republican member of the House of Representatives who voted for the civil rights bill in 1964 lost their bid for re-election in November, yet 10 Republicans who opposed it were defeated.

There was no early indication that conservatism was the wave of the future. The three leading Republican presidential candidates in 1968—Nixon, Rockefeller and Romney—all rejected most of the conservative philosophy. The movement was gathering strength but it was not until Reagan's election as president in 1980 that it became a dominant force.

The Tea Party movement began in 2004 on a set of principles not unlike those of conservative movements that preceded it. Tea Party followers want a smaller government, fewer taxes, less federal debt and adherence to the principles of the U.S. Constitution. While it boasts of having millions of members of all walks of life, there is no official membership list and its followers are predominantly conservative Republicans.

It has what it calls 15 non-negotiable core beliefs:

1. Illegal aliens are here illegally.

2. Pro-domestic employment is indispensable.

3. A strong military is essential.

4. Special interests must be eliminated.

5. Gun ownership is sacred.

6. Government must be downsized.

7. The national budget must be balanced.

8. Deficit spending must end.

9. Bailout and stimulus plans are illegal.

10. Reducing personal income taxes is a must.

11. Reducing business income taxes is mandatory.

12. Political offices must be available to average citizens.

13. Intrusive government must be stopped.

14. English as our core language is required.

15. Traditional family values are encouraged.[14]

"Here we are, 50 years after Goldwater's nomination—54 years after the publication of his book—and every word of *The Conscience of a Conservative* is even more politically relevant than it was when the book was written," wrote author and former Reagan White House political director Jeffrey Lord. "A better rationale of the political success of today's Tea Party could not have been written."[15]

Political commentator Bill Schneider put it this way. "If you are a certain age, the Tea Party movement may evoke a distant memory, the takeover of the Republican Party by Barry Goldwater's supporters in 1964. The two political movements share the same driving force—not personal discontent but ideological outrage."[16]

Nicholas Mills, a professor of American studies at Sarah Lawrence College, writes, "At the center of *The Conscience of a Conservative* were a set of beliefs that Goldwater was prepared to go down to defeat with rather than compromise. On government, taxes and welfare, Goldwater was a Tea Party presidential candidate before there was a Tea Party."[17]

The 1964 Republican National Convention left indelible images on the pages of American history: former president Dwight D. Eisenhower passionately calling for party unity and chastising the press for its bias; New York Governor Nelson Rockefeller being jeered by members of his own party as he tried to speak and convention chairman Thruston Morton banging his gavel in a futile attempt to bring the delegates to order; the attempt by Pennsylvania Governor William Scranton to snatch the nomination from Goldwater; the appearance of Richard Nixon, the fallen leader of 1960, as he introduced Goldwater on Thursday night; and Goldwater's acceptance speech, remembered primarily for 30 words in which he pretty well confirmed what his adversaries had been saying about him.

Through the years, three basic concepts of conservatism have stood the test of time, as Heath Hansen, writing for the Heritage Foundation, has pointed out: (1) ideas matter; (2) core conservative principles should not be compromised; and (3) persistence is critical to success.

It started with Goldwater. He went down to defeat on his own terms—as a choice, not an echo—and, as he titled his autobiography, with no apologies.

Epilogue

Most of the principal characters involved in the politics of 1964 had unique careers in the years ahead.

Lyndon Johnson won a landslide election over Barry Goldwater in November of 1964 but his first full term in office was marred by violent civil rights demonstrations at home and an escalating war in Vietnam overseas. In March of 1968, he announced to the nation that he would not seek another term as president. He retired to his Texas ranch where he stayed out of politics and made few public appearances. He died at his ranch on January 22, 1973. He was 64.

Barry Goldwater was re-elected to his old U.S. Senate seat in 1968 and remained in office until he retired in 1987. In August of 1974, he led a delegation of top Republican officials to the White House to inform President Nixon that he faced certain impeachment if he did not resign. He published two books in his later years. Goldwater died on May 29, 1998, in Paradise Valley, Arizona. He was 89.

William Miller was a well-respected Republican politician and a congressman from New York and was Republican national chairman when he was nominated for vice president in 1964. After the election, he returned to Buffalo, New York, to work in the law firm he started in 1961. He was much sought after as a banquet speaker because of his sharp wit and candid comments. And he was able to laugh at himself and the relative obscurity he was left with after his vice presidential run.

In 1975, Miller was featured in a popular commercial for American Express credit cards in which the gag was that no one recognized him unless he showed his credit card. "Your American Express card—don't leave home without it" was a catch phrase Miller helped make popular.

He was well recognized in many circles, however, as he served on the boards of four corporations and two banks. He died on June 24, 1983, after suffering a stroke.

Nelson Rockefeller never lost his desire to be president. In 1968, without ever announcing his candidacy formally, he made it known he would be available and, similar to Scranton in 1964, made a late attempt to block the nomination of Richard Nixon, to no avail. He continued to be governor of New York, a position he held for four terms, ending in 1973. In 1974, after Nixon resigned and Vice President Gerald Ford became president, he selected Rockefeller as his vice president. The Senate confirmed Rockefeller's appointment to be vice president, with Senator Barry Goldwater voting against him.

In 1976, when Ford was up for a full term as president, he was pressured to drop Rockefeller from the ticket because Rockefeller was disliked by many in the moderate and conservative wings of the party. Sensing the discontent, Rockefeller withdrew from consideration. Ford named Senator Robert Dole of Kansas, a conservative, as his running mate and lost the election to Jimmy Carter.

Rockefeller served on several boards and commissions but otherwise dropped out of public life and continued with his lifelong philanthropic activities. He died on January 26, 1979, at the age of 70.

William Scranton completed his term as governor of Pennsylvania in 1966 and was prevented by law from running for a second term. He later helped revise the state constitution and the revised constitution allowed for second terms for governors. But Scranton vowed he would never again run for public office and he never did.

In 1968, he led a fact-finding mission to the Middle East for President-elect Richard Nixon. In 1970, after a campus war protest at Kent State University resulted in the shooting deaths of students by police, Nixon named Scranton to head a Commission on Campus Unrest which reported back to the administration with recommendations. In 1976, President Ford appointed him U.S. ambassador to the United Nations, a position he held for about a year. Scranton died on July 28, 2013, at the age of 96.

George Romney sought the Republican presidential nomination in 1968 but dropped out of the race prior to the New Hampshire primary. Just as Barry Goldwater had been hurt politically by his use of the term "extremism," Romney's political future was also severely harmed by his choice of words regarding the Vietnam War. In 1967, he told reporters he originally supported the war because he had been "brainwashed" by generals and diplomats during a trip to Vietnam in 1965. He was branded as someone who was easily led or misled because of his reference to being brainwashed and he was never looked on again as a serious national contender.

He served in Nixon's cabinet as secretary of Housing and Urban Development from 1969 through 1972. He retired from public life and did little politically until he campaigned actively for his son, Mitt, in his unsuccessful attempt to defeat Massachusetts' incumbent U.S. Senator Edward "Ted" Kennedy. Romney died on July 26, 1995, at the age of 88.

Henry Cabot Lodge, like Scranton, never sought public office again but resumed his career as a diplomat and served in many capacities. He returned to Vietnam as U.S. ambassador from 1965 to 1967 and then was named by President Johnson as ambassador-at-large in 1967 and 1968. He was ambassador to Germany in 1968 and 1969 and then was appointed by President Nixon to head the American delegation to the Vietnam peace negotiations in 1969 and 1970. His final stint as a diplomat came when Nixon named him as special envoy to the Vatican, a position he held from 1970 to 1977. Lodge died February 27, 1985. He was 82.

Margaret Chase Smith remained in the Senate until 1973 when she was defeated as she sought a fifth term. When she left, she was the longest-serving woman in Congress, a distinction now held by Democrat Barbara McKulski of Maryland who also served in both the House and Senate. Smith remains the longest serving Republican woman. After she left the Senate, she taught at several colleges and universities and was active in many civic activities in Maine. In 1989, she was presented with the Presidential Medal of Freedom by President George H.W. Bush. She died on May 29, 1995, at the age of 97.

Richard Nixon was vice president for eight years under Eisenhower, loser of the 1960 presidential election to John F. Kennedy and loser of the 1962 California gubernatorial election to Edmund "Pat" Brown. He was available, if asked, to run for president in 1964. He wasn't asked.

In 1968, he was the beneficiary of a Democratic implosion when President Johnson chose not to run for a full term; America was embroiled in an unpopular war; racial tensions filled the streets; and Hubert Humphrey became the Democratic nominee after a tumultuous convention marred by police violence outside the convention hall in Chicago.

Nixon was elected that year and re-elected in 1972. During the 1972 campaign, burglars who were later linked to the Nixon White House were caught as they broke into the Democratic National Headquarters in the Watergate building in Washington. After an investigation that lasted two years and resulted in the arrests or resignations of several Nixon aides, Nixon was implicated in a cover-up in which he was accused of obstructing justice. The House of Representatives voted articles of impeachment and the Senate was preparing to hold hearings.

At the height of the scandal, leading Republican senators went to the White House and told Nixon he faced certain conviction in the Senate. One of those senators was Barry Goldwater. To avoid the Senate skirmish, Nixon became the first president to resign from office on August 9, 1974.

In his years after his resignation, Nixon traveled, wrote and made occasional public appearances. Some considered him an elder statesman but his name in history is forever linked with single new word in the American vocabulary—Watergate. Nixon died on April 22, 1994, at the age of 81.

Harold Stassen had a distinguished career in public service beginning with his election as governor of Minnesota in 1938 at the age of 31. He served President Eisenhower in many capacities and was a loyal Republican all of his life. But history remembers him best as a perennial presidential candidate, seeking the Republican nomination for the fifth time in 1964. He also ran in 1968, 1972 and 1988, never having a chance to win the nomination but enjoying his opportunities to try to liberalize the Republican Party, as he put it. Stassen died March 4, 2001, at the age of 93.

Denison Kitchel never denied his disdain for politics. He was a lawyer, a scholar and a loyal friend of Barry Goldwater. As his campaign chairman, he was an organizer and a manager but left the politics to others. After Goldwater's defeat, he returned to Arizona and resumed practicing law in a prestigious firm that produced a future Supreme Court chief justice, William Rehnquist.

Kitchel remained politically aloof but said in an interview late in his life that he and Goldwater spent little time discussing possible Cabinet members because Goldwater was convinced he wouldn't win. But Kitchel said in one conversation they did have about it, Goldwater had suggested Richard Nixon as secretary of state, retired General Electric Board chairman Ralph Cordiner as secretary of the treasury and

Kitchel as attorney general. Kitchel died October 10, 2002, at the age of 94.

Dean Burch was handpicked by Barry Goldwater to be Republican National Chairman and served in that capacity in 1964 and 1965. He was replaced after Goldwater's defeat to Lyndon Johnson and poor showings by many Republicans running for the House and Senate. He returned to Tucson and resumed his work in the law firm in which he was a partner.

In 1969, President Nixon appointed him to the Federal Communications Commission where he served as chairman until 1974 and was credited with being a champion of children's programming and a having a more conservative view toward network programming as a whole. He served as a White House counselor in the last days of the Nixon administration and during the first few months of the Gerald Ford administration and in 1987, became director general of Intelstat, a global satellite consortium that operated a communications network involving 121 nations. He held that position until his death on August 4, 1991, of bladder cancer. He was 63.

Richard Kleindienst returned to Arizona after the 1964 convention and ran unsuccessfully for governor. Two years later, he was campaign director for John Williams and helped him win back the governorship for Republicans. Kleindienst's experience in running campaigns was well known in Republican circles. In 1968, Nixon named him as national director of field operations for his successful campaign for the presidential nomination and he then became deputy campaign director for the general election, with John Mitchell as chairman.

After Nixon was elected, he appointed Mitchell as attorney general and Kleindienst as deputy attorney general. Kleindienst developed a reputation as being a hard-liner and having a heavy handed approach in dealing with protesters of the Vietnam war, even proposing extended detention in special camps for political dissidents. In early 1972, when Mitchell resigned to become director of Nixon's re-election campaign, Kleindienst was nominated to succeed him.

Allegations surfaced in his Senate confirmation hearings that Kleindienst had used his influence to have an antitrust lawsuit against International Telephone and Telegraph Company (ITT) dropped in exchange for the company's making a significant contribution to Nixon's re-election campaign. Kleindienst vigorously denied that and other allegations and was eventually appointed after the longest series of confirmation hearings in Senate history.

He took office with lofty goals for how he wanted the Justice Department to operate but his plans got derailed within the first week when burglars were caught inside the Democratic National Headquarters in the Watergate complex. The scandal that evolved from the burglary eventually led to Nixon's resignation in 1974 and occupied much of Kleindienst's efforts as the Justice Department was caught in the middle of the controversy. Though he was never directly implicated in the Watergate cover-up, Kleindienst resigned in April 1973 because of the pressures the scandal had brought on.

In 1974, the White House taping system that led to Nixon's resignation also proved fateful for Kleindienst. One of the tapes divulged a conversation between Nixon and Kleindienst in 1971 about dropping the antitrust suit against ITT. Kleindienst was charged with giving false testimony to the Senate during his confirmation hearings. He pleaded guilty to the misdemeanor, was fined $100 and received a 30-day suspended sentence. In his later years, he returned to Arizona where he died of lung cancer in February of 2000 at the age of 76.

F. Clifton White resumed his political consulting career after the Goldwater defeat. In 1968, he worked on Ronald Reagan's unsuccessful bid for the Republican presidential nomination. In 1970, he managed the successful campaign of William Buckley's brother, James, who was elected to the U.S. Senate in New York. Two years later, he managed Jesse Helms' race for the U.S. Senate in North Carolina, which Helms won.

In 1976, White broke from his traditional role with conservatives and instead worked for the re-election of President Gerald Ford, who had been challenged for the nomination by Reagan. After Reagan won the presidency in 1981, he named White as director of Radio Marti, a network that broadcast pro–American programming to Communist Cuba.

White was a founding director of the Ashbrook Center for Public Affairs in Ohio, named in honor of White's fellow conservative John Ashbrook, who helped form the Draft Goldwater movement. White also served as president of the International Association of Political Consultants. He died, at age 74, on January 9, 1993.

John Ashbrook, like White one of the founders of the Draft Goldwater movement, remained active in conservative politics until his untimely death on April 24, 1982, at the age of 53. Cause of death was a massive gastric hemorrhage. At the time of his death, Ashbrook, who had been a congressman since 1961, was preparing to run for the U.S. Senate seat held by Howard Metzenbaum, a liberal Democrat.

In 1972, Ashbrook became disenchanted with President Nixon over many of his anticonservative policies including expansion of the federal government with creation of the Environmental Protection Agency and his actions to improve U.S. relations with the Soviet Union and Communist China. He decided to run against Nixon in Republican primaries but dropped out after competing in New Hampshire, Florida and California and failing to get more than 10 percent of the vote in any of those states. In 1974, when Nixon became entangled in the Watergate scandal, Ashbrook was the first Republican congressman to publicly call for his resignation.

William Rusher, who along with Ashbrook and White, started the Draft Goldwater movement, remained active in promoting conservative principles for most of the rest of his life. He was publisher of *National Review*, the magazine started by William F. Buckley, from 1957 to 1988. He wrote a syndicated newspaper column for 36 years, ending in 2009 when he was 85 years old.

In 1972, he opposed the re-election of Nixon because of Nixon's efforts to normalize relations with China. In 1976, he mounted an effort to start a third major political party but it never materialized. He worked for the election of Ronald Reagan in 1980 and considered Reagan's election and re-election a validation of the principles he had advocated for the past 25 years. Rusher, who never married, died on April 16, 2001, at the age of 87.

William J. Baroody, Sr., a key adviser in the Goldwater campaign, was a champion of conservative causes and an adviser to conservative politicians for many years to come. After the unsuccessful Goldwater campaign, Baroody was an unofficial, unpaid adviser to presidents Nixon and Ford.

He became president of the American Enterprise Institute in 1962 and held the position until 1978 when he turned over the reins to his son, William Baroody, Jr. During the elder Baroody's tenure, his organization became the leading conservative think tank, helping to bring conservative values and ideas into the national public policy debate.

It espoused the ideals of free trade, anticommunism and free enterprise dictating economic growth rather than government intervention into private lives and businesses. The American Enterprise Institute brought together many future leaders including Congressman and future Defense Secretary Melvin Laird, future U.N. Ambassador Jeane Kirkpatrick and future national security advisor Bryce Harlow.

One of the keys to Baroody's success was that he was an excellent fund-raiser and enticed many multimillion dollar American corporations to help sponsor the American Enterprise Institute. Started on a shoestring, the organization had a budget of $8 million and 125 employees when Baroody stepped down as president. He served on many boards and commissions and was chairman of the Woodrow Wilson Center for Scholars from 1972 to 1978. He died on July 29, 1980, at the age of 64.

George Hinman, who oversaw Nelson Rockefeller's bids for the Republican presidential nomination in 1964 and 1968, was a lawyer and one of Rockefeller's closest friends and advisers through Rockefeller's entire political career. He was a Rockefeller aide through Rockefeller's tenure as New York governor, which ended in 1973 and was part of the inner circle when Rockefeller was vice president under President Gerald Ford from 1974 to 1977. He was also the lawyer for many of the Rockefeller charitable holdings. Hinman was named to the Republican National Committee in 1959 and remained on the committee through 1977, leaving when Rockefeller's political career ended. Hinman died September 21, 1997. He was 91.

Ronald Reagan, who delivered a speech in support of Goldwater and conservatism on October 27, 1964, that has been misrepresented many times as being the keynote address at the Republican convention three months earlier, became a GOP icon largely because of the speech. He was elected governor of California in 1966, sought the Republican presidential nomination in 1976 and was elected to two terms as president beginning in 1980.

In his later years, he suffered from Alzheimer's disease. When it was first diagnosed, he wrote an open letter to the American people that was, in essence, a good-bye message. He lived many years with the disease, and though he was out of the public eye, his announcement about it and subsequent updates on his condition helped bring awareness and understanding about the disease to an extent not previously known. Reagan died June 5, 2004, at the age of 93.

Appendix A: 1964 Primary Election Results

New Hampshire, March 10
Henry Cabot Lodge	35.55%
Barry Goldwater	22.29
Nelson Rockefeller	21.01
Richard Nixon	16.79
Margaret Chase Smith	2.28
Harold Stassen	1.48
William Scranton	0.11

Wisconsin, April 7
John Byrnes	99.73%
Unpledged	0.27

Illinois, April 14
Barry Goldwater	61.95%
Margaret Chase Smith	25.31
Henry Cabot Lodge	8.23
Richard Nixon	3.66
Nelson Rockefeller	0.25
William Scranton	0.22

New Jersey, April 21
Henry Cabot Lodge	41.71%
Barry Goldwater	28.04
Richard Nixon	22.07
William Scranton	3.34
Nelson Rockefeller	3.23

Massachusetts, April 28
Henry Cabot Lodge	76.85%
Barry Goldwater	10.84
Richard Nixon	5.93
Nelson Rockefeller	2.66
William Scranton	1.86
Margaret Chase Smith	0.46

Pennsylvania, April 28
William Scranton	51.94%
Henry Cabot Lodge	20.47
Richard Nixon	9.80
Barry Goldwater	8.54
Nelson Rockefeller	2.01

Texas, May 2
Barry Goldwater	74.75%
Henry Cabot Lodge	8.85
Nelson Rockefeller	4.46
Richard Nixon	3.87
Harold Stassen	3.79
Margaret Chase Smith	3.46
William Scranton	0.58

Indiana, May 5
Barry Goldwater	67.04%
Harold Stassen	26.81

Ohio, May 5
James Rhodes	100%

Nebraska, May 12
Barry Goldwater	49.13%
Richard Nixon	31.49
Henry Cabot Lodge	16.33
Nelson Rockefeller	1.68
William Scranton	0.42
Margaret Chase Smith	0.18

West Virginia, May 12
Nelson Rockefeller	100%

Oregon, May 15
Nelson Rockefeller	32.83%
Henry Cabot Lodge	27.59
Barry Goldwater	17.46
Richard Nixon	16.83
Margaret Chase Smith	2.82
William Scranton	1.57

Maryland, May 19
Unpledged	58.17%

Florida, May 26
Unpledged	57.77%
Barry Goldwater	42.23

California, June 2
Barry Goldwater	51.57%
Nelson Rockefeller	48.23

South Dakota, June 2
Unpledged	68.4%
Barry Goldwater	31.96

Appendix B: Total Primary Popular Vote

Barry Goldwater	2,267,079	(38.33%)
Nelson Rockefeller	1,304,204	(22.05%)
James A. Rhodes	615,754	(10.41%)
Henry Cabot Lodge	386,661	(6.54%)
John W. Byrnes	299,612	(5.07%)
William Scranton	245,401	(4.15%)
Margaret Chase Smith	227,007	(3.84%)
Richard Nixon	197,212	(3.33%)
Unpledged	173,652	(2.94%)
Harold Stassen	114,083	(1.93%)
Other	58,933	(0.99%)
Lyndon Johnson (write-in)	23,406	(0.40%)
George Romney	1,955	(0.03%)

Appendix C: 1964 Convention First Ballot Vote Count

Barry Goldwater	883
William Scranton	214
Nelson Rockefeller	114
George Romney	41
Margaret Chase Smith	27
Walter Judd	22
Hiram Fong	5
Henry Cabot Lodge	2

Appendix D: Goldwater Acceptance Speech, July 16, 1964

My good friend and great Republican, Dick Nixon, and your charming wife, Pat; my running mate, that wonderful Republican who has served us so well for so long—Bill Miller and his wife Stephanie; to Thruston Morton, who's done such a commendable job in chairmaning this convention; to Mr. Herbert Hoover, who I hope is watching; and to that great American and his wife, General and Mrs. Eisenhower. To my own wife, my family and to all of my fellow Republicans here assembled, and Americans across this great nation:

From this moment, united and determined, we will go forward together dedicated to the ultimate and undeniable greatness of the whole man.

Together we will win.

I accept your nomination with a deep sense of humility. I accept, too, the responsibility that goes with it, and I seek your continued help and your continued guidance. My fellow Republicans, our cause is too great for any man to feel worthy of it. Our task would be too great for any man did he not have with him the heart and the hands of this great Republican Party.

And I promise you tonight that every fiber of my being is consecrated to our cause, that nothing shall be lacking from the struggle that can be brought to it by enthusiasm, by devotion and plain hard work.

In this world, no person, no party can guarantee anything, but what we can do and what we shall do is to deserve victory, and victory will be ours. The Good Lord raised this mighty Republic to be a home for the brave and to flourish as the land of the free—not to stagnate in the swampland of collectivism, not to cringe before the bully of communism.

Now, my fellow Americans, the tide has been running against freedom. Our people have followed false prophets. We must and we shall return to proven ways—not because they are old but because they are true.

We must and we shall set the tide running again in the cause of freedom. And this party, with its every action, every word, every breath and every heartbeat, has but a single resolve, and that is freedom.

Freedom made orderly for this nation by our constitutional government. Freedom under a government limited by laws of nature and of nature's God. Freedom balanced so that order lacking liberty will not become the slavery of the prison cell; balanced so that order lacking liberty will not become the license of the mob and of the jungle.

Now, we Americans understand freedom. We have earned it; we have lived for it; and we have died for it. This nation and its people are freedom's models in a searching world. We can be freedom's missionaries in a doubting world.

But ladies and gentlemen, first we must renew freedom's mission in our own hearts and in our own homes.

During four futile years, the administration which we shall replace has distorted and lost that faith. It has talked and talked and talked and talked the words of freedom but it has failed and failed and failed in the works of freedom.

Now failure cements the wall of shame in Berlin; failures blots the sands of shame at the Bay of Pigs; failures marked the slow death of freedom in Laos; failures infest the jungles of Vietnam; and failures haunt

Appendix D

the houses of our once great alliances and undermine the greatest bulwark ever erected by free nations, the NATO community.

Failures proclaim lost leadership, obscure purpose, weakening wills and the risk of inciting our sworn enemies to new aggressions and to new excesses.

And because of this administration, we are tonight a world divided. We are a nation becalmed. We have lost the brisk pace of diversity and the genius of individual creativity. We are plodding along at a pace set by centralized planning, red tape, rules without responsibility and regimentation without recourse.

Rather than useful jobs in our country, people have been offered bureaucratic makework; rather than moral leadership, they have been given bread and circuses; they have been given spectacles and, yes, they've even been given scandals.

Tonight, there is violence in our streets, corruption in our highest offices, aimlessness among our youth, anxiety among our elderly, and there is a virtual despair among the many who look beyond material success toward the inner meaning of their lives. And where examples of morality should be set, the opposite is seen. Small men seeking great wealth or power have too often and too long turned even the highest levels of public service into mere personal opportunity.

Now, certainly, simple honesty is not too much to demand of men in government. We find it in most. Republicans demand it of everyone. They demand it from everyone no matter how exalted or protected his position might be.

The growing menace in our country tonight, to personal safety, to life, to limb and property, in homes, in churches, on the playgrounds and places of business, particularly in our great cities, is the mounting concern, or should be, of every thoughtful citizen of the United States. Security from domestic violence, no less than from foreign aggression, is the most elementary and fundamental purpose of any government, and a government that cannot fill this purpose is one that can not long command the loyalty of its citizens.

History shows us, demonstrates that nothing, nothing prepares the way for tyranny more than the failure of public officials to keep the streets safe from bullies and marauders.

Now we Republicans see this as more—much more than the result of mere political differences or mere political mistakes. We see this as the result of a fundamentally and absolutely wrong view of man, his nature and his destiny.

Those who seek to live your lives for you, to take your liberty in return for relieving you of yours; those who elevate the state and downgrade the citizen, must see ultimately a world in which earthly power can be substituted for Divine Will, And this nation was founded upon the rejection of that notion and upon the acceptance of God as the author of freedom.

Now those who seek absolute power, even though they seek it to do what they regard as good, are simply demanding the right to enforce their own version of heaven on earth, and let me remind you they are the very ones who always create the most hellish tyranny.

Absolute power does corrupt and those who seek it must be suspect and must be opposed. Their mistaken course stems from false notions, ladies and gentlemen, of equality. Equality, rightly understood as our founding fathers understood it, leads to liberty and to the emancipation of creative differences. Wrongly understood, as it has been so tragically in our time, it leads first to conformity and then to despotism.

Fellow Republicans, it is the cause of Republicanism to resist concentrations of power, private or public, which enforce such conformity and inflict such despotism.

It is the cause of Republicanism to insure that power remains in the hands of the people and, so help us God, that is exactly what a Republican president will do with the help of a Republican Congress.

It is further the cause of Republicanism to restore a clear understanding of the tyranny of man over man in the world at large. It is our cause to dispel the foggy thinking which avoids hard decisions in the delusion that a world of conflict will somehow resolve itself into a world of harmony, if we just don't rock the boat or irritate the forces of aggression—and this is hogwash.

It is, further, the cause of Republicanism to remind ourselves, and the world, that only the strong can remain free; that only the strong can keep the peace.

Now I needn't remind you, or my fellow Americans regardless of party, that Republicans have shouldered this hard responsibility and marched in this cause before. It was Republican leadership under Dwight Eisenhower that kept the peace, and passed along to this administration the mightiest arsenal for defense the world has ever known.

And I needn't remind you that it was the strength and the believable will of the Eisenhower years that kept the peace by using our strength, by using it in the Formosa Strait, and in Lebanon, and by showing it courageously at all times.

It was during those Republican years that the thrust of Communist imperialism was blunted. It was during those years of Republican leadership that this world moved closer not to war but closer to peace than at any other time in the last three decades.

And I needn't remind you, but I will, that it's been during Democratic years that our strength to deter war has been stilled and even gone into a planned decline. It has been during Democratic years that we have weakly stumbled into conflicts, timidly refusing to draw our own lines against aggression, deceitfully refusing to tell even our own people of our full participation and tragically letting our finest men die on battlefields unmarked by purpose, unmarked by pride or the prospect of victory.

Yesterday it was Korea; tonight it is Vietnam. Make no bones of this. Don't try to sweep this under the rug. We are at war in Vietnam. And yet the president, who is commander in chief of our forces, refuses to say, refuses to say, mind you, whether or not the objective over there is victory, and his secretary of defense continues to mislead and misinform the American people, and enough of it has gone by.

And I needn't remind you, but I will, it has been during Democratic years that a billion persons were cast into Communist captivity and their fate cynically sealed.

Today—today in our beloved country, we have an administration which seems eager to deal with Communism in every coin known—from gold to wheat; from consulates to confidence, and even human freedom itself.

Now the Republican cause demands that we brand Communism as the principal disturber of peace in the world today. Indeed, we should brand it as the only significant disturber of peace. And we must make clear that until its goals of conquest are absolutely renounced, and its relations with all nations tempered, Communism and the governments it now controls are enemies of every man on earth who is or wants to be free.

Now, we here in America can keep the peace only if we remain vigilant and only if we remain strong. Only if we keep our eyes open and keep our guard up can we prevent war.

And I want to make this abundantly clear—I don't intend to let peace or freedom be torn from our grasp because of a lack of strength or lack of will—and that I promise you, Americans.

I believe that we must look beyond the defense of freedom today to its extension tomorrow. I believe that the Communism which boasts it will bury us will instead give way to the forces of freedom. And I can see in the distant yet recognizable future the outlines of a world worthy of our dedication, our every risk, our every effort, our every sacrifice along the way. Yes, a world that will redeem the suffering of those who will be liberated from tyranny.

I can seem and I suggest that all thoughtful men must contemplate, the flowering of an Atlantic civilization, the whole world of Europe reunified and free, trading openly across its borders, communicating openly across the world.

This is a goal far, far more meaningful than a moon shot.

It's a truly inspiring goal for all free men to set for themselves during the latter half of the 20th century. I can see and all free men must thrill to the events of this Atlantic civilization joined by a straight ocean highway to the United States. What a destiny! What a destiny can be ours to stand as a great central pillar linking Europe, the Americas and the venerable and vital peoples and cultures of the Pacific.

I can see a day when all the Americas—North and South—will be linked in a mighty system—a system in which the errors and misunderstandings of the past will be submerged one by one in a rising tide of prosperity and independence.

We know that the misunderstandings of centuries are not to be wiped away in a day or wiped away in an hour. But we pledge—we pledge that human sympathy—what our neighbors to the south call an attitude of Sympatico—no less than enlightened self-interest will be our guide.

And I can see this Atlantic civilization galvanizing and guiding emergent nations everywhere. Now I know this freedom is not the fruit of every soil. I know that our own freedom was achieved through centuries by unremitting efforts by brave and wise men, And I know that the road to freedom is a long and challenging road, and I know also that some men may walk away from it, that some men resist challenge, accepting the false security of government paternalism.

And I pledge that the America I envision in the years ahead will extend its hand and help in teaching and in cultivation so that all new nations will be at least encouraged to go our way; so that they will not wander down the dark alleys of tyranny or to the dead-end streets of collectivism.

My fellow Americans, we do no man a service by hiding freedom's light under a bushel of mistaken humility.

I seek an America proud of its past, proud of its ways, proud of its dreams and determined actively to proclaim them. But our examples to the world must, like charity, begin at home.

In our vision of good and decent future, free and peaceful, there must be room, room for the liberation of the energy and the talent of the individual; otherwise our vision is blind at the outset.

We must assure a society here which, while never abandoning the needy or forsaking the helpless, nurtures incentives and opportunity for the creative and the productive.

We must know the whole good is the product of many single contributions. And I cherish the day when our children once again will restore as heroes the sort of men and women who, unafraid and undaunted, pursue the truth, strive to cure disease, subdue and make fruitful our natural environment, and produce the inventive engines of production, science and technology.

This nation, whose creative people have enhanced this entire span of history, should again thrive upon the greatness of all those things which we—we as individual citizens—can and should do.

During Republican years, this again will be a nation of men and women, of families proud of their role, jealous of their responsibilities, unlimited in their aspirations—a nation where all who can will be self-reliant.

We Republicans see in our constitutional form of government the great framework which assures the orderly but dynamic fulfillment of the whole man, and we see the whole man as the great reason for instituting orderly government in the first place.

We see in private property and in economy based upon and fostering private property the one way to make government a durable ally of the whole man rather than his determined enemy. We see in the sanctity of private property the only durable foundation for constitutional government in a free society.

And beyond that, we see and cherish diversity of ways, diversity of thoughts, of motives and accomplishments. We don't seek to live anyone's life for him. We only seek to secure his rights, guarantee him opportunity, guarantee him opportunity to strive with government performing only those needed and constitutionally sanctioned tasks which cannot otherwise be performed.

We Republicans seek a government that attends to its inherent responsibility of maintaining a stable monetary and fiscal climate, encouraging a free and competitive economy and enforcing law and order.

Thus do we seek inventiveness, diversity and creative difference within a stable order, for we Republicans define government's role where needed as many, many levels, preferably though, the one closest to the people involved: our towns and our cities, then our counties, then our states, then our regional contacts and only then the national government.

That, let me remind you, is the land of liberty built by decentralized power. On it also we must have balance between the branches of government at every level.

Balance, diversity, creative difference—these are the elements of the Republican equation. Republicans agree, Republicans agree heartily, to disagree on many, many of their applications. But we have never disagreed on the basic fundamental issues of why you and I are Republicans.

This is a party—this Republican party is a party for free men. Not for blind followers and not for conformists.

Back in 1858, Abraham Lincoln said this of the Republican Party, and I quote him because he probably could have said it during the last week or so: It was composed of strained, discordant and even hostile elements. End of quote, in 1858.

Yet all of these elements agreed on one paramount objective: to arrest the progress of slavery and place it in the course of ultimate extinction.

Today, as then, but more urgently and more broadly than then, the task of preserving and enlarging freedom at home and of safeguarding it from the forces of tyranny abroad is great enough to challenge all our resources and to require all of our strength.

Anyone who joins us in all sincerity we welcome. Those, those who do not care for our cause, we don't expect to enter our ranks in any case. And let our Republicanism so focused and so dedicated not be made fuzzy and futile by unthinking and stupid labels.

I would remind you that extremism in the defense of liberty is no vice! And let me remind you also that moderation in the pursuit of justice is no virtue!

By the—the beauty of the very system we Republicans are pledged to restore and revitalize, the beauty of this federal system of ours, is in its reconciliation of diversity with unity. We must not see malice in honest differences of opinion, and no matter how great, so long as they are not inconsistent with the pledges we have given to each other in and through our Constitution.

Our Republican cause is not to level out the world or make its people conform in computer-regimented sameness. Our Republican cause is to free our people and light the way for liberty throughout the world. Ours is a very human cause for very humane goals. This party, its good people, and its unquestionable devotion to freedom, will not fulfill the purposes of this campaign which we launch here now until our cause has won the day, inspired the world and shown the way to tomorrow worthy of all our yesteryears.

I repeat, I accept your nomination with humbleness, with pride, and you and I are going to fight for the goodness of our land. Thank you.

Chapter Notes

Introduction

1. F. Clifton White, *Suite 3505: The Story of the Draft Goldwater Movement* (Ashland, Ohio: Ashbrook Press, 1992), p. 111.
2. Steven F. Hayward, "From Barry Goldwater to the Tea Party," *The Federalist*, September 23, 2014.
3. J. William Middendorf II, *A Glorious Disaster: Barry Goldwater's Presidential Campaign and the Origins of the Conservative Movement* (New York: Basic Books, 2006).
4. Nick Kotz, *Judgment Days: Lyndon Baines Johnson, Martin Luther King, Jr., and the Laws That Changed America* (New York: Houghton Mifflin, 2005), p. 45.
5. In 1976, the U.S. Senate began investigations into possible illegal government activi ties involving surveillance of private citizens for political purposes. The name of the investigating task force was the Senate Select Committee to Study Governmental Operations with Respect to Intelligence Activities. Mercifully, it came to be known simply as the Church Committee because it was headed by Senator Frank Church, a Democrat from Idaho. The committee's formation was an outgrowth of the Watergate scandal two years earlier in which burglars hired by Republicans broke into the Democratic National Headquarters in the Watergate office complex in Washington. But the committee looked at many other areas of government interference, including President Lyndon Johnson's wiretaps and bugging of rooms at the Democratic convention of 1964. The report concludes that the surveillance may have been intended to try to prevent violence at the convention, which Johnson aides contended, but it undeniably provided "Useful Political Intelligence." Its final conclusion: "Domestic intelligence activity has threatened and undermined the constitutional rights of Americans to free speech, association and privacy." One of the Members of the Church Committee was Barry Goldwater.
6. Kotz, *Judgment Days*, 199–200.
7. Jerry Blizen, "When It Comes to Political Conventions, the 1964 RNC Was Declared 'Ugliest,'" *Tampa Times*, August 12, 2012.
8. *Ibid.*
9. Jackie Robinson, *I Never Had It Made* (New York: Fawcett Press, 1972), p. 340.
10. *Ibid.*
11. Barry Goldwater, *With No Apologies* (New York: William Morrow, 1979), p. 183.

Chapter 1

1. In his speech on the Senate floor on June 18, 1964, a month before the Republican convention, Goldwater explained his vote against the civil rights bill. He said he objected to the provisions of the bill that dealt with public accommodations and with employment. He said, "I find no constitutional basis for federal regulatory in either of these areas; and I believe the attempted usurpation of such power to be a grave threat to the very essence of our basic system of government."
2. F. Clifton White, *Suite 3505*, p. 6.
3. *Ibid.*, P. 7.
4. Jay D. Hartz, "The Impact of the Draft Goldwater Committee on the Republican Party," *Continuity: A Journal of History* (Fall 2000): p. 1.
5. *New York Times*, July 17, 1964.
6. *Washington Post*, July 17, 1964.
7. Robert Novak, *The Agony of the GOP 1964* (New York: Macmillan, 1965) pp. 461–462.
8. White, *Suite 3505*, p. 380.
9. Hartz, "The Impact of the Draft Goldwater Committee," p. 9.
10. *Ibid.*
11. Theodore H. White, *The Making of the President 1964* (New York: Atheneum Publishers, 1965), p. 220.
12. The oft-quoted remark has been attributed to many people. Theodore White, in *The Making of the President 1964*, mentions only that a reporter said it, without naming him or her. A widely-held belief is that it was White himself who said it.

Chapter 2

1. The Kodak camera company developed an advertising campaign in 1961 that included the phrase "Kodak Moment"—a moment in their lives that consumers surely wanted to capture on film, and the phrase became part of the American jargon for many years.
2. Stephen Hess, "The Nixon Sightings, Part I: The 1952 Republican Convention," Brookings Institution Online, December 2014.
3. When Democrats met in Atlantic City, a month after the Republican convention, President Lyndon Johnson feared a floor fight on the convention floor over the seating of the all-white Mississippi delegation. Blacks in Mississippi had organized, elected their own delegation, and went to Atlantic City demanding to be seated. They took their case to the Credentials Committee. Johnson wanted the Credentials Committee to vote his way. He arranged for the FBI to spy on the blacks, bugging their hotel rooms and having imposters pose as television reporters interviewing them. One delegate on the committee was threatened to have a federal judgeship withdrawn, another threatened with a cut-off of federal aid to his district if they didn't support Johnson on the delegate challenge.
4. F. Clifton White, *Suite 3505*, p. xii.
5. Jay D. Hartz. "The Impact of the Draft Goldwater Committee on the Republican Party," 9.
6. Rick Perlstein, *Before the Storm: Barry Goldwater and the Unmaking of the American Consensus* (New York: Nation Books, 2001), p. 173.
7. *Ibid.*
8. Fred Hutchison, "Conservatism Gains Political Traction: From Wilson to Taft, 1912–1952," *RenewAmerica*, May 7, 2008.
9. The Credentials Committee is often a nondescript part of a political convention, away from the glitz of the convention floor, performing tasks the public rarely hears of or sees. But it can wield immense power and even influence the nomination

process and public policy as witnessed by the events with Republicans in 1952 and Democrats in 1964.
  10. Middendorf, *A Glorious Disaster*, p. 113.
  11. Hutchison, "Conservatism Gains Political Traction: From Wilson to Taft," *Renew America*, May 7, 2008.
  12. Lewis L. Gould, "1912 Republican Convention: Return of the Rough Rider," *Smithsonian*, August 2008.
  13. There is an irony in the hardball politics of presidential nominations in that William Howard Taft apparently benefited from what his opponent claimed was the "Stealing" of delegates in 1912 and 40 years later, his son, Robert, claimed he was victimized by the same tactic in being denied the nomination.
  14. Gould, "1912 Republican Convention: Return of the Rough Rider," *Smithsonian*, August 2008.
  15. Novak, *The Agony of the GOP 1964*, p. 18 .
  16. The family trees of the Roosevelts have many branches that extend to the distant relationship of Theodore and Franklin as fifth cousins. They were born a generation apart. Theodore Roosevelt was actually closer to Franklin's wife, Eleanor, who was the daughter of Teddy's brother, Elliot. When Franklin and Eleanor were married, Theodore walked his niece down the aisle.
  17. "Taft Gained Peaks in Unusual Career," *New York Times*, March 9, 1930. While the scars of the bitter Roosevelt-Taft feud of 1912 haunted the Republican Party for generations, the two men at the heart of it had a reconciliation years later. In May of 1918, Taft was at the Blackstone Hotel in Chicago to attend a conference when he was informed Roosevelt was in the dining room. Taft went to the dining room, and upon seeing Roosevelt alone at a table, approached him. The two men embraced and Roosevelt invited Taft to join him. When Taft sat down, other patrons in the dining room broke into applause, recognizing the significance of the moment. Roosevelt died in January 6, 1919. Taft was one of the invited special guests to his funeral. Doris Kearns Goodwin describes the reunion at the hotel in *The Bully Pulpit: Theodore Roosevelt, William Howard Taft and the Golden Age of Journalism* (New York: Simon & Schuster, 2013), pp. 743–745.

Chapter 3

  1. Though the joke about not paying for a landslide is often attributed to the presidential election, it actually originated after the West Virginia primary, when Kennedy defeated Senator Hubert Humphrey of Minnesota and was a witticism that Jack Kennedy himself used to deflect questions about his father's influence.
  2. At a press conference in 1960, Charles Mohr of *Time* magazine asked President Eisenhower if he could give an example of a major idea of Vice President Nixon that he had followed through on in his role as the decision maker. Eisenhower replied, "If you give me a week, I might be able to think of one," a remark he later regretted. Senator Kennedy used a film clip of Eisenhower's comment to attack Nixon's leadership capabilities. Just prior to the ill-fated remark, Eisenhower had told reporters Nixon was involved in every high-level discussion at the White House for more than seven years and that his advice was sought and appreciated. That part of the press conference is rarely acknowledged or referenced.
  3. Novak, *The Agony of the GOP 1964*, p. 8.
  4. *Ibid.*, p. 9.
  5. Hartz, "The Impact of the Draft Goldwater Committee."
  6. Middendorf, *A Glorious Disaster*. P. 12.
  7. Theodore H. White, *The Making of the President 1964*, p. 62.
  8. Novak, *The Agony of the GOP 1964*, p. 156.

9. Hartz, "The Impact of the Draft Goldwater Committee."
10. *Ibid.*
11. *Ibid.*
12. *Ibid.*
13. Perlstein, *Before the Storm*, p. 142.
14. Rusher remained publisher of the *National Review* for 30 years. He was also a well-known nationally syndicated newspaper columnist. He died April 16, 2011, in San Francisco at the age of 87.
15. Ashbrook served in Congress from 1961 until his untimely death at the age of 53 on April 24, 1982. At the time, he had announced his candidacy to run against Howard Metzenbaum, a liberal Democrat incumbent United States senator from Ohio.
16. F. Clifton White, *Suite 3505*, p. 24.
17. "Salesman for a Cause," *Time*, June 23, 1961.
18. Barry Goldwater, *The Conscience of a Conservative* (New York: Stellar, 2013), p. 13. (Reprint of book originally published in 1960.)
19. *Ibid.*
20. Hartz, "The Impact of the Draft Goldwater Committee."
21. Novak, *The Agony of the GOP 1964*, p. 119.

Chapter 4

1. Perlstein, *Before the Storm*, p. 24.
2. The political curve involving McFarland, Goldwater and Johnson went full circle in 1964 when Johnson and Goldwater were both presidential candidates. Neither probably would have reached that plateau had Goldwater not started his Washington career by defeating McFarland in 1952, which provided the opportunity for Johnson to advance his career by replacing McFarland as Senate minority leader and later majority leader. By losing one election, McFarland catapulted the careers of two people who wound up running for president against each other.
3. *New York Daily News*, January 27, 1979.
4. Goldwater, *With No Apologies*, p. 96.
5. *New York Daily News*, January 27, 1979.
6. "Retrospect: The Death of Nelson Rockefeller," *New York Daily News*, January 27, 2015.
7. *New York Times*, July 27, 1988.
8. *Fortune*, June 1964.
9. *Ibid.*
10. *Ibid.*
11. Perlstein, *Before the Storm*, p. 275.
12. *Ibid.*
13. *Ibid.*, p. 277.
14. The Kennedy-Lodge connections have a long history in Massachusetts. In 1916, Lodge's grandfather, for whom he was named, defeated John F. Kennedy's grandfather, John "Honey" Fitzgerald, for the same Senate seat. In 1962, in an election to fill the vacancy created by JFK's election to the presidency, the president's brother, Edward "Ted" Kennedy, defeated George Lodge, Henry Cabot Lodge's son.
15. Eisenhower's role in the 1964 presidential race is intriguing. Still widely admired for his role as a general in World War II, and the only Republican president in 36 years, his opinions were highly regarded in GOP circles and his support was coveted. Ike sought to remain neutral prior to the Republican convention and favored a wide open race for the nomination. In so doing, he openly encouraged two potential candidates, Scranton and Lodge, to run and Scranton mistakenly took that as an endorsement, which it was not.

16. Theodore H. White, *The Making of the President 1964*, pp. 33–34.
17. A detailed account of the Nixon-Voorhis race is found in American President: A Reference Source, http://millercenter.org/president/nixon/essays/biography/2.
18. Goldwater, *With No Apologies*, p. 103.

Chapter 5

1. *Greenville Times Examiner*, May 18, 2011.
2. F. Clifton White, *Suite 3505*, p. 31.
3. *Ibid.*
4. *Ibid.*
5. Theodore H. White, *The Making of the President 1964*, p. 131.
6. *Ibid.*
7. Perlstein, *Before the Storm*, p. 181.
8. *Ibid.*
9. Middendorf, *A Glorious Disaster*, p. 5.
10. *Ibid.*, p. 21.
11. F. Clifton White, *Suite 3505*, pp. 91–92.
12. *Ibid.*, p. 105.
13. Perlstein, *Before the Storm*, p. 191.
14. Hughes' call to "Draft the Son of a Bitch" is found in many resources. The author cites F. Clifton White's *Suite 3505* and Middendorf's *A Glorious Disaster* as two of them.

Chapter 6

1. Theodore H. White, *The Making of the President 1964*, p. 93.
2. *Ibid.*
3. Obviously, it wasn't his last press conference. Nixon rose from the political graveyard to not only win the Republican presidential nomination in 1968 but to be elected and re-elected president. His true political obituary came in 1974 when he became the only president ever to resign; he faced impeachment and probable conviction for his role in the cover-up of the Watergate scandal involving a break-in at the Democratic national headquarters.
4. The committee wanted to have a Washington presence but did not have a Washington office yet. Clif White wanted to continue to keep a low profile on his work at Suite 3505 so the decision was made to get a post office box in Washington where correspondence and, hopefully, contributions could be picked up.
5. *New York Times*, April 15, 1963.
6. In 2008, Barack Obama became the third sitting senator to be elected president.
7. In the early 1960s, there was no such thing as the Internet or email or word processors. Mass mailings took a lot of paper, a lot of postage and a lot of time.
8. Middendorf provides a brief outline of his fundraising techniques in his book, *Glorious Disaster*, pp. 32–33. Examples of ways in which these techniques can be used are the author's.
9. *Wall Street Journal*, December 10, 1962.

Chapter 7

1. Widely quoted. The author's reference is from Middendorf, *A Glorious Disaster*, p. 38.

2. In 1980, Ronald Reagan became the first divorced person to be elected president. He was divorced from his first wife, actress Jane Wyman in 1949, 31 years earlier, and had married Nancy Davis in 1952. Times had changed in America and divorce did not carry the stigma in 1980 that it did for Rockefeller 16 years earlier.
 3. www.ourcampaigns.com/CandidateDetail.html?CandidateD=37552.
 4. Novak, *The Agony of the GOP 1964*, p. 144.
 5. *Ibid.*
 6. *New York Times*, October 27, 2014.
 7. Novak, *The Agony of the GOP 1964*, pp. 145–146.
 8. Seth Kaplan, "Rocky and His Friends," *Harvard Crimson*, July 30, 1976.
 9. *New York Journal-American*, July 15, 1963.
 10. *Congressional Record*, July 15, 1963.
 11. Kaplan, "Rocky and His Friends," *Harvard Crimson*, July 30, 1976.
 12. Novak, *The Agony of the GOP 1964*, p. 146.
 13. Kaplan, "Rocky and His Friends," *Harvard Crimson*, July 30, 1976.
 14. Theodore H. White, *The Making of the President 1964*, p. 95.
 15. Arthur M. Schlesinger, Jr., *Robert Kennedy and His Times* (New York: Ballantine Books, 1978), p. 651.
 16. Middendorf, *A Glorious Disaster*, P. 55.
 17. Schlesinger, *Robert Kennedy and His Times*, p. 661.
 18. *Detroit News*, May 3, 1963.

Chapter 8

 1. The author was among those students in the Douglas Hall dormitory on campus.
 2. In the first telecast of *Gilligan's Island*, an American flag is seen in the background, flying at half staff.
 3. *Lansing Journal*, November 22, 1963.
 4. *Dallas Morning News*, November 22, 1963.
 5. More detailed accounts of the wedding couple in Florida, the hunter in Michigan and the politicians can be found in "Where We Were," a *People* magazine article published November 28, 1988, in observance of the 25th anniversary of the Kennedy assassination.
 6. The investigation went on for nearly two years. Reynolds produced receipts for the allegations he made against Johnson. But in further testimony, months after the assassination, accusations he made about Johnson and others could not be substantiated and the majority report coming out of the committee described Reynolds as having no credibility. Much of the information about Reynolds' testimony on November 22, 1963, is based on recollections of those involved and there are inconsistencies. No written record of the proceedings has been found. At the same time the investigation was going on, *Life* magazine was preparing a series of stories on Lyndon Johnson's wealth and how he attained it. When Kennedy was assassinated and Johnson became president, the magazine editors chose to put the project on hold and it never came into fruition.
 7. Novak, *The Agony of the GOP 1964*, p. 251.
 8. *Ibid.*
 9. Goldwater, *With No Apologies*, p. 118–119.
 10. Novak, *The Agony of the GOP 1964*, p. 252.
 11. Goldwater, *With No Apologies*, p. 156.
 12. *Ibid.*
 13. *Ibid.*, p. 160.
 14. *U.S. News & World Report*, December 21, 1964.

15. F. Clifton White, *Suite 3505*, p. 236.
16. Barndollar, *Martyr to the Cause*, p. 149.
17. Goldwater, *With No Apologies*, p. 156.
18. *Ibid.*, pp. 160–161.
19. John B. Judis, "The Man Who Knew Too Little," *Washington Post*, September 24, 1995.

Chapter 9

1. Middendorf, *The Glorious Disaster*, p. 68.
2. *Ibid.*, p. 50.
3. Gilman Barndollar, *Martyr to the Cause: The Goldwater Campaign of 1964* (Concord: The Concord Review, 1998), p. 147.
4. Novak, *The Agony of the GOP 1964*, pp. 246–247.
5. As an adult, those who knew Kleindienst well said he had the ability to curse in two languages—English and Navajo.

Chapter 10

1. *New York Times*, August 25, 1997.
2. Novak, *The Agony of the GOP 1964*, p. 72.
3. Theodore H. White, *The Making of the President 1964*, p. 73.
4. Perlstein, *Before the Storm*, p. 263.
5. Michigan Governor George Romney, a potential Republican candidate in 1968, told the press he had been "brain-washed" by American military personnel who had briefed him on the war in Vietnam. The remark haunted him because it made him appear to be naïve or easily misled and his potential candidacy fizzled. In 1988, rumors swirled about the social life of Colorado Senator Gary Hart, a candidate for the Democratic presidential nomination. Hart, a married man with a family, dared reporters to follow him. Some did and photographed the senator in the company of a young lady on a boat with the unfortunate (for Hart) name— "Monkey Business." His campaign nose-dived.
6. Novak, *The Agony of the GOP 1964*, p. 238.

Chapter 11

1. Kotz, *Judgment Days*, p. 12.
2. When Johnson was president, he appointed Fortas to the Supreme Court.
3. Doris Kearns Goodwin, *Lyndon Johnson and the American Dream* (New York: St. Martin's Press, 1991), pp. 74–75.
4. McFarland's political career was not over. He was later elected governor of Arizona.
5. Goldwater, *With No Apologies*, p. 192.
6. Robert Dallek, *Lyndon Johnson: Portrait of a President* (New York: Oxford University Press USA, 2005), p. 87.
7. Goodwin, *Lyndon Johnson and the American Dream*, p. 50.
8. Hubert Humphrey. *The Education of a Public Man: My Life in Politics* (Minneapolis: University of Minnesota Press, 1991), pp. 181, 216–218.
9. Goldwater, *With No Apologies*, p. 120.

10. Vice presidents who later became president are John Adams, George Washington's vice president; Thomas Jefferson, John Adams' vice president; Martin Van Buren, Andrew Jackson's vice president; John Tyler, William Henry Harrison's vice president; Millard Fillmore, Zachary Taylor's vice president; Andrew Johnson, Abraham Lincoln's vice president; Chester Arthur, James Garfield's vice president; Theodore Roosevelt, William McKinley's vice president; Calvin Coolidge; Warren Harding's vice president; and Harry Truman, Franklin Roosevelt's vice president. Johnson became the 11th vice president to later become president and most recently, George Herbert Walker Bush, Ronald Reagan's vice president, became the 12th.

11. Goldwater, *With No Apologies*, p. 121.

Chapter 12

1. Theodore White, *The Making of the President 1964*, p. 101.
2. *Ibid.*, p. 103.
3. Novak, *The Agony of the GOP 1964*, p. 307.
4. Politicians in those days did not have to contend with modern media that now include Cable News Network (CNN), Fox News, MSNBC, other 24-hour news sources in which Americans can watch, hear or read about what a candidate said somewhere in the morning and said the same thing somewhere else that afternoon and evening. When former New Jersey Senator Bill Bradley sought the Democratic presidential nomination in 2000, he campaigned in the South and told the touching story of being in a school room of youngsters and asking how many of them didn't have breakfast that morning. One little boy raised his hand. Bradley asked him why and the boy said, "Because it wasn't my turn." It was a poignant story and Bradley told it most everywhere he went, but because it had been aired so many times as he traveled from city to city, most people had heard it by the time he reached their town.
5. Perlstein, *Before the Storm*, p. 267.
6. *Ibid.*, 274.
7. Smith competed in several primaries, not coming close to winning any of them. She allowed her name to be placed in nomination at the Republican convention in San Francisco and then refused to withdraw even after Goldwater's nomination was assured, thus preventing him from being the unanimous choice.
8. Stassen ran five other times for president—in 1968, 1980, 1984, 1988 and 1992—making it 10 times altogether. He also made another run for governor of Pennsylvania and additional runs for the U.S. House and Senate, losing them all.
9. *New York Herald Tribune*, December 24, 1963.
10. Theodore H. White, *The Making of the President 1964*, p. 110.
11. Perlstein, *Before the Storm*, p. 292.
12. F. Clifton White, *Suite 3505*, p. 272.
13. *Manchester Union Leader*, May 3, 2011.
14. Perlstein, *Before the Storm*, p. 298.
15. F. Clifton White, *Suite 3505*, p. 208.
16. Middendorf, *A Glorious Disaster*, p. 66.

Chapter 13

1. Novak, *The Agony of the GOP 1964*, p. 329.
2. Theodore H. White, *The Making of the President 1964*, p. 83.
3. Goldwater, *With No Apologies*, p. 176.
4. *New York Herald Tribune*, December 5, 1963.
5. This particular luncheon was held on November 8, 1963.

6. *New York Herald Tribune*, December 23, 1963. The next day, the same newspaper published the Roscoe Drummond column that included the false information about the nationwide momentum for Henry Cabot Lodge.
   7. G. Terry Madonna, *Pivotal Pennsylvania: Presidential Politics from FDR to the 21st Century* (Mansfield: Pennsylvania Historical Association, 2008), p. 89.
   8. Theodore H. White, *The Making of the President 1964*, p. 91.
   9. Perlstein, *Before the Storm*, p. 279.
   10. *New York Times*, May 3, 1964.
   11. Perlstein, *Before the Storm*, p. 274.
   12. Novak, *The Agony of the GOP 1964*, p. 160–161.
   13. *Detroit News*, May 3, 1963.

Chapter 14

   1. Evan Thomas, *Ike's Bluff: President Eisenhower's Secret Battle to Save the World* (New York: Little, 2012), p. 416.
   2. Theodore H. White, *In Search of History* (New York: Warner Books, 1978), p. 408.
   3. Stephen Ambrose, *Eisenhower: Soldier and President* (New York: Simon & Schuster, 1991), p. 573.
   4. Beschloss, *Taking Charge*, p. 195.
   5. Former president Herbert Hoover was 16 years older than Eisenhower and was in failing health and was no longer an active participant or spokesman for Republican causes.
   6. Anderson was in trouble with the law many years after he served Eisenhower. In 1987, at the age of 78, he was sentenced to one month in prison and five months' house arrest after pleading guilty to federal charges of tax evasion that occurred in 1983 and 1984 as well as operating an illegal offshore bank.
   7. *New York Times*, May 2, 1963.
   8. Theodore H. White, *The Making of the President 1964*, p. 71.
   9. *New York Times*, December 8, 1963.
   10. Perlstein, *Before the Storm*, p. 277.
   11. *Ibid.*, pp. 347–48.
   12. Goldwater, *With No Apologies*, p. 177.
   13. *Ibid.*
   14. *New York Times*, May 31, 1983.
   15. Anything could happen, and in baseball in 1964, the unbelievable did occur. The Philadelphia Phillies, in the National League, had a 6½ game lead with 12 to play and lost 11 out of the 12, losing the pennant to the St. Louis Cardinals.

Chapter 15

   1. Perlstein, *Before the Storm*, p. 313.
   2. *New York Herald Tribune*, May 7, 1964.
   3. Novak, *The Agony of the GOP 1964*, p. 335.
   4. *Ibid.*, p. 357.
   5. The Wisconsin crossover rule and the Illinois law not requiring the counting of write-in votes as well as the powers given to the gubernatorial nominee are two examples of what Clif White had preached to the Draft Goldwater neophytes in 1961—the importance of knowing the nuances of the laws in individual states.
   6. A generation later, the author interviewed Walter Mondale, who as candidate for vice president and president, had experienced the caucus and primary election

grind three times—in 1976 and 1980 as Jimmy Carter's running mate and in 1984 when he ran for president. In 1984, he received 49 percent support to win the Iowa caucuses. Gary Hart was a distant second at 17 percent. Yet Mondale said Hart got more favorable press than he did because of media expectations. Mondale was expected to win big but Hart exceeded expectations and was therefore the big story. Also, said Mondale, the media focuses on the second-place finisher because if there's no opponent, there's no story.

 7. *Washington Star*, April 16, 1964.
 8. Novak, *The Agony of the GOP 1964*, p. 372.
 9. *Portland Oregonian*, April 6, 1964.
 10. *National Review*, June 2, 1964.

Chapter 16

 1. Novak, *The Agony of the GOP*, p. 386.
 2. F. Clifton White, *Suite 3505*, pp. 311–312.
 3. Theodore H. White, *The Making of the President 1964*, p. 121.
 4. Goldwater, *With No Apologies*, p. 178.
 5. F. Clifton White, *Suite 3505*, p. 323.
 6. Middendorf, *A Glorious Disaster*, p. 101.

Chapter 17

 1. The phrase "It ain't over till it's over" is actually attributed to baseball catcher, coach and manager Yogi Berra when he was a coach for the New York Mets in 1969. He was talking about the Mets being seven games behind the Chicago Cubs in the National League in August. The Mets had a torrid September, overtook the Cubs and then beat the Baltimore Orioles in the World Series. Five years earlier, the anti–Goldwater faction of the Republican Party was looking for something similar to happen.

 2. Gary Donaldson, *Liberalism's Last Hurrah: The Presidential Campaign of 1964* (New York: Routledge, 2003), p. 137.

 3. Novak, *The Agony of the GOP 1964*, p. 421.

 4. After the convention that nominated Goldwater, Romney was even more focused on the effects it might have on his re-election chances in November. The *San Francisco Chronicle* reported on July, 16, 1964, "Michigan Governor George Romney said he had strong reservations about Goldwater's positions on civil rights and political extremists and would not associate himself with the ticket in his campaign for re-election this year."

 5. *Face the Nation* television broadcast, June 7, 1964.
 6. *Ibid.*

Chapter 18

 1. Audio and text versions of the Kennedy speech are available at www.americanrhetoric.com.

 2. www.senate.gov/artandhistory/common/generic/CivilRightsAct1964.htm.

 3. *The Texas Observer*, June 10, 1960.

 4. Congressional Record, 84th Congress, second session, v. 102, pt. 4, March 12, 1956, Washington, D.C.: Government Printing Office.

 5. George H.W. Bush, a candidate for the U.S. Senate from Texas and son of Connecticut Senator Prescott Bush, was also opposed to the bill.

6. Middendorf, *A Glorious Disaster*, p. 105.
7. *Newsweek*, June 22, 1964.
8. G. Terry Madonna, *Pivotal Pennsylvania: Presidential Politics from FDR to the 21st Century* (Mansfield: Pennsylvania Historical Association, 2008), p. 21.
9. *New York Times*, June 17, 1964.
10. *Pittsburgh Post-Gazette*, April 22, 1964.
11. *Saturday Evening Post*, January 18, 1964.

Chapter 19

1. www.cowpalace.com/about/cow-palace-history.html.
2. Theodore H. White, *The Making of the President 1964*, p. 192.
3. Goldwater, *With No Apologies*, p. 182.
4. *Convention News*, July 13, 1964.
5. *Newsweek*, July 13, 1964. Moley was the chief speech writer for Roosevelt whom historians credit with writing the 1933 inaugural address in which the president told the country, "The only thing we have to fear is fear itself" although that particular line was inserted after Moley had completed his work.
6. In Clif Smith's elaborate plans to control the communications flow at the convention, he had underestimated the presence of the media. On the weekend before the convention, as he stood on the floor of the convention, he was amazed when he looked up and saw huge rectangular booths, the size of railroad cars that ABC, NBC and CBS had erected on the second level of the Cow Palace, similar to press boxes in Major League ballparks, only much larger. There would be no control over what was transmitted from those alcoves.
7. Theodore White, *The Making of the President 1964*, p. 198.
8. Smith, *On His Own Terms*, p. 245.
9. *Ibid.*
10. *Washington Star*, July 15, 1964.
11. Perlstein, *Before the Storm*, p. 389.
12. In his autobiography *With No Apologies*, Goldwater makes no mention of Miller.

Chapter 20

1. Clif White wanted to be national chairman and believed he deserved it. Goldwater was the Republican nominee largely because of the grassroots Draft Goldwater movement started by White in a Chicago hotel room in 1961. Goldwater did not inform White of his decision. White learned about it in a casual conversation with someone in an elevator at the Mark Hopkins Hotel. He was deeply hurt but accepted a much more minor role in the campaign after the convention was over.
2. Goldwater, *With No Apologies*, p. 179.
3. *Ibid.*
4. As noted in Chapter One, the widely-quoted line is unattributed but many believe the man who said it was Theodore White.
5. *New York Times*, July 16, 1964.
6. Transcript of White House tapes, available at the LBJ Library in Austin, Texas. Also quoted in *Taking Charge*, pp. 456–457.
7. Benjamin Bradlee, *A Good Life: Newspapering and Other Adventures* (New York: Simon & Schuster, 1995), p. 264.
8. Goodwin, *Lyndon Johnson and the American Dream*, p. 206.
9. Goldwater, *With No Apologies*, p. 179.

Chapter 21

1. The references mentioned are included in "Making Mitt: The Myth of George Romney," *BuzzFeed*, October 15, 2012.
2. *Ibid.*
3. *Human Events*, August 1966.
4. Perlstein, *Before the Storm*, p. 123.
5. A full account of the Reagan staged speech can be found in Perlstein, *Before the Storm*, pp. 499–504.
6. The text of Reagan's speech can be found in many resources including www.americanrhetoric.com.
7. Scott Bomboy, "The Myth of Reagan's GOP Convention Speech," *National Convention Center*, August 13, 2012.
8. Jerry Blizin, "When It Comes to Political Conventions, the 1964 RNC Was Declared Ugliest," *Tampa Bay Times*, August 7, 2012.

Chapter 22

1. Phyllis Schlafly, *Eagle Forum*, June 1998.
2. Lee Edwards, "Barry M. Goldwater: The Most Consequential Loser in American Politics," *Heritage*, July 3, 2014.
3. Barry Goldwater, Jr., told the story when he was the featured speaker at a dinner marking the 50th anniversary of the Draft Goldwater Movement on November 18, 2014.
4. Michael Kazin, *A Godly Hero: The Life of William Jennings Bryan* (New York: Alfred A. Knopf, 2007) p. 17.
5. R. Hal Williams, *Realigning America: McKinley, Bryan and the Remarkable Election of 1896* (Lawrence: University Press of Kansas, 2010), p. 88.
6. William D. Harpine, *From the Front Porch to the Front Page: McKinley and Bryan in the 1896 Presidential Campaign* (College Station: Texas A&M University Press, 2005), p. 52.
7. Steven F. Hayward, "From Barry Goldwater to the Tea Party," *The Federalist*, September 23, 2014.
8. Four years later, McCarthy did essentially the same thing Scranton did when he launched an 11th-hour attempt to stop Hubert Humphrey from getting the Democratic nomination when Humphrey's nomination was all but assured.
9. Hayward, "From Barry Goldwater to the Tea Party," *The Federalist*, September 23, 2014.
10. Ed Hubbard, "Statesmanship and the Goldwater Legacy," BigJollyPolitics.com, April 29, 2015.
11. Edwards, "Barry M. Goldwater, the Most Consequential Loser."
12. Middendorf, *A Glorious Disaster*, pp. ix, xi.
13. A similar circumstance occurred with Barack Obama. He was a state senator from Illinois running for the U.S. Senate when Democrats saw him as a rising young star in their party. He delivered the keynote address at the 2004 Democratic convention, was elected to the Senate later that year and was elected president for the first time in 2008. But he had been a relative political unknown until he made that one speech in 2004.
14. www.teaparty.org/about-us/.
15. Jeffrey Lord, "The Vindication of Barry Goldwater," *The American Spectator*, July 24, 2014.
16. Bill Schneider, "The Tea Party: Goldwater," *National Journal*, April 24, 2010.
17. Nicolaus Mills, "Barry Goldwater: Father of the Tea Party," *The Daily Beast*, July 16 2014.

Bibliography

Books

Ambrose, Stephen. *Eisenhower: Soldier and President*. New York: Simon & Schuster, 1991.
Barone, Michael. *Our Country: The Shaping of America from Roosevelt to Reagan*. New York: Free Press, 1990.
Beschloss, Michael R. *Taking Charge: The Johnson White House Tapes, 1963–1964*. New York: Touchtone, 1997.
Bradlee, Benjamin. *A Good Life: Newspapering and Other Adventures*. New York: Simon & Schuster, 1995.
Broder, David, Lou Cannon, Haynes Johnson, Martin Schram, Richard Harwood, and *Washington Post* staff. *The Pursuit of the Presidency 1980*. New York: Berkley Books, 1980.
Caro, Robert. *The Years of Lyndon Johnson, Master of the Senate*. New York: Knopf, 2002.
Crawford, Alan. *Thunder on the Right*. New York: Pantheon Books, 1980.
Dallek, Robert. *Lyndon B. Johnson: Portrait of a President*. New York: Oxford University Press, 2005.
Diamond, Sara. *Roads to Dominion*. New York: Guilford Press, 1995.
Donaldson, Gary. *Liberalism's Last Hurrah: The Presidential Campaign of 1964*. New York: Routledge, 2003.
Faber, Harold. *The Road to the White House*. New York: McGraw-Hill, 1965.
Fein, Kim Phillips. *Invisible Hands: The Businessman's Crusade Against the New Deal*. New York: W.W. Norton, 2010.
Frisk, David. *If Not Us, Who: William Rusher, National Review and the Conservative Movement*. New York: ISI Books, 1965.
Goldberg, Robert Alan. *Barry Goldwater*. New Haven: Yale University Press, 1995.
Goldwater, Barry. *The Conscience of a Conservative*. New York: Hillman Books, 1961.
_____. *With No Apologies*. New York: William Morrow, 1979.
Goodwin, Doris Kearns. *The Bully Pulpit: Theodore Roosevelt, William Howard Taft and the Golden Age of Journalism*. New York: Simon & Schuster, 2013.
_____. *Lyndon Johnson and the American Dream*. New York: St. Martin's Griffin, 1976.

Harpine, William D. *From the Front Porch to the Front Page: McKinley and Bryan in the 1896 Presidential Campaign*. College Station: Texas A&M University Press, 2005.
Kazan, Michael. *A Godly Hero: The Life of William Jennings Bryan*. New York: Alfred A. Knopf, 2007.
Madonna, G. Terry. *Pivotal Pennsylvania: Presidential Politics from FDR to the 21st Century*. Mansfield: Pennsylvania Historical Association, 2008.
Middendorf, J. William II. *A Glorious Disaster: Barry Goldwater's Presidential Campaign and the Origins of the Conservative Movement*. New York: Basic Books, 2006.
Novak, Robert. *The Agony of the GOP 1964*. New York: Macmillan, 1964.
Perlstein, Rick. *Before the Storm: Barry Goldwater and the Unmaking of the American Consensus*. New York: Nation Books, 2009.
Robinson, Jackie. *I Never Had It Made*. New York: Fawcett, 1972
Rumbaugh, Stanley M., Jr. *Citizens for Eisenhower: The 1952 Presidential Campaign—Lessons for the Future*. McLean, Va.: International Publishers, 2013.
Rusher, William. *Rise of the Right*. New York: William Morrow, 1984.
Schlesinger, Arthur. *Robert Kennedy and His Times*. New York: Ballantine Books, 1978.
Shadegg, Stephen. *What Happened to Barry Goldwater?* New York: Holt, Rinehart and Winston, 1965.
Smith, Hedrick. *Who Stole the American Dream?* New York: Random House, 2013.
Smith, Richard Norton. *On His Own Terms: A Life of Nelson Rockefeller*. New York: Random House, 2014.
Stricherz, Mark. *Why the Democrats Are Blue*. New York: Encounter Books, 2007.
Troy, Gil. *See How They Run*. New York: Free Press, 1991.
White, F. Clifton. *Suite 3505: The Story of the Draft Goldwater Movement*. New York: Arlington House, 1967.
White, Theodore H. *In Search of History*. New York: Warner Books, 1978.
_____. *The Making of the President 1964*. New York: Atheneum Publishers, 1965.
Williams R. Hal. *Realigning America: McKinley, Bryan and the Remarkable Election of 1896*. Lawrence: University Press of Kansas, 2010.

Articles

Blizen, Jerry. "When it comes to political conventions, the 1964 RNC was declared ugliest." *Tampa Bay Times*, August 7, 2012.
Bomboy, Scott. "The Myth of Reagan's GOP Convention Speech." *National Convention Center*, August 13, 2012.
Burns, Alexander. "The Myth of George Romney's Walkout." Politico.com, October 15, 2012.
Cityscape. Iowa League of Cities, January 2015.
Clark, Kenneth R. "NBC's John Chancellor Leaving TV After 43 Years." *Chicago Tribune*, June 20, 1993.
Edwards, Lee. "Barry M. Goldwater: The Most Consequential Loser in American Politics." *Heritage*, July 3, 2014.
"Former New York Governor and U.S. Vice President Nelson Rockefeller Dies at 70." *New York Daily News*, January 27, 1979.
"George Romney: Businessman in Political Jungle." *Fortune*, June 1964.

"George Romney Dies at 88; A Leading GOP Figure." *New York Times*, July 27, 1995.
Gould, Lewis L. "1912 Republican Convention: Return of the Rough Rider." *Smithsonian*, August 2008.
Hartz, Jay D. "The Impact of the Draft Goldwater Committee on the Republican Party." Ashland, Ohio: John M. Ashbrook Center for Public Affairs, Ashland University, Fall 2000.
Hayward Steven F. "From Barry Goldwater to the Tea Party." *The Federalist*, September 23, 2014.
Hubbard, Ed. "Statesmanship and the Goldwater Legacy." BigJollyPolitics.com, April 29, 2015.
Judis, John B. "The Man Who Knew Too Little." *Washington Post*, September 24, 1995.
Kaplan, Seth. "Rocky and His Friends." *Harvard Crimson*, July 30, 1976.
Kempton, Murray. "The GOP Disestablishment." *The New Republic*, July 12, 1964.
Lord, Jeffrey. "The Vindication of Barry Goldwater." *The American Spectator*, July 24, 2014.
Mills, Nicolaus. "Barry Goldwater: Father of the Tea Party." *The Daily Beast*, July 16, 2014.
"1964: Lodge's Write-in Victory." *Manchester Union Leader*, May 3, 2011.
Plumer, William, David Grogan, and Denise Lynch. "Where We Were." *People*, November 28, 1988.
"Republicans: Salesman for a Cause." *Time*, June 23, 1961.
Roberts, Sam. "Capturing the Life of a Striver Who Fell Short of the White House." *New York Times*, October 17, 2014.
Schneider, William. "The Tea Party: Goldwater." *National Journal*, April 24, 2010.
Smith, Richard Norton. "Nelson Rockefeller's Last Stand." Politico.com, October 21, 2014.
"Stephen Shadegg. Goldwater Adviser and Alter Ego, 80." *New York Times*, May 24, 1990.
Sullivan, Ronald. "Nixon Reportedly Giving Up Hope on Nomination." *New York Times*, July 3, 1964.
"Taft Gained Peaks in Unusual Career." *New York Times*, March 9, 1930.
"William W. Scranton, 96, GOP Prodigy Who Led Pennsylvania, Is Dead." *New York Times*, July 29, 2013.

Index

Abbott, Gordon 50
The Agony of the GOP 1964 27
Aiken, George 176
Alcorn, Meade 119, 170
Alda, Alan 1
Aldrich, Nelson 37
Alessandroni, Walter 138
Ali, Muhammad 3
Alsop, Stewart 163
Ambrose, Stephen 123
American Automobile Association 38
American Conservative Union 46
American Enterprise Institute 129, 205, 206
American Express 199
American Football League 50
American Motors 38, 39, 60, 120, 152
American Red Cross 124
American Veterans Committee 20, 21, 52
Anderson, John 135, 136, 150
Anderson, Robert 123, 124
Andy Griffith Show 18
"Antsy Pants" 36
Appling, Howell 137, 138
Aristotle 16
"Arizona Mafia" 80, 113, 114, 130, 130, 144, 180
Ashbrook, John 30, 31, 32, 34, 35, 45, 48, 55, 61, 204, 205
Ashbrook Center 204
Autry, Gene 165
Avenue Hotel 45, 49

Babcock, Tim 150
Baker, Robert "Bobby" 74
Barnes, Sam 50
Barnes, Sullivan 50
Baroody, William 78, 80, 129, 181, 182, 205
Barr, Charles 31, 32, 46, 47, 57
Batista, Fulgencio 29

Battle Hymn of the Republic 183
Bay of Pigs 29, 65, 75, 94, 123, 162
Beatles 3, 13, 165
Beck, Glenn 191
Belafonte, Harry 5
Bell & Howell 133
Bellow, Saul 73
Belmon, Henry 132, 150
Blizen, Jerry 191
Bonanza 18
Boston Strangler 3
Boyce, James 46
Bozell, L. Brent 32, 80
Bradlee, Ben 98, 185
Brave New World 72
Breakfast at Tiffany's 142
Bree, Rita 52
Brennan, Walter 61
Broglio, Ernie 13
Brooklyn Dodgers 142
Brown, Edmund "Pat" 44, 59, 143, 201
Brown vs. Board of Education 143, 157
Brownell, Herbert 118
Bruce, Don 46
Buchanan, James 96
Buckley, James 204
Buckley, William F. 30, 57, 204, 205
"Bull Moose" 24, 25, 174
Burch, Dean 78, 80, 83, 86, 87, 133, 180, 203
Burstyn, Ellen 1
Burton, Richard 3
Bush, George H.W. 201
Bush, George W. 195
Bush, Prescott 66
Byrd, Harry 98–100
Byrne, John 132

Cabot, George 41
Car 54, Where Are You? 142

235

Carpentier, Charles 133, 134
Carroll, John 58
Carter, Andy 57
Carter, Jimmy 84, 200
Castro, Fidel 29, 162
CBS News 170, 171
Chafee, John 150
Chancellor, John 8, 176
Chapman, Robert 47
"Checkers" speech 43, 116
Chicago Bears 72
Chicago Cubs 13
Christopher, George 144
Civil Rights Act 8, 14, 101, 155–165, 169, 175, 185, 196
Claremont College 16
Clay, Cassius 3
Clay, Lucius 124, 150
Cleopatra 3
Cleveland, Grover 64
Clyde, George 152
Coleman, J.D. "Stets" 54
Columbia University 122
Columbus Dispatch 55
Commodore Hotel 31
Connally, John 73
The Conscience of a Conservative 32, 153, 154, 195, 197
"Contract with America" 195, 196
Convention News 169
Cordiner, Ralph 202
Cornell University 20
Cotton, Norris 78, 159
Cow Palace 2, 12, 13, 15, 17, 165, 166, 167, 169, 172, 173, 174, 177, 183, 184, 185
Creole Petroleum 37
Cronkite, Walter 111
Curtis, Carl 65, 69, 78
Cushing, Charles "Ned" 48

Dallas Morning News 73
Davidson, John 72
Davis, John 41
DeBloom, Carl 55
deGaulle, Charles 39
Dennis, Lahoma 136
Denver, Bob 73
DeSalvo, Albert 3
Detroit News 71, 121
DeVries, Walt, 187
Dewey, Thomas E. 20, 23, 28–29, 64, 68, 83, 88, 118, 149
Dillworth, Richardson 40, 60
Dirksen, Everett 19, 23, 36, 133, 158, 175
"Dixie" 16, 177
Dr. Kildare 142
Dole, Robert 135, 200
Dominick, Peter 58
"Dominique" 72
Douglas, Helen Gahagen 43

"Draft Goldwater" movement 6, 8, 33, 46, 58, 60, 61, 79, 80, 82, 83, 84, 85, 89, 92, 94, 95, 113, 133, 162, 204, 205
Drennan, Lorin 74
Drummond, Roscoe 110
Duke, Paul 63
Duke University 42
Dulles, John Foster 40

Eastland, James 157
Edson, Arthur 55
Eisenhower, Dwight 7, 11, 12, 18, 21, 22, 23, 26, 29, 36, 37, 39, 41, 43, 47, 49, 66, 73, 76, 83, 85, 86, 97, 116, 118, 119, 120, 121, 122–127, 139, 145, 149, 150, 151, 152, 153, 154, 160, 161, 165, 170, 171, 173, 174, 175, 180, 182, 184, 188, 197, 201, 202
Eisenhower, Milton 124, 125, 176
Emporia Gazette 135
Environmental Protection Agency 205
Ethell, Edward 50
Extremism 9, 14, 15, 16, 68, 69, 75, 76, 89, 92, 93, 145, 171, 174, 175, 11, 182, 184, 187, 200

Face the Nation 151, 153
Fair Deal 29, 37, 183
Fannin, Paul 61, 150
Farley, Jim 90
"favorite son" 8, 9, 53, 117, 132, 161, 162
Fay, Albert 50
Fiddler on the Roof 3
Fifth Avenue Compact 4
Fisk, Carlton 103
Fong, Hiram 176
Ford, Gerald 40, 176, 186, 195–196, 200, 203, 204, 205, 206
Ford Motor Company 90
Forsythe, Robert 176
Fortas, Abe 96, 99
Foss, Joe 50
Frontline 187
Frost, Robert 103
The Fugitive 18
Fulbright, J. William 159
Funny Girl 3

Gallup Poll 61, 67, 70, 128, 129, 146, 161, 177
Gandhi, Mahatma 14
Garner, John Nance 73, 95
Gaston, Robert 144
Gates, Thomas 118
GE Theater 189
General Electric 188–189, 195
"Gilligan's Island" 73
Gingrich, Newton 2, 195, 196
A Glorious Disaster 2, 195
Goldberg, David 109, 112, 138–139, 145
Goldwater, Baron 35

Index

Goldwater, Barry 1, 6, 7, 8, 9, 12, 13, 14, 15, 16, 17, 18, 20, 27, 28, 29, 30, 32, 33, 34 35, 36, 37, 38, 40, 41, 44, 45, 47, 48, 49, 50, 51, 53, 54, 55, 56, 58, 59, 61, 62, 63, 65, 67, 68, 69, 70, 71, 73, 75, 76, 77, 79, 80, 81, 82, 83, 84, 85, 86, 87, 88, 89, 90, 91, 92, 93, 97, 98, 100, 103, 105, 106, 107, 108, 109, 110, 111, 112, 115, 1116, 117, 118, 119, 120, 121, 126, 128, 129, 130, 131, 132, 133, 134, 135, 136, 139, 143, 144, 145, 146, 147, 149, 150, 151, 152, 153, 154, 155, 158, 159, 160, 161, 163, 165, 166, 167, 168, 169, 170 171, 172, 174, 176, 177, 178, 180, 181, 182, 183, 184, 185, 186, 187, 188, 189, 190, 196, 198, 199, 200, 202, 203, 204
Goldwater, Barry, Jr. 192
Goldwater, Morris 35
Goodwin, Doris Kearns 98, 185–186
Gore, Albert, Sr. 159
Graham, Billy 39
Greeley, Horace 103
Green Bay Packers 72
Greenville Times-Examiner 47
Grindle, Paul 109, 110, 112, 138–139
Gruenther, Alfred 124
Gubbrud, Archie 150

Hagerty, James 119
Hale, Alan 73
Hall, Jay 78
Hall, Len 119
Halleck, Charles 176
Hansen, Clifford 150
Hansen, Heath 197
"Hard Day's Night" 13
Harding, Warren 11, 39, 62
Harlow, Bryce 205
Harriman, W. Averill 38
Harrington, Tom 60
Harris, Louis 146
Harris Poll 161
Harvard University 160
Hatfield, Mark 150, 152, 154, 172–173, 175, 191
Hay, Samuel 48
Hayward, Steven 194
Hello, Dolly 3
Helms, Jesse 204
"Henry Sabotage" 110, 116
Heritage Foundation 197–198
Herter, Christian 40
Hess, Karl 16, 78, 129, 130, 181
Hickenlooper, Bourke 159
Hinman, George 90, 144, 206
Hiss, Alger 43
Holland, Cecil 175
Hoover, Herbert 23, 40, 73, 184
House Un-American Activities Committee 43

Hruska, Roman 47, 65
Hubbard, Ed 195
Hudson Motor Company 38
Hughes, Bob 57
Hughes, Charles Evans 64
Hughes, Robert 47
Hugus, Paul 118–119, 162, 163
Humphrey, George 118
Humphrey, Hubert 5, 98, 100, 108, 158, 201
The Hustler 142
Huxley, Aldous 72

"If I Had a Hammer" 73
International Telephone & Telegraph 203, 204
Irvin, Sam 159
Issues and Answers 45

Jackson, Andrew 84
Jaffa, Harry 16, 181, 182
Jasper, Claude 65
Javits, Jacob 55, 60, 69, 170
"Joe Glotz" 5
John Birch Society 75, 76
Johns Hopkins University 124
Johnson, Ann Eve 80, 83
Johnson, Lady Bird 74, 98
Johnson, Lyndon 1, 3, 4, 5, 12, 14, 36, 42, 56, 59, 73, 74, 75, 78, 79, 94–102, 103, 108, 110, 112, 116, 123, 124, 125, 155, 156, 157, 158, 159, 163, 172, 175, 177, 178, 184, 185, 186, 199, 201, 203
"Johnson Treatment" 97–100
Jordan, Hamilton 84
Judd, Walter 176

Kansas State University 124
Kasselbaum, Nancy 135
Katz, Nick 4
Keating, Kenneth 69, 176
Kefauver, Estes 178
Kendall, David 119
Kennedy, Edward "Ted" 109, 201
Kennedy, John F. 2, 3, 12, 26, 29, 30, 32, 5, 36, 40, 41, 42, 44, 62, 64, 65, 66–67, 69, 70, 71, 73, 74, 77, 79, 94, 95, 100, 101, 107 112, 115, 116, 119, 123, 124, 125, 128, 140, 155, 156, 162, 163, 178, 186, 195, 201
Kennedy, Joseph 26
Kennedy, Robert 70–71, 77, 125
Khruschev, Nikita 107
King, Martin Luther, Jr. 2
King Edward VIII 66
Kirkpatrick, Jeane 205
Kissinger, Henry 90
Kitchel, Denison 56, 78, 80, 82, 83, 84, 85, 86, 87, 139, 202, 203
"kitchen cabinet" 84

Index

Kleberg, Richard 95
Kleindienst, Richard 80, 83, 84, 85, 86, 139, 203, 204
Knight, Goodwin 143
Knowland, William 78, 143, 145, 176
"Kodak moment" 19
Kuchel, Thomas 144

Laird, Melvin 166, 174, 205
Lance, Bert 84
Landon, Alf 23, 135
"Landslide Lyndon" 96, 101
Lansing State Journal 73
LaRue, Fred 54
Lawrence, David 134
League of Nations 41
Leland, LaRaine 73
LePage, Norman 109
Lewis, C.S. 73
Life 73, 117, 165
Lincoln, Abraham 40, 153, 160, 168, 171
Lindsay, John 175
Linen, James 117
Lippman, Walter 159, 160
Liston, Sonny 3
Littleton, Roger 73
Lodge, George 109, 112
Lodge, Henry Cabot 6, 9, 28, 41, 42, 70, 109–113, 116, 125, 126, 128, 129, 130, 133, 134, 138, 140, 141, 145, 152, 161, 165, 170, 176, 177, 186, 194, 201
Loeb, William 108, 115
Long, Huey 3, 95, 100, 101
Long, Russell 108
Lord, Jeffrey 197
Los Angeles Angels 143
Los Angeles Dodgers 143
Los Angeles Rams 143
Love, John 150
Loyola University 147
Luce, Clare Booth 176
Lundigan, William 61
Lupton, John 50

Manchester Union Leader 105, 108
Mansfield, Mike 157–158
Mark Hopkins Hotel 165, 166, 167, 168, 181
Marriott, J. Willard 120
Mathias, Charles 66
Matthews, Robert 47, 57
Mayflower Hotel 61, 82
McCabe, Edward 86
McCabe, Thomas 118, 119, 162
McCarthy, Eugene 194
McCarthy, Joseph 21, 108
McElroy, Neil 119
McFadzean, William 50
McFarland, Ernest 36, 97
McKinley, William 11, 135

McKulski, Barbara 201
McManus, Robert 90
"Me-too-ism" 9, 23, 26, 27, 28, 36, 37, 43, 53, 62, 80, 88, 92, 195
Mecham, Edwin 159
Mencken, H.L. 19
Mere Christianity 72
Meet the Press 106
Metzenbaum, Howard 204
Middendorf, J. William 2, 27, 54, 59, 60, 62, 82, 84, 85, 131, 159, 195
Milbank, Jerry 54
Miller, William 119, 178–179, 181, 182, 199, 200
Milliken, Gerrish 47
Milliken, Roger 47, 50
Mills, Elijah 41
Mills, Nicholas 197
Mr. Smith Goes to Washington 20
Mitchell, John 203
Moley, Raymond 113, 170
Mondale, Walter 5
Mones, Robert 48
Moore, Charles F. 90
Moore, Roger 47
Morgenthau, Hans 107
Morgenthau, Robert 59
Morton, Thruston 67, 174, 197
Mullen, Robert 110
Murphy, James Slater 65

Nash-Kelvinator Corporation 38, 39
Nashua Telegraph 103
National Governors Conference 149
National Press Club 6, 71, 119, 120
National Public Radio 172
National Review 16, 30, 47, 205
National Youth Administration 96
NBC News 176
New Deal 25, 27, 29, 34, 37, 183, 188
New England Journal of Medicine 13
New Frontier 61
New Republic 159, 187
New York Giants 142
New York Herald Tribune 55, 110, 117, 118, 126, 129, 145, 160
New York Journal-American 69
New York Mets 13
New York Times 16, 61, 66, 120, 125, 185, 187, 194
New York World 159, 194
New York Yankees 3
Newsweek 98, 107, 113, 170
Nichols, Dave 48
Niven, Paul 153
Nixon, Arthur 42
Nixon, Harold 42
Nixon, Richard 2, 6, 7, 12, 14, 25, 26, 27, 28, 32, 33, 35, 41, 42, 43, 44, 46, 48, 51, 59, 61, 62, 64, 69, 70, 73, 90, 94, 109,

111, 115, 116, 120, 125, 128, 130, 133, 134, 18, 140, 141, 143, 145, 152, 154, 165, 182–183, 184, 186, 195, 196, 197, 199, 200, 201, 202, 203, 204, 205
Nixon, Thelma "Pat" 42
Nobel Peace Prize 2
Novak, Robert 16, 27, 34, 90, 120, 130, 138
Nutter, Donald 50, 52

O'Donnell, Peter 57, 58, 60, 61, 78, 83, 113
Ohio State University 30
Oswald, Lee Harvey 3, 162
Otten, Alan 153

Paine, Thomas 16
Paley, William 118
Palmer House 45
Parks, Rosa 157
Pasek, Leonard 48
Peace Corps 40
Pearl Harbor 42
Penn State University 124
Percy, Charles 133–134
Perkins, Roswell 90
Peter, Paul & Mary 73
Philadelphia Eagles 72
Pinchot, Gifford 24
Pittsburgh Post-Gazette 163
Poitier, Sidney 2
Portland Oregonian 139
Powell, Jody 84
Proctor & Gamble 119
Progressive political party 24, 25
Pyle, Howard 36

Reagan, Ronald 2, 19, 123, 188, 189, 190, 191, 195, 196, 204, 205, 206
The Real McCoys 61
Reavis, Speed, Jr. 48
Reed, John 150
Reedy, George 185
Rehmann, John Keith 48
Rehnquist, William 202
Republican National Committee 82, 117, 119
Reston, James 16
Reynolds, Donald 74
Rhodes, James 150
Rhodes, John 78, 84
Rights of Man 16
Robertson, Hayes 133, 134
Robinson, Jackie 8, 19, 176
Rockefeller, John D. 36
Rockefeller, Margaretta "Happy" 65, 66, 67, 92, 148
Rockefeller, Mary 37, 65, 67
Rockefeller, Nelson 6, 7, 8, 13, 18–19, 26, 27, 28, 34, 36, 37, 38, 41, 43, 50, 55, 59, 61, 62, 64, 65, 67, 68, 69, 70, 71, 88, 89,

90, 91, 92, 93, 94, 103, 104, 105, 106, 107, 108, 109, 110, 111, 112, 115, 117, 118, 120, 126, 130, 131, 132, 133, 134, 135, 136, 137, 138, 140, 141, 143, 144, 145, 146, 147, 150, 152, 161, 168, 170, 172, 174, 176, 177, 180, 185, 186, 187, 194, 196, 197, 200, 206
Rockefeller, Nelson, Jr. 146
Rockefeller Institute 65
Romney, George 6, 28, 38, 60, 61, 62, 63, 67, 70, 71, 109, 117, 119, 120, 121, 125, 126, 130, 131, 137, 138, 145, 151, 152, 153, 154, 168, 172, 175, 176, 177, 184, 186, 187, 188, 194, 196, 200, 201
Romney, Mitt 187, 201
Ronan, William 90
Roosevelt, Franklin 23, 24, 29, 37, 64, 84, 90, 96, 113, 135, 170, 188
Roosevelt, Theodore 7, 23, 24, 25, 27, 64, 69, 84, 135, 153, 174
Rusher, William 30, 31, 32, 33, 34, 35, 57, 148, 205

St. Francis Hotel 168
St. Louis Cardinals 3, 13
St. Petersburg Times 191
Saltonstall, Sally 109
Same Time Next Year 1
San Francisco Examiner 54
San Francisco Exposition Company 166
San Francisco 49ers 143
San Francisco Giants 143
Saturday Evening Post 163
Schneider, Bill 197
Schorr, Daniel 170, 171
Scott, Hugh 66, 170
Scott, William 133–134
Scott Paper Company 118, 119, 162
Scranton, Mary 40, 117, 160
Scranton, William 6, 28, 39, 41, 60, 61, 62, 63, 67, 70, 109, 113, 116, 117, 119, 125, 126, 130, 131, 133, 134, 137, 138, 140, 145, 150, 151, 152, 153, 160, 161, 162, 163, 164, 166, 168, 169, 170, 174, 176, 177, 181, 184, 186, 187, 194, 197, 200, 201
Scranton, Worthington 39
Screen Actors Guild 188
Semple, Effie 136
77 Sunset Strip 61
Shadegg, Steve 16, 80, 139, 140, 141
Shasta College 126
Shepard, Alan 103
Sherman House 45
Shoemaker, Mervin 139
Shorey, Greg 47
Shriver, Sargent 40
Simpson, Millard 159
Simpson, Wallis 66
Singing Nuns 72

Smith, Clyde 108
Smith, Margaret Chase 9, 108, 109, 133, 134, 137, 140, 176, 177, 201
Smith, Tad 50, 57
Smith, Tony 76
Smylie Robert 150
Snodgrass, Bob 132
Der Spiegel 170
Spivak, Lawrence 107
Stassen, Harold 109, 202
Stevenson, Adlai 66, 178
Stevenson, Coke 96
Stewart, James 20
Stewart, Potter 40
Stookey, Noel "Paul" 73
Suite 3505 52
Summerfield, Arthur 85
Supremes 13
Swainson, John R. 39, 60

Taft, Robert 11, 28, 33, 68, 149, 171, 182
Taft, William Howard 7, 21, 23, 24, 25, 27, 69, 174
Tampa Bay Times 191
Taylor, Elizabeth 3
Tea Party 2, 195, 196, 197
Thayer, Walter 118
Thomas, Evan 122
Time 32, 117
"A Time for Choosing" 189
Today 89, 103
Tope, John 50
Tower, John 59, 61, 78, 159, 176
Travers, Mary 73
Truman, Harry 23, 25, 29, 37, 68, 73
Tyler, Gus 20, 21

United Nations 41
University of Alabama 150, 155
University of California–Los Angeles 143
University of Dallas 48

Van Buren, Martin 64
Vance, Cyrus 40
VanKirk, Burkett 74
Van Susteren, Greta 191

Voorhis, Jerry 42, 43
Waldorf-Astoria Hotel 73
Wall Street Journal 63, 153
Wallace, George 150, 155
Walsh, David 38
War on Poverty 173
Warner, Jack 144
Warren, Earl 3, 12, 43, 143
Warren Commission 3
Washington Post 16, 98, 185
Washington Redskins 72
Washington Star 134, 175
Watergate 202, 204, 205
"We Shall Overcome" 16, 177
Webster, Daniel 103
Welch, Robert 76
"When the Saints Coming Marching In" 176
"Where Did Our Love Go?" 13
"Where Have All the Flowers Gone?" 73
Whetson, Frank 47, 48, 52, 57
White, Byron 40
White, Frederick Clifton ("Clif") 15, 16, 18, 19, 20, 21, 23, 25, 28, 29, 30, 31, 32, 33, 34, 35, 45, 46, 48, 50, 51, 52, 53, 54, 55, 56, 58, 60, 62, 63, 68, 76, 77, 78, 115, 118, 129, 130, 131, 132, 133 134, 135, 136, 147–148, 153, 161, 162, 163, 164, 166, 167, 168, 169, 170, 174, 176, 177, 181, 182, 184, 185, 186, 204
White, Theodore 59, 105, 116, 119, 122, 123, 144, 163, 165, 172, 176, 177
White, William Allen 135
Wilkie, Wendell 121
Williams, Caroline 109
Williams, John 203
Wills, Chill 61
Wilson, Woodrow 174
Wooden, John 143

Yarborough, Ralph 73
Yarrow, Peter 73
Young Americans for Freedom 53
Young Republicans 30, 31, 45, 47, 48, 50, 144

Zimbalist, Efram, Jr. 61

www.ingramcontent.com/pod-product-compliance
Ingram Content Group UK Ltd.
Pitfield, Milton Keynes, MK11 3LW, UK
UKHW041940140426
5217IPUK00014B/580